PROGRAMMING IN FORTRAN

by

William F. Schallert

Carol Reedy Clark

St. Louis Community College at Florissant Valley

ADDISON-WESLEY PUBLISHING COMPANY
Reading, Massachusetts • Menlo Park, California
London • Amsterdam • Don Mills, Ontario • Sydney

To our families

Bill	Mary Ellen
Reid	Bill
Todd	Chris
Clark	Schallert

Reproduced by Addison-Wesley from camera-ready copy
prepared by the authors.

 Printed in the United States of America.
Library of Congress Catalog Card
No. 78-74039

Second printing, January 1981

ISBN 0-201-06716-1
ABCDEFGHIJ-AL-8987654321

PREFACE

This book is intended as a text and problem set for a first course in Scientific and Engineering Computer Programming. It contains instructional information for programming in the FORTRAN language and a graduated problem set providing programming experience starting at the beginning of the course.

The book is designed for students majoring in Science, Engineering or Technology. By suitable problem modification and selection of topics, it is adaptable to students majoring in the engineering technologies and in business. The only previous knowledge required is that of basic algebra with an introduction to the basic trigonometric functions.

The material contained provides an orderly approach to learning FORTRAN language. Generally, each chapter corresponds to the equivalent of one week of course work. Each section provides the necessary instructional content, examples, and practice for the student. This sequence is intended to satisfy the objectives specified for each section.

The approach used was developed over a twelve year period at St. Louis Community College at Florissant Valley. Materials were designed to provide a learning situation to enable students with a wide range of interest and prior preparations to learn sufficient knowledge of the FORTRAN language to be able to write programs related to their major field. Information is also included to provide an understanding of what is needed to communicate with professional programmers. Starting with the first chapter, program statements are used to provide an early introduction to FORTRAN language. The student is not expected to understand fully the meaning and construction of the language during this early exposure.

Our purpose in producing this text is to provide useful instructional materials for FORTRAN programming students. We feel that we have succeeded in providing a text for an introductory course that is sufficiently indepth for science and engineering majors, but does so in a way that attrition is reduced to a minimum.

The problem set is designed for maximum programming experience. Each problem is carefully geared to the chapter lesson. The student begins programming at Chapter 2 with a complete program to keypunch and run. Each successive program has the student supply the portion of a program previously covered with the remainder supplied. By Chapter 6 the student has covered enough material to write complete programs. Chapter 7 introduces the student to a five-step approach to problem solving to aid in his design of the remaining programs in the text. This approach has been successful in utilization of written text material. By the end of the course the student is programming complete problems related to practice. Chapter 15 is optional and includes an exercise in project programming.

Standards have been established to make the FORTRAN language universal so that programs are compatible with different computed systems. The standards adopted by the American National Standards Institute (ANSI) in 1966 have set the minimum standards for the FORTRAN language until recently. This prior standard is referred to as ANSI X3.9 1966, ANSI Standard FORTRAN or simply as FORTRAN 66 in the text. In 1977 new proposed standards, referred to as FORTRAN 77 were drafted and are the new American National Standards for the FORTRAN language.

Because FORTRAN 66 is still widely used, those standards are incorporated in this text. However, since many computer systems have expanded versions of FORTRAN 66 with added capabilities which are now standard in FORTRAN 77, both standards are frequently presented and the user can adopt whichever method is used on his/her computer.

The authors wish to express their appreciation to the many individuals who have contributed to this book. Dr. Virgil Griffith and Vincent J. Cavanaugh provided earlier materials and notes that have been included. Marlin Greer, Ben Hall, Andrew Lindberg, Herb McMahon, Ken Smith, Jerry Stapleton, and Paul Wilson have provided numerous suggestions, examples, and materials that have been helpful in completing this effort. The staff of the Engineering Division at Florissant Valley provided assistance throughout this effort. A special thanks should be extended to the divisional support staff coordinated by Anne Zuius: Rose Watt, Debra Lowe, Audrey Huhmann, and Carol E. Zacher.

Appreciation is also extended to Betty J. Butler, W.F. Schallert II, Lynn Ellen Smith, Melvin Hayden Jr., Ken Hansen and Arthur Kriewall for program suggestions, critical review and proof reading.

Cartoons and PT's were created by Carol Reedy Clark. Graphic production was done by Robert R. Bay, Chairman, and Dennis Kossman, Graphics Department-St. Louis Community College at Florissant Valley, with assistance from Hashimoto Masahiko and Tom Ries.

The book was typeset in Theme 11 point bold on an IBM Electronic Selectric Composer. Output Formats, Source Program Listings and Statements were produced on an IBM Selectric II typewriter to simulate computer 'Printed Characters.' All type was provided by Press Typography, 8720 White Avenue, St. Louis, Missouri, 63144, (314) 962-8311.

Ferguson, Missouri - 1978 WFS/CRC

CONTENTS

FORTRAN 1

1.1 . . . state the functions performed by a computer and identify the six features that enable a computer to perform them.

1.2 . . . state the four basic parts of a computer system and the function of each, and . . . state the composition and function of a basic computer system.

1.3 . . . define the following terms: programming, program, coding a program, programmer, machine language and . . . define FORTRAN and give the advantages of coding in FORTRAN over machine language.

1.4 . . . identify the meaning and function of each of the following terms: compiler, source program, object program.

1.5 . . . state the meaning of the following terms: execution, normal order of execution, and non-executable statement.

1.6 . . . identify FORTRAN keywords and state the purpose of using keywords in a statement.

1.7 . . . identify the meaning of the following: job, control cards, monitor, and deck setup. . . arrange a deck in accordance with the deck setup of your installation.

1.1

OBJECTIVE: . . . state the functions performed by a computer and identify the six features that enable a computer to perform them.

The computer has become an indispensable aid to modern man. It has taken over tasks that were previously very tedious and feats that were once thought impossible. Computers prepare bank statements, monitor life support systems in hospitals, provide current airline reservation information, and monitor world-wide weather patterns via weather satellites. They allowed man to walk on the moon!

The basic operation of a computer working in each of these diverse fields can be expressed in the simple diagram shown in Figure 1.1-1.

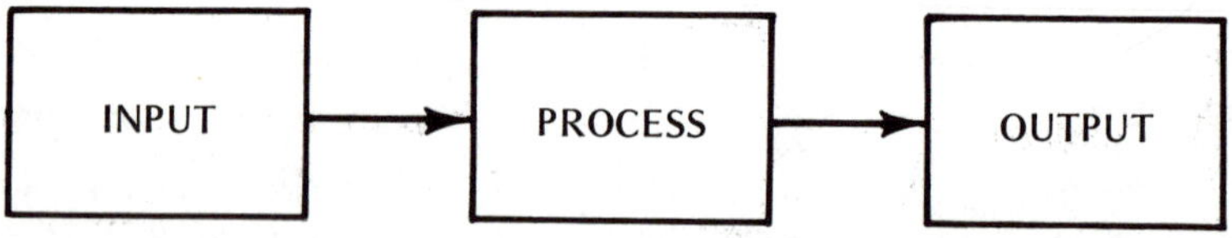

Figure 1.1-1 Computer System

Information or data is entered into the computer, such as the previous month's bank balance and each transaction that was made during the month. Instructions are entered telling how the information is to be processed, such as: add each deposit, subtract the amount of each check, and subtract the service charge from the previous balance. The computer processes the data according to the instructions and outputs the results of the processing, namely, the current bank balance.

In order for a computer to perform the input-process-output operation, it must have the following features:

- an input medium
- a storage capability
- a calculating capability
- an output medium
- a decision capability
- the ability to store instructions as well as data

The first five of these features were set forth as early as 1830 by Charles Babbage in a description of a machine which he called the Analytical Engine. Babbage, an English mathematician, tired of laboriously grinding out mathematical tables on a desk calculator, spent his life in a futile attempt to build the machine he described.

His ideas were a hundred years ahead of the technology to enable such a machine to be built. Not until 1939, when the MARK I computer was built at Harvard University, were Babbage's ideas actually realized. The completion of the MARK I in 1944 launched the computer era.

The MARK I was primarily electromechanical. In 1943, a contract was awarded to the University of Pennsylvania to develop a digital computer using vacuum tubes, which made it considerably faster than MARK I, which used switches and relays. This new computer, named ENIAC, was the world's first electronic digital computer. In order to use the ENIAC, it was necessary to wire the instructions for each new task to be performed. Because this wiring was so tedious, Professor John von Newmann of Princeton proposed the sixth feature on the list, the idea of storing the instructions in the computer in the same manner as the data. A punched card system for representing letters and numbers with machines that could sense the holes in the card had been developed by a statistician named Herman Hollerith in 1889, working for the U.S. Census. Newmann's concept of the stored program was included in the first commercially produced computer, UNIVAC I, and in most subsequent computers.

1.2

OBJECTIVE: . . . state the four basic physical parts of a computer system and the function of each, and . . . state the composition and functions of a basic computer system.

A typical computer system has four basic physical components. Each component is listed here with its function.

Physical Part	Function
1. input devices	provide an input media for instructions and data
2. memory or storage unit	provides storage capability for data and instructions
3. central processing unit (CPU)	
a. control section	decision capability
b. arithmetic logic section	calculating capability
4. output devices	provide an output media

A diagram of a basic computer system is shown in Figure 1.2-1. At least one input and one output device are needed, but any combination of devices may be used.

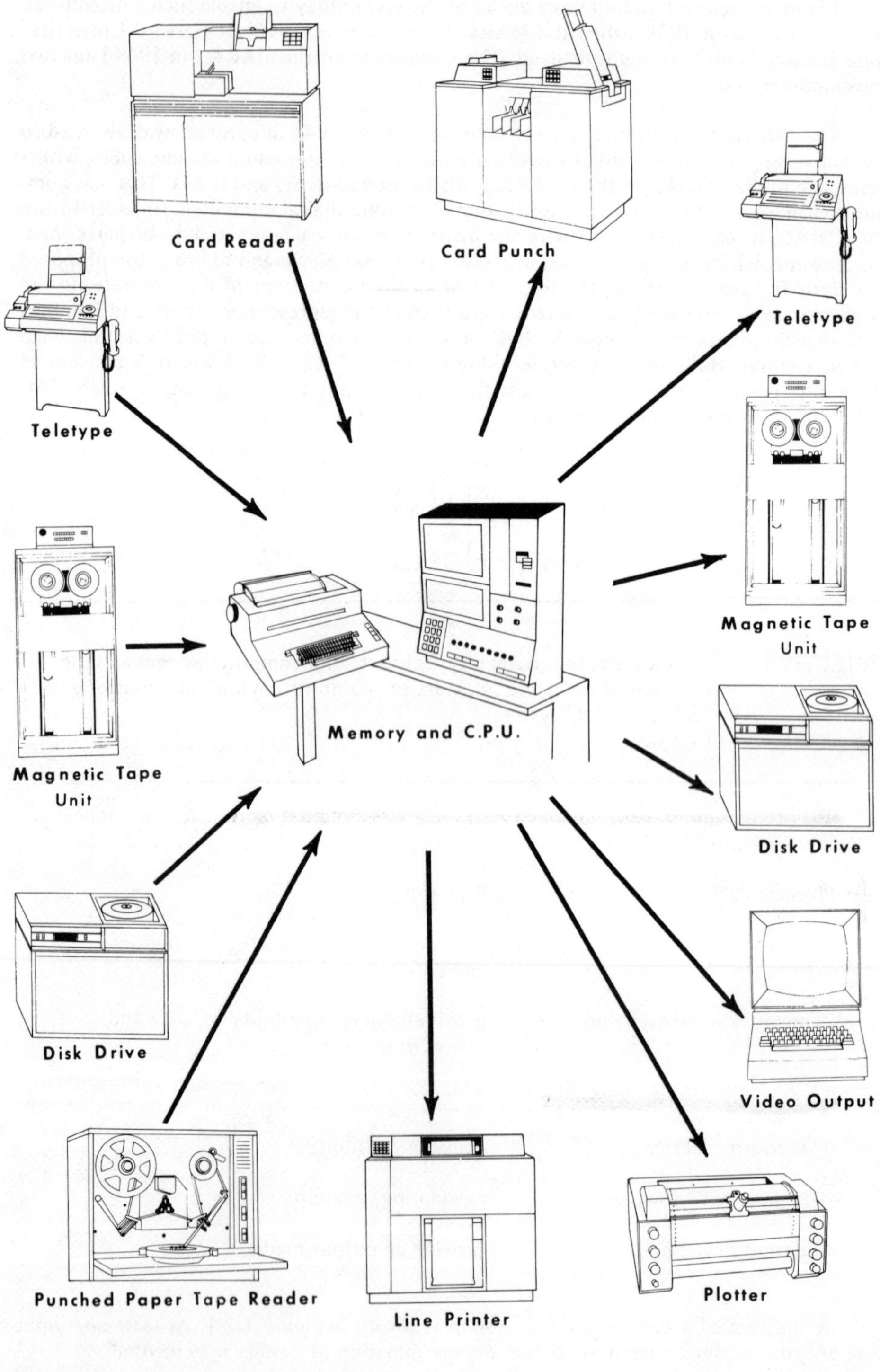

Figure 1.2-1. Basic Computer System.

Input refers to the process of entering any information into the computer. Each individual piece of information is called an input data item, and collectively, the information is called input data. Input data consists of both data to be processed and instructions to the computer on how to process it. Input data has the form of numbers, letters, and special characters.

The computer cannot read or process numbers or letters written on paper. However, it can handle patterns of electrical pulses which represent them. Several input devices and input media have been designed to communicate information to the computer. One commonly used device is the card reader, which is shown in Figure 1.2-1. It reads punched cards which have had holes punched in them by a special machine called a key punch machine, shown in Figure A-1 of Appendix A. Appendix A shows detailed pictures of a key punch machine and describes its operation.

Figure 1.2-2 shows a picture of a punched card.

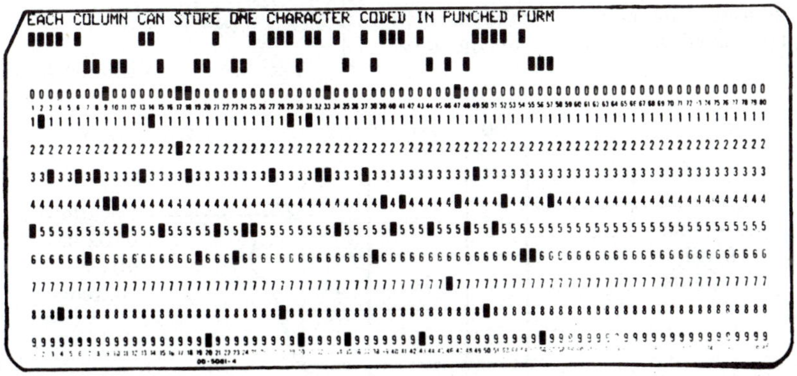

Figure 1.2-2. Punched card.

Each of the 80 columns on the card stores one character of information coded by a combination of punches. The card reader 'reads' the cards by sensing the punches. It translates the punches into electronic pulses in accordance with a universal code, the Extended Binary Coded Decimal Interchange Code (EBCDIC).

A second device frequently used for input is the remote terminal. The terminal may be a teletype machine or a keyboard with a video screen for displaying information, as shown in Figure 1.2-1. Time-sharing systems use several terminals operating simultaneously with the computer, each receiving a share of the memory and a share or slice of the central processing unit's time on an alternating basis. In many systems, the communication link between the terminal and the computer is the telephone line. The computer may be hundreds of miles away from the terminal. The user dials the number of the computer in the same way that he dials other telephone numbers, and he interfaces with the computer as if it were in the same room.

Other input media that are used are paper tape, magnetic tape, disk,and light pens.

The memory is a storage unit that can store data. It consists of many cells or locations each of which is capable of storing a number in the binary number system. This is a number system in which numbers are represented by combinations of 0's and 1's.

The fundamental unit of the cell which stores a 0 or a 1 is called a bit, an acronym for binary digit. The number of bits in each cell varies with the computer system. Complete the following:

> The number of bits in each memory cell of my computer is 36 !!.

The numbers stored in memory can be data values or number coded instructions to the computer. In order to locate information stored in memory, each location is assigned a unique number called the memory address. The total number of memory locations is referred to as the storage capacity of the computer, a number generally in the tens of thousands. Figure 1.2-3 shows twelve locations of memory, each with a unique 4-digit address. The number stored in each location is called the contents of the location.

Each Box Has a Unique Address

	00	01	02
00	-5	572	3.2
01	16	-87.1	90
02	0	19	24
03	27	-300	0

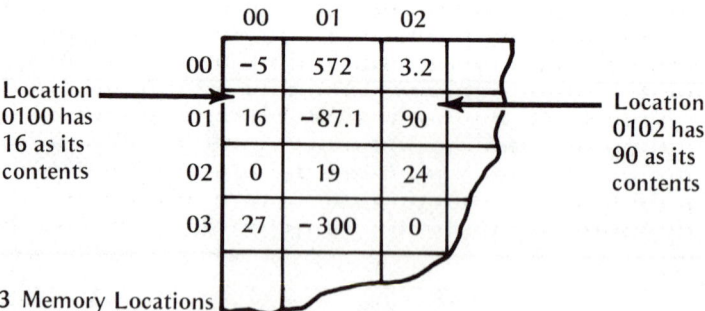

Location 0100 has 16 as its contents

Location 0102 has 90 as its contents

Figure 1.2-3 Memory Locations

To make it easier for the user, computer languages use symbolic names for locations instead of addresses. In Figure 1.2-3 if the name A is assigned to location 0100, then A contains 16. One data item can be assigned to each location. Reading a data item from an input device and assigning it to a location destroys the previous contents of the location assigned to that data item. Other locations remain unchanged. Every location contains numbers; however, only those locations which have had data assigned to them by the current user contain meaningful numbers to that user.

The central processing unit or CPU consists of a control section and an arithmetic/logic section. The control section of the CPU coordinates the various tasks within the computer system. The arithmetic section performs the arithmetic functions and the logic section performs comparisons.

Output refers to the process of transferring data from the computer's memory to an output device. Each individual piece of data so transferred is called an output data item. The contents of the location from which a data item is transferred is not destroyed after the output data has been transferred.

The most commonly used output device is the line printer, which prints the output data on continuous paper forms. A picture of a line printer is shown in Figure 1.2-1. The terminal, described above, is also used for output data in a time-sharing system. Other commonly used output media are punched cards, which are punched by an output device called a card punch, paper or magnetic tape, and the disk.

1.3

OBJECTIVE: . . . define the following terms: programming, program, coding a program, programmer, machine language . . . define FORTRAN and give the advantages of coding in FORTRAN over machine language.

For all its speed and power, the computer cannot perform its functions alone. It must be told exactly what to do and in a language that it can understand. The person who writes instructions to tell the computer what to do is called a programmer, and the process of writing this program on paper is called coding the program. The program is the organized sequence of instructions to the computer to perform a specific task. Programming refers to the process of writing the program.

A Programmer Programming A Program

The instructions that the computer can understand and perform are called machine language instructions. Writing in machine language has many disadvantages. Besides being very tedious, it is computer-oriented and requires that a programmer be familiar with the internal organization of a computer. Therefore, languages were developed which were machine independent, required little knowledge of the internal workings of the computer, and which were problem-oriented. These 'high-level' languages resemble as nearly as possible the humanly-used languages that would be used to solve the problem. FORTRAN is an acronym contracted from FORmula TRANslation, which was developed by IBM as a high-level language in which a mathematical formula can be represented by a single, closely analogous program instruction. The mathematical formula, $A=1/2h(b_1+b_2)$, would be written in FORTRAN as follows: A=H*(B1+B2)/2. This single program instruction in FORTRAN is called a FORTRAN statement.

Each FORTRAN statement is coded on special paper called FORTRAN coding paper. Each line of the coding paper is punched into one data card. For input by terminal each line is separately typed in and then entered by pressing the Return Key. Figure 1.3-1 shows a FORTRAN coding sheet on which a program has been coded. The coding is on ten lines, and hence, it would be punched into ten punched cards, as is shown in Figure 1.3-2.

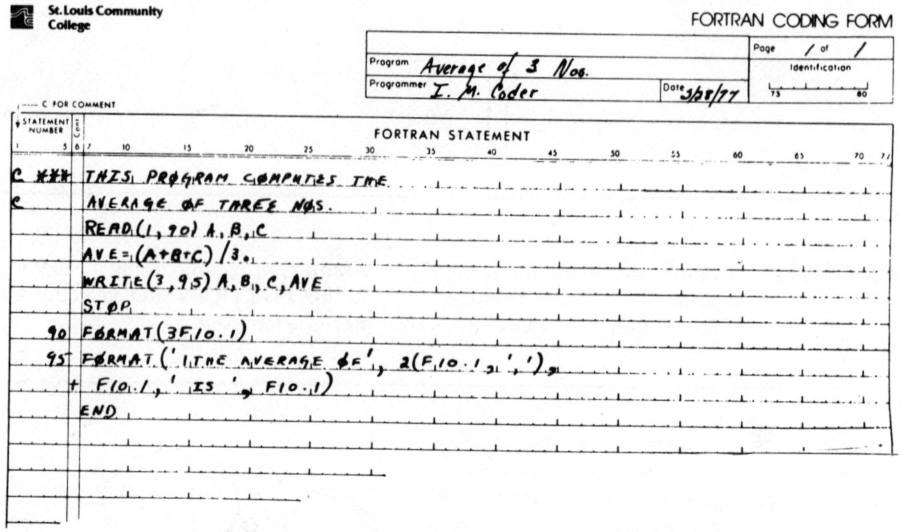

Figure 1.3-1. A Program Coded on Coding Paper

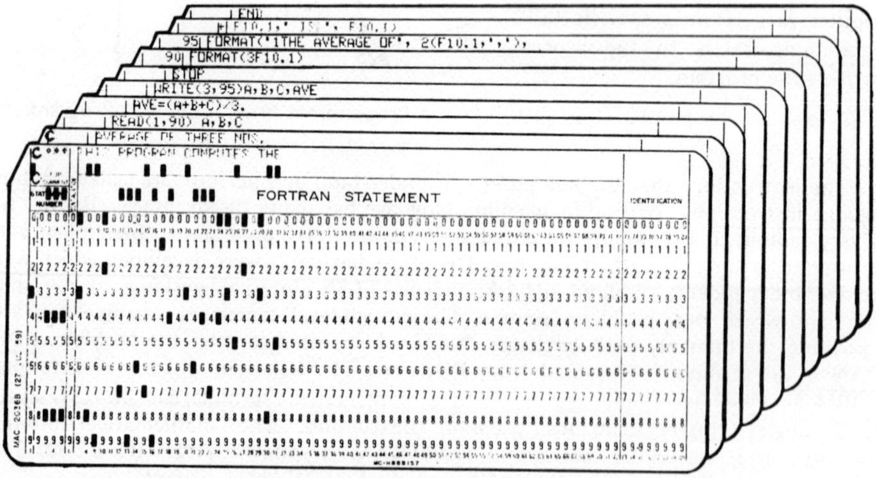

Figure 1.3-2. A Program Punched on Cards

1.4

OBJECTIVE: . . . identify the meaning and function of each of the following terms: compiler, source program, object program.

Although it is easier to write in FORTRAN, the computer cannot execute instructions unless they are in its machine language. A compiler is a special program which translates each FORTRAN statement into the machine language instructions needed to perform the instruction. Before translating a FORTRAN statement, the compiler checks the statement to see if all the rules of the language have been followed. If any error has been made, the compiler does not generate the machine language instructions for the statement, but it does continue to check the remaining FORTRAN statements. The set of all FORTRAN language instructions to perform a specific task is called the source program. When the source program has been compiled without FORTRAN language errors, a new program has been generated that is the machine language equivalent of the FORTRAN source program. This program is called the object program. This process by the FORTRAN compiler of generating the object program is referred to as compiling the program or the compilation. When a program is completed and checked out, the object program is frequently saved on punched cards or other output media for later use to save the time and cost of recompiling.

In addition to the object program, the compiler generates a listing of the program. Figure 1.4-1 shows a listing of the 'Average of Three Numbers' program.

```
                C THIS PROGRAM COMPUTES THE AVERAGE
                C  OF THREE NUMBERS
C001                  READ(1,9C) A,B,C
C002                  AVE=(A+B+C)/3.
0003                  WRITE(3,95)A,B,C,AVE
0004                  STOP
0005               90 FORMAT(3F1C.1)
0006               95 FORMAT('1THE AVERAGE OF', 2(F10.1,','),
                     + F10.1,' IS',F10.1 )
0007                  END
```

Figure 1.4-1. A Program Listing

If any errors were made during the compilation, diagnostic error messages are printed with the listing.

1.5

OBJECTIVE: . . . state the meaning of the following terms: execution, normal order of execution, and non-executable statement.

When a program has compiled without errors so that a good object program has been produced, the next step is the execution of the object program. Execution refers to the process of performing the machine language instructions of the object program. It is during the execution phase that any input data is read into memory, if it is requested by the program in a statement called a READ statement.

Figure 1.5-1 shows the input data for the 'Average of Three Numbers' program.

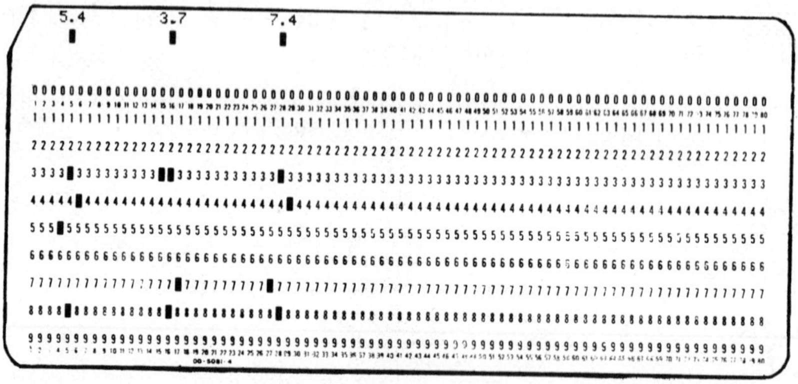

Figure 1.5-1. Input Data.

During execution, a WRITE statement in the program causes the results of the processing to be printed out. Figure 1.5-2 shows the output of the 'Average of Three Numbers' program.

```
THE AVERAGE OF        5.4,        3.7,        7.4 IS        5.5
```

Figure 1.5-2. Output Data.

Turn back to the program listing in Figure 1.4-1. Can you guess --

- which statement causes input data to be read? ______________________

- how many data items are read? ______________________

- what statement halts execution? ______________________

Instructions that supply information for the execution of the program but do not themselves translate into machine instructions are called non-executable statements. An example of a non-executable statement is a FORMAT statement which gives information as to how input or output is to be read or written but does not itself cause the data to be read or written.

Look again at Figure 1.4-1. How many FORMAT statements are in the program?

____

The normal order of execution of the instructions is sequentially in the order that the FORTRAN statements were submitted to the computer. However, there are three types of FORTRAN statements that alter the normal order; namely,

1. statements that cause a branch to another statement

2. statements that halt the execution of the program

3. certain informational statements which are non-executable

1.6

OBJECTIVE: . . . identify FORTRAN keywords and state the purpose of using keywords in a statement.

If you were able to find the READ statement and FORMAT statements in Figure 1.4-1, you were identifying a certain type of FORTRAN statement called a keyword statement. FORTRAN uses a pre-defined set of keywords to identify the type of operation to be performed by a statement or to supply information about the data used. Examples of keywords are READ, WRITE, END. If a keyword appears first in the statement, it identifies the type of statement. For example, when a READ statement is referred to, it means a statement beginning with the keyword, READ. The compiler recognizes a keyword by its placement in the statement as well as by its unique spelling. The keywords that will be used in the first programming problems are given in Table 1.6-1, along with a brief explanation of their meaning. Detailed information on using each of these keywords will be presented in the following chapters.

Table 1.6-1
Examples of Keywords

KEYWORD	MEANING
READ	Supplies a list of symbolic names of data items that are to be read.
WRITE	Supplies a list of symbolic names of data items that are to be written out.
FØRMAT	Supplies information on how the data is structured on the card or how it should be written on the output medium.
STØP	Terminates the execution of the program.
END	Signifies the end of the source program.

One type of statement, the assignment statement, does not have a keyword. Look back at Figure 1.4-1 again. Can you find the only statement in the program that does not contain one of the keywords? . . . If you chose the statement,

```
AVE=(A+B+C)/3.
```

you are correct. It does not contain a keyword but rather has the special character, =. You will learn about this statement, called an assignment statement, in Chapter 4. You might have chosen the first two lines as they also do not have a keyword. However, these two lines are informational statements, called comment statements, which you will read about in Chapter 2.

1.7

OBJECTIVE: . . . identify the meaning of the following: job, control cards, monitor, deck setup. . . arrange a deck in accordance with the deck setup of your installation.

The set of all information submitted to the computer for processing a particular task is referred to as a job. The job includes the FORTRAN source program, the input data cards required by the program, and informational cards to the computer to enable it to process the job.

These informational cards are called control cards, and they supply information, such as the language in which the program is coded, what functions are to be performed, input and output requirements of the job, as well as the programmer's name and account number for accounting purposes. The control cards are unique to a computer installation so a user should check the local installation for control card requirements. A special control program, called the monitor or supervisor, supervises the operations within the computer, using the information supplied on control cards. Other tasks performed by the monitor are supervising input/output operations and controlling the execution of a number of programs, either sequentially in batch processing systems, or concurrently, in time-sharing systems so as to require a minimum of operator intervention. Batch processing refers to the sequential processing of jobs as in card input systems.

Figure 1.7-1 shows the interaction of the monitor and the compiler programs with your program.

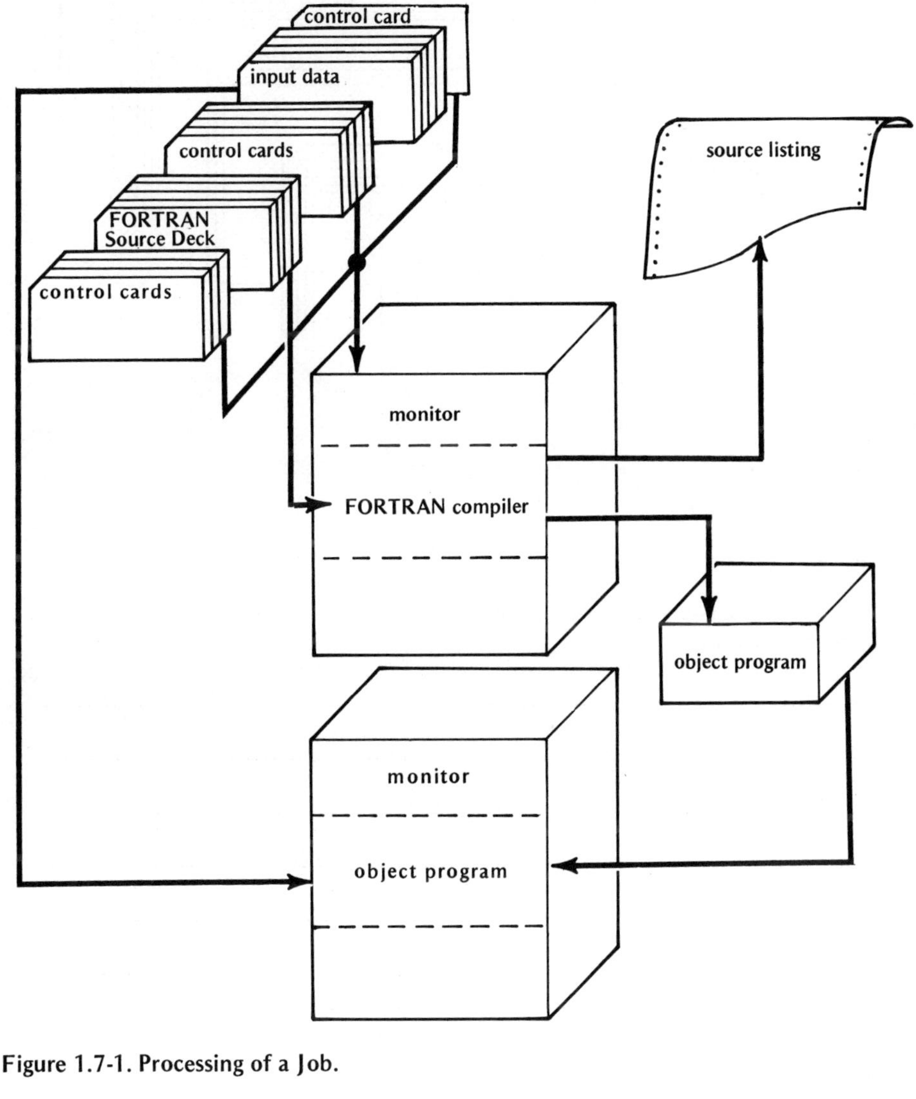

Figure 1.7-1. Processing of a Job.

Earlier it was stated that input data consists of both input data and instructions on how to process it. Figure 1.7-1 shows how this is so. Your entire job, consisting of control cards, FORTRAN statements, and input data is input data to the computer. The monitor reads the control cards, the FORTRAN compiler[1] reads the FORTRAN program and generates the object program, and the object program reads your input data.

The physical arrangement of the control cards, the source program and/or object program and the input data is called the deck setup. As in the case of control cards, the deck setup is unique to the installation. A typical deck setup is shown in Figure 1.7-2.

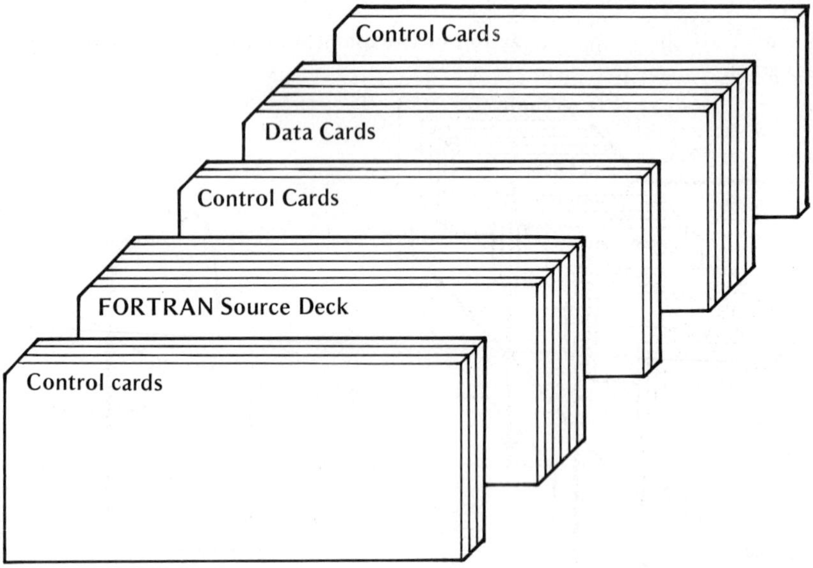

Figure 1.7-2. Deck Setup.

EXERCISE

Find out what control cards are required to execute a job on your computer, and show the deck setup.

____

____

____

____

____

____

[1] Some installations may use processors and some use interpreters instead of compilers. Although this would affect the manner in which the job is processed, the details of FORTRAN presented in this book would be the same.

CHAPTER EXERCISES

1. Match the definitions on the left with the correct words on the right.

   ___7___ a. mnemonic for binary digit
   ___4___ b. storage unit
   ___1___ c. control and arithmetic unit
   ___10___ d. organized sequence of instructions
   ___2___ e. informational cards
   ___5___ f. values supplied external to the program
   ___3___ g. sequential execution of several jobs.
   ___6___ h. control program
   ___8___ i. FORTRAN program
   ___9___ j. machine language program

   1. CPU
   2. control cards
   3. batch processing
   4. memory
   5. data
   6. supervisor
   7. bit
   8. source program
   9. object program
   10. program

2. State two advantages of FORTRAN over machine language.

   a.____

   ____

   b.____

   ____

3. What is FORTRAN?

   ____

   ____

   ____

4. What does the name FORTRAN mean?

   ____

   ____

5. What is the function of a FORTRAN compiler?

   ____

   ____

   ____

   ____

If you use punched card input, do the following exercises on a keypunch.

6. Punch a single card.

Example problem: Punch one card containing the following: the alphabetic characters A-Z in columns 1-26, punch digits 0-9 in columns 30-39, punch +-*/,.()'=$ in column 50-60.

a. If the keypunch is not on, flip the main switch located on the front panel under the keyboard.

b. Place switches in the following settings: (setting of unnamed switches does not matter)

Auto Feed	OFF
Print	ON
Clear	OFF

c. Place an unpunched stack of cards in the card hopper. Be sure they are secured firmly by the pressure bar.

d. Press the FEED key to feed a card from the card hopper into the punching station.

e. Press the REG key to register the card in the punch station.

f. Punch your information by pressing the proper keys of the keyboard.

g. When you are finished punching column 60, press the REL key to release that card. The card is now in the read station. (If a card is punched in column 80, the card will release without pressing the REL key.)

h. Clear the card by either of the following:

   a. feed another card by pressing FEED
   b. if you are done punching, press REG and REL or flip the CLEAR switch

7. Correct a card

Example problem: Punch a new card that is the same as Exercise 1, except in columns 30-39 punch digits in reverse order 9-0.

a. Repeat steps a-c of Exercise 6.

b. Place the mispunched card in the read station.

c. Feed an unpunched card into the punching station by pressing FEED.

d. Press the REG key to register the new card.

e. Hold the DUP key while watching in the column indicator until you have duplicated up to the incorrect column. (Stop when the column indicator points to column 30) indicating that column 30 is the next column to be punched.

f. Make the correction by pressing the keyboard keys.

g. Repeat steps e and f above to make any other corrections needed. (In this example, all letters would be punched at one time and there are no further corrections.)

h. Clear the cards as indicated in steps g and h of Exercise 6.

8. Add information to a punched card in a blank field.

Example problem: Add your name in columns 61-72 of the card punched in Exercise 6.

a. Repeat steps a and b of Exercise 6.

b. Place the punched card in the card hopper in front of all unpunched cards.

c. Feed this card into the punching station by pressing FEED.

d. Register this card by pressing REG.

e. Press the space bar while watching the card column indicator until you are up to column desired (column 60).

f. Punch your new information (your name).

g. Clear the card as indicated in steps g and h of Exercise 6.

9. Punch several cards sequentially.

Example problem: Punch the program given in Figure 1.3-1.

a. Place the AUTO FEED in ON and otherwise, repeat steps a-d of Exercise 6.

b. Press FEED to register one card and feed a second card.

c. Punch information in the first card.

d. Release the card (Card 2 will register and a new card will be fed).

e. Repeat steps c and d above until all cards have been punched.

f. Clear all cards to the stacker by flipping the CLEAR switch.

FORTRAN 2

2.1 ... identify the members of the FORTRAN character set.

2.2 ... recognize the use of each of the characters in the FORTRAN character set.

2.3 ... identify the parts of a FORTRAN instruction and ... state the card columns associated with each part.

2.4 ... use conventions to reduce errors in writing ambiguous characters.

2.5 ... define the term 'debugging' and ... locate and correct compilation errors by rescanning the pre-coded program.

2.6 ... define and state the advantages of using the flow diagram as an aid in programming, and ... draw flow diagrams for normal sequential operations.

2.1

OBJECTIVE: . . . identify the members of the FORTRAN character set.

The FORTRAN language is written using a set of alphabetic characters, numeric characters, and special characters. A term used frequently in referring to the alphabetic, numeric and special characters is alphanumeric.

Alphabetic characters:	ABCDEFGHIJKLMNOPQRSTUVWXYZ
Numeric characters:	0123456789
Special characters:	+-*/=().,'b$ (b stands for blank)

These are the only characters which may be used in writing FORTRAN statements. Figure 2.1-1 shows these characters as they appear when punched on a card.

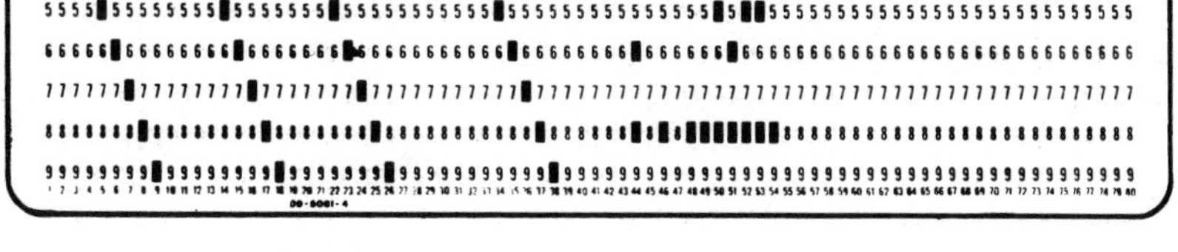

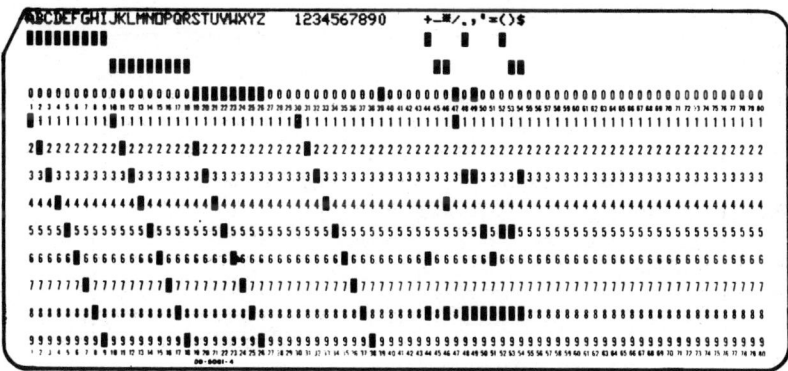

Figure 2.1-1. FORTRAN Character Set.

All of the characters given in Figure 2.1-1 can also be used as input data for a FORTRAN program. There are additional special characters that can be read as data even though they are not a part of the FORTRAN character set. However, as some printers cannot print all of the special data characters, only the FORTRAN character set will be given and used in this book.

2.2

OBJECTIVE: . . . recognize the use of each of the characters in the FORTRAN character set.

Alphabetic characters: A-Z

The alphabetic character set is composed of the upper case letters of the alphabet only. Alphabetic characters are used alone or with the numeric characters to form FORTRAN symbolic names according to special rules.

Numeric characters: 0123456789

Numeric characters or digits are used to form numbers, such as 100 and 10.2, as well as being used with alphabetic characters to form symbolic names.

Special characters: +-/*=().,'$b   b indicates blank

Special characters are used to denote arithmetic operations, indicate decimal numbers and signed numbers, assign values, and separate parts of a statement.

The special characters that are used to designate the arithmetic operations are given in Table 2.2-1.

Table 2.2-1
Arithmetic Operators

CHARACTER	OPERATION
+	Addition
-	Subtraction
*	Multiplication
/	Division
**	Exponentiation

The following examples illustrate their use.

X + Y means X plus Y

X - Y means X minus Y

X * Y means X times Y

X / Y means X divided by Y

X ** 3 means X raised to the third power

The characters + and - are also used to denote signed numbers. For example, +2 is a positive 2 and -3 is a negative 3.

Assignment

The character "=" is used to assign a value to a data item referenced by its symbolic name. The statement

A = 3.0

means assign the value 3.0 to the data item whose symbolic name is A. The statement containing "=" is called an assignment statement.

Separators

FORTRAN statements must be written according to precise rules. The following special characters are used as separators between the different parts of a statement: +-*/=,'.() They are used in a manner similar to the way punctuation marks are used in English.

In the statement

```
1 2 3 4 5|6|7 8 9 . . .
         | |READ(1,5)X,Y
```

the characters (,) and , are separators.

The arithmetic operators indicate the operation to be performed, as well as separating the operators. For example, in the statement

```
1 2 3 4 5|6|7 8 9 . . .
         | |M=N+1
```

the + indicates addition as well as separating the addends. Similarly, the = indicates assignment and separates the two parts of the statement.

The Blank

The special character, blank, is used in FORTRAN to make statements easier to read, but unless specifically stated, it has no other significance. Blanks are important when they occur in data that is read by a program. Blanks in data are discussed in the input section. When it is important to emphasize a blank throughout this book in FORTRAN statements, a lower case b is used to denote a blank.

2.3

OBJECTIVE: . . . identify the parts of a FORTRAN instruction and . . . state the card columns associated with each part.

The use of coding paper, which was shown in Figure 1.3-1, simplifies coding a program because it has the card columns marked with vertical lines to aid the programmer in using the correct columns.

The card columns used for a FORTRAN instruction are:

Table 2.3-1
FORTRAN Card Columns

COLUMNS	USE
7-72	FORTRAN statement
1	C for comment
1-5	Statement label
6	Continuation
73-80	Sequence number or program identification (optional)

The FORTRAN Statement

The FORTRAN statement uses columns 7 through 72 of a card, and it may be continued in these same columns on subsequent cards by using the continuation column described later in the chapter. Blanks are ignored within the FORTRAN statement, but may be inserted for easier reading. The following statements are equivalent:

```
1 2 3 4 5|6|7 8 9 ...
         | |READ(1,10) X,Y
         | |READ (1, 10) X, Y
         | |  R E A D ( 1, 10 ) X , Y
```

Comment Statements

Comment statements are used to supply information such as identification of the program and the programmer and details of the methods used throughout the program. Comment statements appear in the listing of the source program, but the FORTRAN compiler ignores them. Comments may be inserted any place throughout a program by placing a C in column 1 of each card containing the comment. Columns 2-80 may contain comment information. If a comment is continued on additional cards, a C is placed in column 1 of each card. Any of the characters in the FORTRAN character set may be used on comment statements. Turn to the program in Figure 1.4-1. Which statements are comment statements?

PT'S*

. Comments should identify all logical units of coding and provide heading information for all program units.
. Too many comments embedded within the code can obscure the flow of code's logic.
. The use of self-defining symbolic names minimizes the need for embedded comments.

*Programmer Techniques

Statement Label

A statement label is given to any FORTRAN statement which is referenced by other statements. A statement label is an unsigned positive integer placed anywhere within columns 1 through 5. Any statement may have a label. (Note: the END is not an executable FORTRAN statement and only signifies the end of the source program. It cannot be referenced and should not have a label.) Only the statements which are referred by other statements must have labels, and only these statements are usually given labels. Each statement label must be unique. Blanks are ignored in the statement label. The following are all statement 102.

```
1 2 3 4 5|6|7 8 9 ...
102      | |X=Y
      102| |X=Y
1   0   2| |X=Y
```

PT's*

. Statement labels do not need to be in numerical order.
  However, consecutive numbering aids readability.
. Start numbering in increments of 10 to allow for later 'in order' additions.

*Pretty Touches

Continuation

If a FORTRAN statement is too long to be contained in columns 7 through 72, it may be continued to column 7 through 72 of another card by placing any FORTRAN characters, other than a blank or zero, in column 6. Column 6 is not a part of the FORTRAN statement. Format 40 below is continued to the second card by the '+' in column 6.

```
12345|6|789...
   40| |FØRMAT(/'bVØLUMEb',F8.2,'bSTØRAGEb',I3,
     |+|'bVØLUME PER BØXb',F6.2)
```

Comments are not FORTRAN statements, and they are not continued by means of column 6, but rather by a C in column 1 of each line of the comment. A FORTRAN statement may have up to 19 continuation cards.

Sequence Number

Columns 73 through 80 are ignored by the FORTRAN compiler. These columns are optionally used for card sequencing or program identification.

2.4

OBJECTIVE:. . . use conventions to reduce errors in writing ambiguous characters.

FORTRAN requires characters to be used according to precise rules. Because of the similarity in writing certain characters, such as I and 1, or the alphabetic character, O, and the numeric character, zero, care should be taken in the coding and punching so these characters are not interchanged. One convention for distinguishing the alphabetic O from the zero is to write the alphabetic O with a slash through it, as follows: Ø. As some installations reverse this convention, it is important to check with the local installation before one has hand-written coding submitted for keypunching.

Another convention used to call attention to a blank is to use a small b for blank, as is shown in the following statement.

```
12345|6|789...
   10| |FØRMAT('b',F10.0)
```

2.5

OBJECTIVE: . . . define the term 'debugging' and . . . locate and correct compilation errors by rescanning the pre-coded program.

Debugging is the name used to refer to the process of finding the errors (bugs) in the program. There are two categories of errors that are made depending on which stage, compilation or execution, the program is in when the error occurs.

Compilation Errors

Compilation errors are very common to the beginning programmer (and the experienced programmer as well). They are errors that violate the FORTRAN language rules. They are detected by the FORTRAN compiler, and a diagnostic error message is printed with the program listing.

A few of the common compilation errors are listed below to give examples of the type of error you should look for:

1. Invalid or misspelled keyword
2. Non-FORTRAN character
3. Mismatched parentheses
4. Missing comma
5. Missing statement number
6. Missing continuation character

Debugging

If there are no compiler errors, an object program (machine language program) is saved, and the program goes into execution if so requested by the control cards.

2.6

OBJECTIVE: . . . state the advantage of using the flow diagram as an aid in programming and . . . draw flow diagrams for normal sequential operations.

The flow diagram provides a graphic representation of the operations required to solve a given problem. The first step in scientific, engineering or business problem solving is to define the problem itself.

A set of models, mathematical techniques and/or design procedures are then specified. The applications of these to the specific problem results in a set of instructions to complete the required analysis. The set of instructions can be written with processes and inter-relationships specified in a flow diagram, where operations are represented by symbols, and inter-relationships represented by joining lines. The flow diagram provides a simplified symbolic means of representing the required set of instructions. As problems grow in complexity, so does the need for using the flow diagram.

The flow diagram used in this book will be a detailed flow diagram that will indicate all the steps, decisions, and details of the program. From it one should be able to code each statement of the program. When equations have been given in the problem statement, verbal descriptions, such as "compute volume" may be used which reference the actual equations in the problem statement.

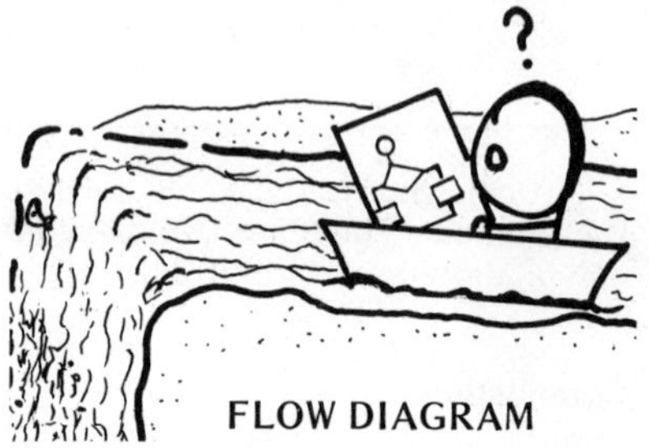

In designing a complex program, a programmer does not simply draw a detailed flow diagram on the first attempt. In Chapter 7, some preliminary steps in arriving at a detailed flow diagram are presented. A detailed flow diagram will be given with some of the problem exercises. It will be your guide in putting together the steps of a program before you are ready to design and write a complete program on your own. The symbols used in the flow diagrams in this book are given in Figure 2.6-1.

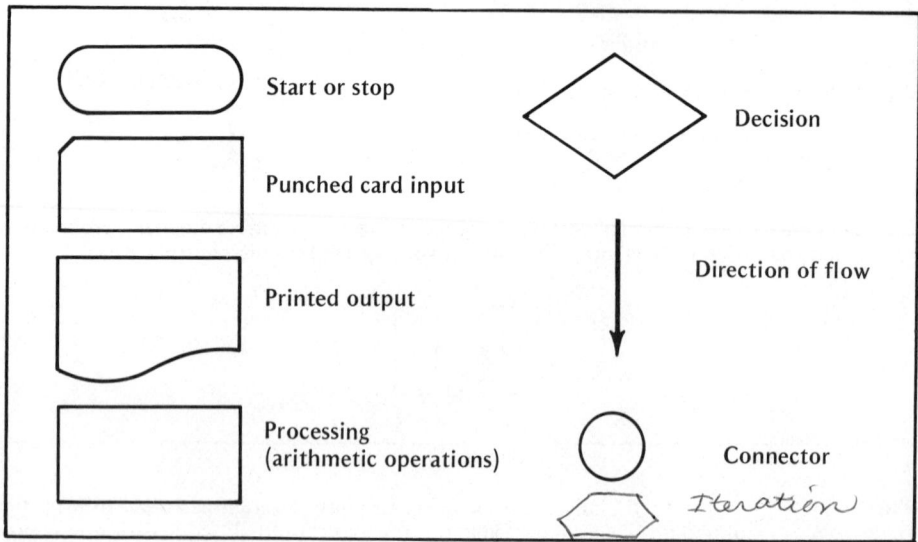

Figure 2.6-1. Flow Diagram Symbols

The most elementary programs involve the use of statements in a sequential form, as represented in Figure 2.6-2. Numerous examples of this basic process are given in the following chapters and problems. Branching (Chapter 10) and looping (Chapter 4) instructions will modify this normal sequence.

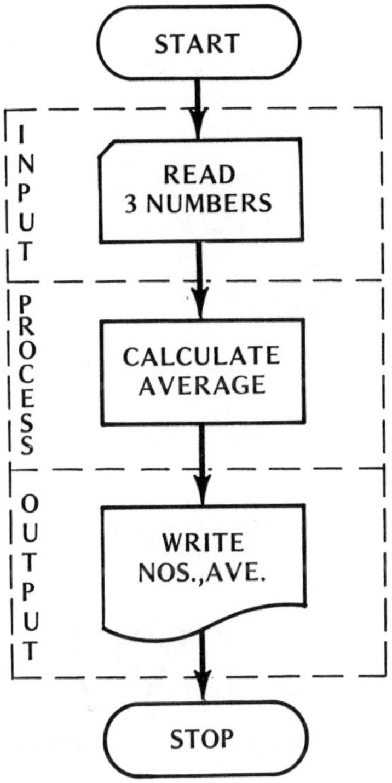

Figure 2.6-2. Flow Diagram

CHAPTER EXERCISES

1. Circle the characters which are not part of the FORTRAN character set.

   * B b $ % (= ' @ 0 Ø

2. Give the special character used for each of the following operations.

Addition	_____
Subtraction	_____
Multiplication	_____
Division	_____
Exponentiation	_____

3. Answer T for True, F for False

   a. The = in N=N+1 means equal in the algebraic sense. _____

   b. A blank is a separator. _____

   c. Blanks are ignored in data fields. _____

   d. Blanks are ignored in FORTRAN statements. _____

   e. Blanks are ignored in statement labels. _____

   f. All statements must have a statement label. _____

   g. The % is a special character in FORTRAN. _____

   h. Columns 7-80 are used for the FORTRAN statement. _____

   i. Column 1 is used for continuation. _____

   j. Comment cards do not use column 6 for continuation. _____

4. Indicate the card columns used for FORTRAN statements.

USE	COLUMNS
a. The FORTRAN statement	_____
b. C for comment card	_____
c. label (statement number)	_____
d. continuation	_____
e. sequence number (when used)	_____

5. What does the term 'debugging' mean? ______________________________

   ____

TOPIC APPLICATION
a) Keypunching
b) Computer Operational Procedures
c) FORTRAN Coding Sheet
d) Comment Statement

STATEMENTS SUPPLIED
All necessary statements are supplied
a) READ
b) ARITHMETIC
c) CONTROL
d) WRITE

Problem Number 2.1

PROBLEM STATEMENT

Programmer N. T. Carton has written a program to compute the lateral surface (S), the total surface (T), and the volume (V) for the figure shown below.

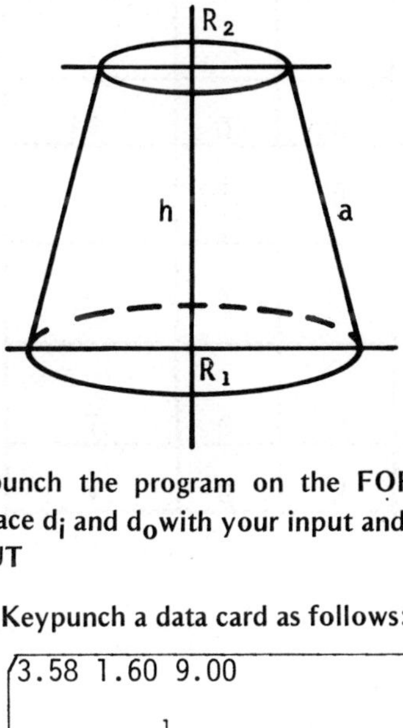

$$a = \sqrt{(R_1 - R_2)^2 + h^2}$$

$$S = \pi (R_1 + R_2) a$$

$$T = \pi [R_1{}^2 + R_2{}^2 + (R_1 + R_2) a]$$

$$V = \frac{1}{3}\pi h (R_1{}^2 + R_2{}^2 + R_1 R_2)$$

Keypunch the program on the FORTRAN coding sheet provided below. Replace d_i and d_o with your input and output device number.

INPUT

Keypunch a data card as follows:

```
3.58 1.60 9.00

         1
1234567890123345678 . . .
```

note that

h = 9.00

R_1 = 3.58

R_2 = 1.60

OUTPUT

The successful printout will have the form

```
         1         2         3
123456789012345678901234567890123...
1       LATERAL SURFACE AREA   =nnn.nn
2       TØTAL SURFACE AREA     =nnn.nn
3       VØLUME                 =nnn.nn
```

FORTRAN DATA TABLE

PROBLEM NO. 2.1 PROGRAMMER N. T. Carton

DATA ITEM	DEFINITION	UNIT	DATA TYPE	USE	FORTRAN NAME
R_1	radius of cone	m	R	I	R1
R_2	radius of cone	m	R	I	R2
h	height of cone	m	R	I	H
π	value of π	-	R	C	PI
a	temporary calculation	m	R	T	A
S	lateral surface area of cone	m^2	R	Ø	S
T	total surface area of cone	m^2	R	Ø	T
V	volume of cone	m^3	R	Ø	V

Assemble a program deck and run it on your computer.

Program NØ. 2.1

Programmer N.T. CARTØN   Date 7-13-18

Page 1 of

Identification 73–80

C FOR COMMENT

STATEMENT NUMBER | Cont. | FORTRAN STATEMENT

```
C     PRØBLEM NØ 2.1
C     READ IN VALUES ØF R1, R2, AND H
      READ(di,10)R1,R2,H
   10 FØRMAT(3F5.2)
C     SET VALUE ØF PI
      PI=3.1416
C     CALCULATE S, T, AND V
      A=SQRT((R1-R2)**2+H**2)
      S=PI*(R1+R2)*A
      T=PI*(R1**2+R2**2+(R1+R2)*A)
      V=PI*H*(R1**2+R2**2+R1*R2)/3.
C     ØUTPUT VALUES
      WRITE(do,20)S
   20 FØRMAT('1',T6,'LATERALbSURFACEbAREAbb=',F6.2)
      WRITE(do,30)T
   30 FØRMAT('b',T6,'TØTALbSURFACEbAREAbbbb=',F6.2)
      WRITE(do,40)V
   40 FØRMAT('b',T6,'VØLUME',T28,'=',F6.2)
      STØP
      END
```

Problem 2.2

PROBLEM STATEMENT

Keypunch the source program contained on the FORTRAN Coding Sheet. Run this program on your computer using necessary control cards as specified by your instructor or computer center. Replace d_o with the device number for your computer.

INPUT

No data cards are required.

OUTPUT

A sample printout is shown .

INCHES	CENTIMETERS	INCHES	CENTIMETERS
1	2.5	51	129.5
2	5.1	52	132.1
3	7.6	53	134.6
4	10.2	54	137.2
5	12.7	55	139.7
6	15.2	56	142.2
7	17.8	57	144.8
8	20.3	58	147.3
9	22.9	59	149.9
10	25.4	60	152.4
11	27.9	61	154.9
12	30.5	62	157.5
13	33.0	63	160.0
14	35.6	64	162.6
15	38.1	65	165.1
16	40.6	66	
17	43.2		203.2
18	45.7	81	205.7
19	48.3	82	208.3
20	50.8	83	210.8
21	53	84	213.4
22	[illegible]	85	215.9
23	[illegible].4	86	218.4
24	94.0	87	221.0
25	96.5	88	223.5
26	99.1	89	226.1
2[illegible]	101.6	90	228.6
	104.1	91	231.1
[illegible]2	106.7	92	233.7
43	109.2	93	236.2
44	111.8	94	238.8
45	114.3	95	241.3
46	116.8	96	243.8
47	119.4	97	246.4
48	121.9	98	248.9

C FOR COMMENT

```
STATEMENT
NUMBER   Cont.                FORTRAN STATEMENT
C PROBLEM NO 2.2
C PROGRAM TØ PRØDUCE A METRIC CØNVERSIØN TABLE
C FRØM INCHES TØ CENTIMETERS
C   - NO DATA CARDS ARE REQUIRED
C     SET CONVERSIØN FACTØR
      CF=2.54
C     PRINT HEADING
      WRITE(do,10)
   10 FØRMAT('1',T10,'INCHES CENTIMETERS      INCHES  CENTIMETERS'/)
C     CALCULATE AND PRINT VALUES
      DØ 20 I=1,50
      J=I+50
      CMI=CF*FLØAT(I)
      CMJ=CF*FLØAT(J)
      WRITE(do,15)I,CMI,J,CMJ
   15 FØRMAT('b',T12,I3,T21,F5.1,T34,I3,T42,F5.1)
   20 CØNTINUE
      STØP
      END
```

Problem 2.3

PROGRAM STATEMENT

The program below reads in the dimensions of length, width, and height of a box and computes the volume. The three dimensions symbolically called XL, W, and H, and the volume, VOL, are printed.

EXERCISE

The program was not coded on coding paper. Rewrite the program on the FORTRAN coding paper on the next page observing the FORTRAN column requirements. Fill in the flow diagram with word descriptions of each step. Punch the program from the coding paper and the data card given below. Run the program on your computer.

NOTE: Replace d_i and d_o with your input and output device numbers.

```
C THIS PRØGRAM CØMPUTES VØLUME
C
5 READ (di,90) XL,W,H
VØL=XL*W*H
WRITE (do,95) XL,W,H,VØL
90 FØRMAT (3F10.1)
95 FØRMAT (4F10.1)
10 STOP
END
```

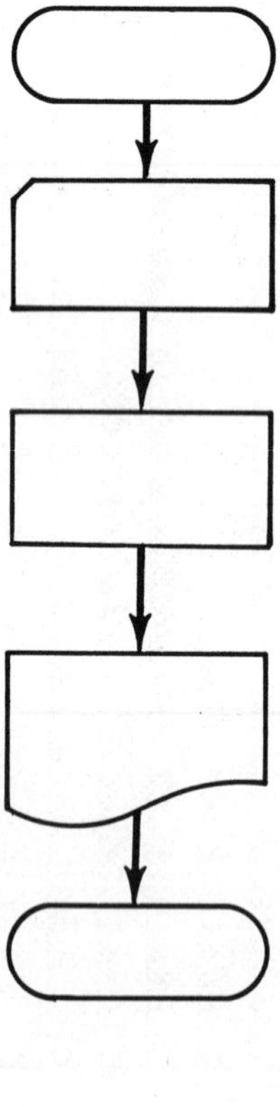

CODING FORM

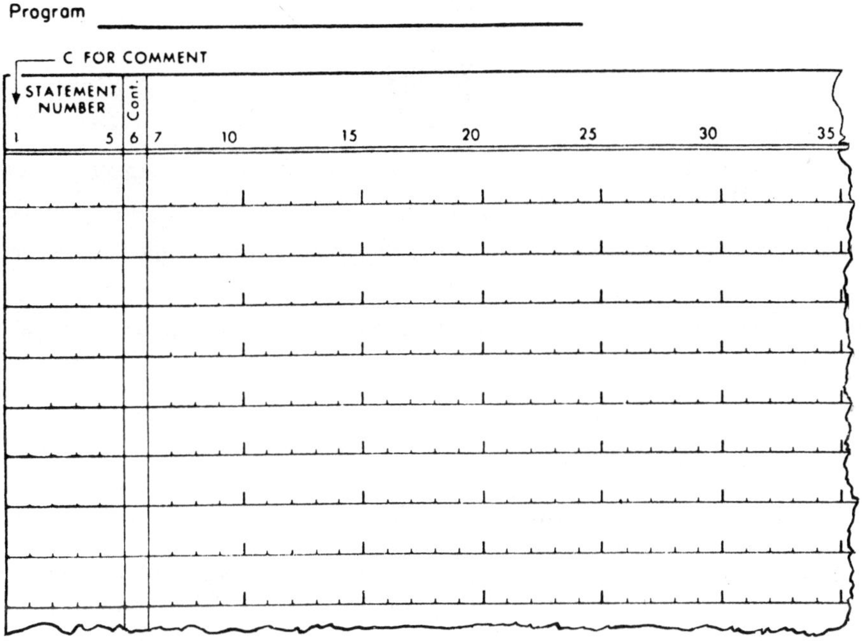

INPUT

Punch one data card as shown below.

```
23.5      48.0       6.2
                  1                   2                   3
1 2 3 4 5 6 7 8 9 0 1 2 3 4 5 6 7 8 9 0 1 2 3 4 5 6 7 8 9 0 . . .
```

3 FORTRAN

3.1 . . . define a constant and . . . identify and write the two main types of numerical constants: integers and reals.

3.2 . . . identify the terms magnitude and precision of real constants . . . and specify how real constants are stored in memory.

3.3 . . . specify two forms of real numbers, without an exponent and with an exponent.

3.4 . . . specify a 'double precision' real number.

3.5 . . . define a FORTRAN variable.

3.6 . . . specify rules for implicitly naming variables.

3.7 . . . override the implicit specification of the type of a variable by means of the explicit type specification statements, REAL and INTEGER.

3.8 . . . initialize a variable by means of a DATA statement.

3.9 . . . define an arithmetic expression and . . . form arithmetic expressions in accordance with the rules for writing them.

3.10 . . . specify data by means of a data table.

Everything but X

3.1

OBJECTIVE: . . . define a constant and . . . identify and write the two main types of numerical constants: integers and reals.

An arithmetic number, such as 340 or 21.5, is called a constant in FORTRAN because its value does not change. The computer stores each constant in a program in one memory location in an area reserved for program constants.

CONSTANT
A constant is a fixed quantity whose value does not change. There are two main types of numerical constants used in FORTRAN to specify decimal numbers: integer and real.

INTEGER CONSTANT
An integer constant or integer is a whole number written without a decimal point.

The following rules apply to writing integers:

1. An integer must be written without a decimal point.
   Examples: 55, -10
2. An integer may be positive, negative, or zero.
3. A positive integer may be preceded by a + sign or it may be written as an unsigned non-zero number.
4. A negative number must be preceded by a - sign.
5. Leading zeros do not effect the integer value. 0010 and 10 are equivalent.
6. Embedded commas are not allowed.
7. The magnitude of an integer may not exceed the maximum value allowed.
8. An integer may not contain any non-numeric characters except the + and - signs.

EXAMPLE

Examples of valid and invalid integers are as follows:

VALID INTEGERS	INVALID INTEGERS	
10	10.	(rule 1)
-40	$10	(rule 8)
025	15FT.	(rule 8)
+12345	1,257,892	(rule 6)
0	10%	(rule 8)

An integer is stored in one memory location as a binary number with a sign, as shown below:

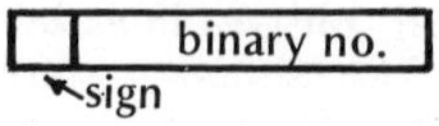

Integer numbers are used to represent whole quantities or discrete data, such as: chairs in a classroom, number of bolts in a box, number of students taking a programming course, etc. Real numbers are used to represent quantities with fractional parts or continuous data, such as: speed of an automobile, length of a room, temperature, etc. In the FORTRAN language real numbers are called real constants.

REAL CONSTANT

A real constant is a measuring number which can be expressed in any of the following forms:

1. An integer and a decimal point, such as 5.0.
2. An integer, a decimal point, and a fractional part, such as 15.125.
3. A decimal point and a fractional part, such as .875.
4. Any of the above followed by an exponent or as an integer followed by an exponent. The exponent consists of the letter E followed by a signed or unsigned integer, such as 5.5E2, 5E-20. The exponent represents the power of 10 to which the real or integer constant is to be raised; i.e., 7.1E+12 means $7.1 * 10^{12}$.

The following rules apply to writing real constants:

1. A real constant must be written in one of the four ways above.
2. A real constant contains a decimal, except when it is written as an integer with an exponent; e.g. 5E-20.

FORTRAN 66 did not permit this form. Does your compiler?

Yes ___ No ___

3. A real constant may be positive, negative, or zero.

4. A positive real constant is preceded by a plus sign or is an unsigned, non-zero real number.

5. A negative real constant must be preceded by a minus sign.

6. Leading zeros do not effect the value of the real number.

7. Embedded commas are not allowed.

8. A real constant may not contain any non-numeric character, except + - . E and D.

9. The magnitude of the real constant must be within the range allowed for the computer used.

EXAMPLE

Examples of valid and invalid real constants are as follows:

VALID REAL NUMBERS	INVALID REAL NUMBERS	
.123	0	(rule 1)
+987.123	2,300.1	(rule 7)
8.E2 ($8.0*10^2 = 800.$)	\$1.20	(rule 8)
+8.0E+02 (same as above)	5.E	(rule 1)
-8.E-4 ($-8.0*10^{-4} = -.0008$)	10E.45	(rule 1)

The magnitude and number of digits of precision of integer and real constants vary with the number of bits per memory location of a computer. Table 3.1-1 gives a table of several computers with the associated limits for integers and reals. Complete the table for your computer.

Table 3.1-1
Magnitude and Precision of Constants
For Several Computers

		INTEGERS		REALS	
COMPUTER	# BITS /MEMORY CELL	MAX. # DIGITS OF PRECISION	MAX. MAG.	MAX. DIGITS OF PRECISION	MAX. MAG.
IBM 1130	16	5	$2^{15}-1$	7	10^{38}
IBM 360/370	32	10	$2^{31}-1$	7	10^{75}
UNIVAC 1108	36	11	$2^{35}-1$	9	10^{38}
CDC 6000/7000	60	15	$2^{48}-1$	14	10^{322}
Your computer	36				

3.2

OBJECTIVE: . . . identify the terms magnitude and precision of real constants . . . and specify how real constants are stored in memory.

Real numbers are used to express measurements of physical quantities. Measurements are not exact, but are subject to the instruments used and the person using them. Therefore, the term, precision, is used in discussing real numbers, in addition to the magnitude or size of the measurement.

The real numbers, .0000001 and 1000000., represent measurements of relatively small and large quantities, respectively; hence, they are numbers of considerable difference in magnitude. Each of these measurements is expressed with the same degree of precision, however, namely, one digit. The precision of a real number is the number of significant digits in the internal representation of the number. Internally (in memory), all real numbers, whether written with or without an exponent, are expressed in the same form, namely a sign, an exponent and a fractional part. To store a non-zero number, the number is expressed in a manner similar to scientific notation, i.e., as a decimal fraction (equal to or greater than .1 but less than 1.0) and an exponent. Table 3.2-1 shows a decimal representation of the two numbers as they would be expressed internally. Note the fractional part of both, which gives the precision, is the same.

Table 3.2-1
Internal Storage of Real Numbers

REAL NUMBER	SHIFTED FOR INTERNAL STORAGE	DECIMAL REPRESENTATION OF INTERNAL FORM		
		SIGN	EXPONENT	FRACTIONAL PART
.0000001	$.1*10^{-6}$	+	-6	.1
1000000.	$.1*10^{7}$	+	7	.1

3.3

OBJECTIVE: . . . specify two forms of real numbers, without an exponent and with an exponent.

The E form of a real number facilitates writing a very large or very small number in FORTRAN without using a large number of zeros. The following number .0000001, written without an exponent, could be written in any of the following ways using an exponent:

```
 0.000001E-1
  .00001E-2
  .0001E-3
  .1E-6
 1.0E-7
10000.E-11
```

The internal form of all of these numbers would be as is shown in Table 3.2-1. The precision or fractional part would be the same; only the exponent differs. To increase the precision of the number, additional digits are used. The numbers, 1.0E-7, 1.1E-7, 1.14789E-7 express numbers of increasing precision.

The definition for a real constant (Section 3.1) gives four permissible forms, but the number of digits permitted varies with the computer. Complete the statements below so they define each type of real constant on your computer, consulting Table 3.1-1.

> Without an exponent
>
> A real constant consists of an optionally signed string of up to ___digits with a decimal anywhere in the string.
>
> Examples: 34.5 -.345
>
> With an exponent
>
> The exponent of a real constant consists of the letter E followed by an optionally signed one to____________digit integer. The exponent indicates an integer power of 10 by which the precision part or mantissa is to be multiplied. The mantissa may be a_______ constant or a___________constant.

Examples:

5.0E + 2 means +5.0 times 10^2

-.7E-2 means -0.7 times 10^{-2}

+.7E-2 means +0.7 times 10^{-2}

500.E12 means 500 times 10^{12}

3.4

OBJECTIVE: . . . specify a 'double precision' real number.

Sometimes the precision of the real numbers is not sufficient to handle the arithmetic of real numbers. For example, when numbers which are very nearly equal are subtracted, erroneous results may be obtained because, due to the round off errors inherent in real numbers, there are not significant digits to compute the difference. In such cases, it may be necessary to use double precision real constants.

A double precision real constant has the same permissible forms as the real constant described above except that the number of digits of precision is increased and the letter E in the exponent is changed to a D.

Examples of double precision real numbers are:

-21.987654D-8
123456.78D+02

It should be noted that double precision increases the precision of a real number but the range of the magnitude is the same as a single precision real number. The magnitude and number of digits of precision vary with the computer.

Because double precision numbers require twice as much storage, and because arithmetic operations using double precision are slower than single precision, double precision number should be used only when the measurements or computations justify such precision. In the vast majority of measurements, four or five digits of precision is quite adequate. All of the examples done in this book use single precision real numbers.

3.5

OBJECTIVE: . . . define a FORTRAN variable.

In Chapter 1, we called each individual piece of information stored in a memory location a data item. So as not to 'boggle' the programmer's mind with actual memory locations, symbolic names are used instead. This symbolic name, chosen according to the rules of FORTRAN, is called a FORTRAN variable name or simply a variable.

FORTRAN VARIABLE
A FORTRAN variable is identified by a name, has a type, occupies a memory location, and has a value that may change. The type of a variable is integer or real.

Variables are used in FORTRAN in a manner similar to the use of symbolic names in an algebraic formula. In the algebraic formula, d = rt, d, r, and t are symbolic names used to represent the values of distance, rate and time. Similarly, in the FORTRAN statement

```
D=R*T
```

D, R, and T are FORTRAN variable names selected to represent the values of the variable quantities.

One memory location is reserved for each variable used in a program. The current value stored in the location is the value of the variable. In the above example, D, R, and T each have a unique memory location. The values of R and T must have been determined prior to this statement. The value of D is determined by the values of R and T.

A variable is defined when it is given a value. Three ways of defining a variable in a program are:

1. Read its value in from a data card,
2. Assign it a value in an assignment statement, such as A = 1.3 or A = B + 2.7,and
3. Initialize it by means of a DATA statement,which is discussed in Section 3.8.

Before a variable is defined, its value is undefined and the variable may not be referenced except in a statement which will assign it a value.

There are two kinds of variables: integers and reals. The type of variable depends on which type of value the variable represents.

3.6

OBJECTIVE: . . . specify rules for implicitly naming variables.

The choice of the name for a variable is up to the programmer. However, one must follow the rules for naming FORTRAN variables that are given below. Mnemonic names are generally chosen to aid the programmer in remembering the meaning of the variables. The statement, D = R * T, is more meaningful than the statement X = Y * Z in which X, Y and Z are used to represent distance, rate and time.

Names of variables must satisfy the following rules:

1. Names must be six characters or less in length.

2. The first character of a name must be a letter of the alphabet.

3. Characters after the first must be letters or digits. No special characters are allowed.

4. Variable names beginning with I, J, K, L, M, or N are implicitly integer variables. This rule is called the I-N rule for naming integers. All variable names beginning with the remaining letters are implicitly real variables. There are some special statements given in the next section which will alter these implicit assignments.

Integer variable names are given to variables that represent integer numbers. For example, the number of rows in a classroom has an integer value with no fractional part, such as 5; therefore, an integer name, such as NROW, would be used to represent the integer value.

EXAMPLE

The following examples show valid and invalid integer names.

VALID integer names	INVALID integer names	
I	S	(rule 4)
JØHN	JØHNATHAN	(rule 1)
LITTLE	AREA	(rule 4)
JKL2	2JKL	(rule 2)
KLM123	M.N	(rule 3)

Real variable names represent quantities that will be assigned real constant values, such as PI represents the real number 3.14. Real variable names should be used to represent quantities whose value is determined by measurement to some degree of precision, such as temperature, velocity, or volume.

EXAMPLE

Examples of valid and invalid real variable names are as follows:

VALID	INVALID	
X		
AREA	I	(rule 4)
ENERGY	LENGTH	(rule 4)
Z1234	ELECTRIC	(rule 1)
TINT	Z12/4	(rule 3)
V LUME (blanks are ignored)	8 BALL	(rule 2)

PICKING A NAME

3.7

OBJECTIVE: . . . override the implicit specification of the type of variable by means of the explicit type specification statements, REAL and INTEGER.

In many situations it is desirable to override the type specification defined by the variable name. If, for example, the variable name 'I' is to be used to represent an electrical current, it must be defined as a real variable. The REAL statement will provide this specification and override the integer type specification defined by the integer variable name.

GENERAL FORM

```
12345|6|789...
     | |REAL in1,in2,in3, ...
     | |     \______________/
     | |           list
```

COMPONENTS

REAL is the keyword

list is a sequence of integer names to be retyped as real variable names

EXAMPLES

```
12345|6|789...
     | |REAL I
     | |REAL ITEM,NO,ID,I1,I2,L
```

In a similar manner, real variable names can be retyped by the INTEGER statement.

GENERAL FORM

```
123456789 ...

      INTEGER rn1,rn2,rn3,...
              \_____________/
                   list
```

COMPONENTS

INTEGER is the keyword

list is a sequence of real names to be retyped as integer variable names

EXAMPLES

```
123456789 ...

      INTEGER RØW
      INTEGER A, B, C
```

The REAL and INTEGER statements retype variables for the complete program unit. The redesignated type applies in each case the variable name appears in the program unit.

The implicit length of each variable is assumed to be single precision unless explicitly declared double precision in a statement, DOUBLE PRECISION, whose form and use is similar to the REAL and INTEGER statements above.

> PT's*
>
> . Variable names should be self-defining, such as AREA.
>
> . Which is better, using implicit I-N rule or explicit typing of variables?
> Each has advantages:
> I-N rule makes the type of a variable clearly known without looking for a declaration.
> Explicit declaration of all variables 'frees' up one letter for more descriptive names.
>
> *Phenomenal Tactics

3.8

OBJECTIVE: . . . initialize a variable by means of a DATA statement.

The DATA statement can be used to assign an initial value to a variable at the start of the program.

GENERAL FORM
1 2 3 4 5 6 7 8 9 • • • DATA $k_1/d_1/,k_2/d_2/,...k_n/d_n/$ or DATA $k_1,k_2,k_3...k_n/d_1,d_2,d_3,...d_n/$
COMPONENTS
k is a list of variable names d is a list of initial values, integer or real, according to the variable type DATA is the keyword
EXAMPLES
1 2 3 4 5 6 7 8 9 • • • DATA A/1./,B/2./,C/3./ DATA A,B,C/1.,2.,3./

There must be a one-to-one correspondence between the list of variables and the list of initial values. The DATA statement is not an executable statement. It assigns the values to the variables before the start of program execution. It must be placed before any executable statements. The type of the variable and the type of constant assigned must be the same.

Write

```
123456789...
      DATA X/1./
```

not

```
123456789...
      DATA X/1/
```

In a DATA statement, the symbol, *, can appear before a constant to indicate that the constant is specified a number of times. The general form is i*k where i is the number of times the constant k is repeated.

EXAMPLE

The following DATA statement assigns initial values of 5.0 to A, 6.0 to B, 7 to M, and sets X, Y, and Z to 0.

```
123456789...
      DATA A,B,M/5.,6.,7/,X,Y,Z/0.,0.,0./
                       or
      DATA A/5./,B/6./,M/7/,X,Y,Z/3*0./
```

3.9

OBJECTIVE: . . . define an arithmetic expression and . . . form arithmetic expressions in accordance with the rules for writing them.

Arithmetic Expression
An arithmetic expression is used in FORTRAN to specify computations. An arithmetic expression consists of a single constant or a single variable or combinations of these used with the arithmetic operators. The value of an arithmetic expression is always a number whose type is integer or real.

The arithmetic operators are as follows:

Operator	Meaning
**	Exponentiation
*	Multiplication
/	Division
+	Addition
-	Subtraction

Examples of valid arithmetic expressions are as follows:

432	a single constant
AREA	a single variable
AREA/2	combinations of the above with
A+B*C/D	arithmetic operators

Arithmetic expressions are formed in accordance with the following rules:

1. All computations must be explicitly specified. There are no implied operations. The algebraic formula, $A=3.14r^2$ would be written in FORTRAN with the multiplication of 3.14 and r explicitly stated as follows:

   A = 3.14 * R **2

2. Only one operator may be used between two variable names. The following are invalid:

   X*-Y X*/B

   In order to multiply X by -Y either the order can be reversed to be -Y * X or else parentheses can be used as follows:

   X * (-Y)

An expression can begin with a + sign or – sign but no other symbol. The unary operation –Y is permitted and is equivalent to 0.–Y. Two asterisks (**) representing exponentiation are considered as a single symbol.

3. If two or more arithmetic operations appear in an expression, the computations are performed in accordance with a hierarchy of operations as follows:

> PT's*
>
> X**2 is preferred to X**2. X**2 is usually evaluated as X*X whereas many compilers evaluate X**2. by logarithms resulting in a less accurate answer.
>
> *Pointed Tip

HIERARCHY	OPERATION	SYMBOL
1st	exponentiation	**
2nd	multiplication, division	*, /
3rd	addition, subtraction	+, -

When two operations which are of the same order appear in an expression, they are evaluated left to right. The following example shows how an expression is evaluated.

a. D**2 is performed, call the result X

b. A*B is performed, call the result Y

c. C/X is performed, call the result Z

d. Y is added to Z to give the result.

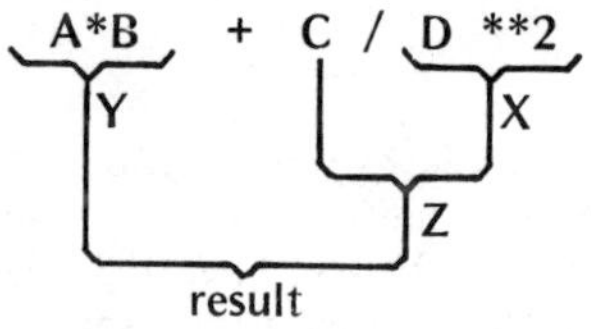

There is an exception to the left to right order for operations of the same order. If there are two sequential exponentiation operators, the evaluation is from right to left. The following expression, 2**3**2, has the meaning 2**(3**2) and would be evaluated as shown below according to FORTRAN 77. As not all computers do it this way, check how it is done on your computer.

3**2	gives 9
2**9	gives 512

Special attention needs to be paid to the results of division of two integer constants. (Note: The other operations with integer operands all give exact results.) When an integer is divided by an integer, the result is truncated to an integer, that is, any fractional part is dropped.

TRUNCATION

Thus,

1/2 = 0

4/5 = 0

5/4 = 1

7/4 = 1

The result of the expression

(1/3)*3 is 0

since

(1/3)=0 and 0*3=0

Remember: The result of the division of two integers is predictable and precise. The fractional part is always dropped. This is not the case if both operands are reals.

For example,

1./2. = .5

4./5. = .8

5./4. = 1.25

7./4. = 1.75

(1./3.)*3 = .9999999≠1.0

The last example above shows a second problem area. The computer cannot exactly represent the result of 1./3. other than as .33333. . . to the maximum precision of the computer. Hence, (1./3.)*3=.99999 . . . and not 1. as might be expected. However, in printing out a data item value of .999 . . . , many computers round off the results to the nearest whole number, and this result would appear as 1.0. Yet, if a comparison of this item is made with 1.0, they would not be equal!

In addition to the repeating fraction, which you are familiar with, many other real constants (i.e., .2) and quotients of real constants (i.e., 1./5.) cannot be represented exactly in the computer, which represents all numbers in the binary number system.

'Round off error' is the error introduced during a computer operation when only a finite number of significant digits in computations can be stored. Each computer will have a specified accuracy that will limit the accuracy of computer operations. While individual errors will be small, a significant error can be accumulated through many repetitive arithmetic operations. Round-off errors can arise in different ways:

a) non-terminating fractions

b) magnitude faults through additions or subtractions of very large and very small numbers.

c) combinations of (a) and (b)

Appendix E has a further discussion of round-off errors entitled 'Round-Off Error Sources'.

How then are we able to deal with the unexpected results? Simply suspect that all real numbers may not be exact even though their printed value appears to be.

4. Parentheses are used in expressions to specify the order in which operations are to be performed. When present, parentheses are evaluated before the other operations are performed. Parentheses within parentheses are evaluated beginning with the innermost. Thus, the expression

A/((B+C)*D)

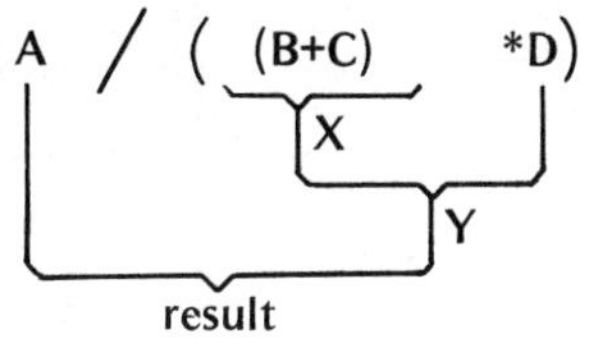

is evaluated in the following manner:

a. B+C call the result X
b. X*D call the result Y
c. A/Y gives the final result

5. All operands in an expression should be of the same type. Thus, X=X+1 should be X=X+1.0. We use the word 'should' instead of 'must' in Rule 5 because many compilers have permitted the use of mixed mode expressions; that is, an expression containing operands of different types, and FORTRAN 1977 permits them.

> PT's*
>
> Use additional parentheses whenever they add clarity and might avert an error. There is no virtue in writing complicated expressions with the minimum of parentheses if clarity is clouded or errors emerge.
>
> *Perspicuous Techniques

If your compiler does not permit mixed mode expression or if you wish to avoid additional rules for expressions and the pitfalls which mixed expressions frequently cause, skip the rest of this section.

Complete the following:

My computer [does / does not] permit mixed-mode expressions.

BUT, for those whose computer permits them and who are likely to encounter them in the programs with which you work, the rules governing the evaluation of mixed-mode expressions are presented here.

Table 3.9-1 shows what type the result will be for all combinations of two operands for the operation +,-,*, and /.

Table 3.9-1
Type Determination in Arithmetic Operations

+-*/		OPERAND 2: Integer	S. P. Real	D.P. Real
OPERAND 1	Integer	Integer	S. P. Real	D.P. Real
	S. P. Real	S. P. Real	S. P. Real	D.P. Real
	D.P. Real	D.P. Real	D.P. Real	D.P. Real

Note: S. P. is single precision real; D. P. is double precision real.

Thus, if we consider the types, integer, single precision real and double precision to be in a hierarchy with integer the lowest and double precision the highest, the result of an expression will be the highest type present in the expression. However, each operation in the expression will be evaluated according to the types of the two operands involved. The following illustrates this:

Evaluate 2.3*(I/2)-I/M when I=9 and M=4

1. Evaluate the expression in parentheses first

   I/2 or 9/2=4 (integer divided by integer gives integer)

2. Perform * and / next (they are of the same hierarchial order so evaluate them left to right)

   2.3*4=9.2 (real times integer gives real)

   I/M or 9/4=2 (integer/integer gives integer)

3. Perform subtraction last

   9.2-2=7.2 (real - integer gives real)

3.10

OBJECTIVE: . . . specify data by means of a data table.

Most problems look very complex at the start. However, since all processing is done on data items, one method of attacking the 'complex' problem is to spell out the data requirements of the problem including both input data and output data. This specification may take several forms, and the form we shall use for our applications is the Data Table shown in Table 3.10-1.

Table 3.10-1
FORTRAN DATA TABLE

DATA ITEM	DEFINITION	UNIT	DATA TYPE[1]	USE[2]	FORTRAN NAME

[1] DATA TYPE: I = Integer, R = Real
[2] USE: I = Input, Ø = Output, T = Temporary, C = Constant

The DATA ITEM column consists of the mathematical symbol or any other symbol or word used to designate a single piece of information. Each symbol in the formula A=lw would be listed as a data item. In some cases where no formula is present, there may be no symbolic designation, and this column would be left blank.

The DEFINITION and UNITS columns contain verbal descriptions of the data item with units specified when applicable.

The next column, DATA TYPE, specifies whether the data item is an integer, I, or a real, R. Additional types will be added later.

The column entitled USE, refers to the main use of this data item in the program. I is for input, O is for output. Since it will be our practice to always print out all our input data for debugging purposes, the O will not be put on the data item if its main use or source is input. C is used if the data item is used to store a program constant, such as PI for 3.14. A temporary T is for a data item which stores a value computed in the program but which is neither an input nor an output data item.

The FORTRAN NAME is the name you choose in keeping with the rules for naming FORTRAN variables.

You start with the data specification because when you begin a problem you generally have a good idea about the results that you want to obtain. The list of items that you want to know is your output data. Next, ask yourselves, 'What information do I need to supply in order to achieve the results?' This is your input data. In Chapter 7, it will be shown that making the Data Table is one step in a step-by-step approach to problem solving.

CHAPTER EXERCISES

1. Indicate which of the following are valid integers with I, valid real numbers with R, and invalid numbers with X.

a)	1E1	______	f)	-1.1E11	______
b)	1,000	______	g)	0	______
c)	100	______	h)	0.0	______
d)	100.	______	i)	5E	______
e)	$100.0	______	j)	2.302	______

2. Indicate which of the following are valid integer variable names with I, valid real variable names with R, invalid variable names with X.

a)	H	______	f)	CU7&5	______
b)	I	______	g)	7ABX	______
c)	HELLØ	______	h)	A1B	______
d)	GØØDBYE	______	i)	ARbEA	______
e)	CU	______	j)	M.Z	______

3. Evaluate each of the following expressions:

a) 7/2+4*3**2 ________

b) 7./2+4**2/2 -10/3 ________

c) 24/((2+3)*2/5)**2 ________

d) 1.E2+.1E-1+1.1E1 ________

e) 12.0*2.0/3.0*.5 ________

f) (1/2+2)**3+1 ________

g) (1./2)**2+1. ________

h) (2.0*(3+4)-2)/5-2 ________

4. Indicate which of the following is an integer (I) quantity and which is a real (R) quantity.

a) rotational speed of an engine ________

b) number of peas in a pod ________

c) number of players on a team ________

d) number of storage bins on a shelf ________

e) displacement of a piston ________

f) number of days in a week ________

5. In the expression X+Y*Z, which operation is performed first?

____

6. What keyword supplies a list of variable names into which data is to be read and stored?

____

7. What value is calculated for the expression I/K if I = 1 and K = 3?

____

8. Write a DATA statement to initialize PI to 3.14159, SUM = 0.0, and A, B, and C each to −1.0.

1 2 3 4 5	6	7 8 9 ...

TOPIC APPLICATION

a) Assign appropriate and meaningful names to integer and real variables.
b) Perform arithmetic operations using the proper mode.

STATEMENTS SUPPLIED

All necessary statements are supplied with variable names to be assigned.

a) READ
b) ARITHMETIC
c) CONTROL
d) WRITE

Problem 3.1

PROBLEM STATEMENT

A room of length 20.2 ft., width 15.35 ft., and height 30.0 ft. contains box storage space consisting of 6 rows, 5 columns, and 8 decks. A program has been written to calculate the volume, storage capacity, and volume per box in the room. The program is complete but lower case letters have been used to indicate the necessary FORTRAN variables as follows:

a = length
b = width
c = height
d = number of rows
e = number of columns
f = number of decks
g = volume of the room
h = storage capacity of the room as an integer variable
i = storage capacity of the room as a real variable
j = cubic feet per box

EXERCISE

Assign proper FORTRAN names to these variables using the data table below, keypunch the program, and process on your computer. Replace d_i and d_o with your input and output unit numbers.

INPUT

Data card arrangement:

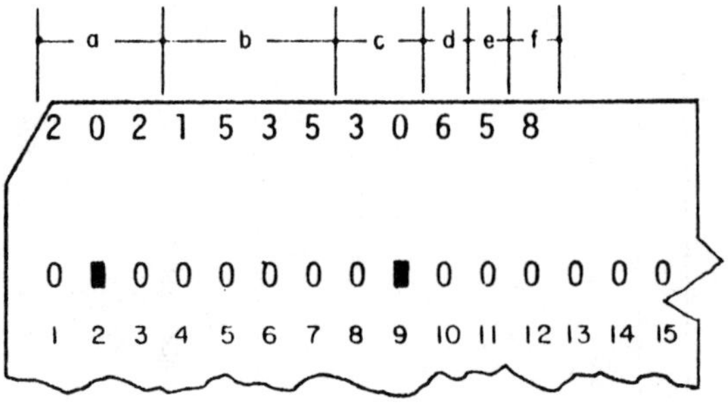

FORTRAN DATA TABLE

DATA ITEM	DEFINITION	UNIT	DATA TYPE[1]	USE[2]	FORTRAN NAME

[1] DATA TYPE: I = Integer, R = Real
[2] USE: I = Input, Ø = Output, T = Temporary, C = Constant

OUTPUT

The printout should appear as follows:

VOLUME 9302.09 STORAGE 240 VOLUME PER BOX 38.76

Program PRØBLEM NØ. 3.1

Programmer I. M. SMART II   Date 12/20/72

FORTRAN STATEMENT

```
C PROBLEM NØ 3.1
C    READ IN VALUES ØF LENGTH, WIDTH, HEIGHT, RØWS, CØLUMNS, AND DECKS
C    IN ØRDER LISTED
      READ(di,4,END=99) a,b,c,d,e,f
    4 FØRMAT(F3.1,F4.2,F2.0,I1,I1,I1)
C    CALCULATE THE VØLUME ØF THE RØØM
      g=a*b*c
C    CALCULATE THE STØRAGE CAPACITY ØF THE RØØM
      h=d*e*f
C    CHANGE THE INTEGER VARIABLE FØR STØRAGE CAPACITY TØ A REAL VARIABLE
      i=h
C    CALCULATE THE NUMBER ØF CUBIC FEET PER BØX
      j=g/i
C    PRINT THE VØLUME, STØRAGE CAPACITY, AND VØLUME PER BØX IN THE ØRDER
C    LISTED
      WRITE(do,5)g,h,j
    5 FØRMAT(//' VØLUME     ',F8.2,' STØRAGE     ',I3,' VØLUME PER BØX  '
     +,F6.2)
      STØP
   99
      END
```

Problem 3.2

Write a program which reads in a data card which is a sample of data collected on each student at a college. Print out this information. A description of the data card is given in the FORTRAN Data Table below.

EXERCISE

a) Assign each data item a FORTRAN name in the table

b) Replace each small letter in the list of the READ and WRITE statements in the program below with the FORTRAN name you select. Rewrite the program on a FORTRAN Coding Form, keypunch, and process on your computer using a data card keypunched as shown.

FORTRAN DATA TABLE

PROBLEM NO. __________ PROGRAMMER ____________________

DATA ITEM	DEFINITION	UNIT	DATA TYPE[1]	USE [2]	FORTRAN NAME
a	student ID number				
b	class code: 1-Fresh; 2-Soph; 3-Jr.;				
	4-Sr.				
c	number of credit hours (whole				
	number)				
d	GPA (nearest tenth)				
e	height (nearest tenth in inches)				
f	weight (nearest tenth in pounds)				

[1] DATA TYPE: I = Integer, R = Real
[2] USE: I = Input, Ø = Output, T = Temporary, C = Constant

PROGRAM

```
123456789...

C   READ AND WRITE STUDENT DATA
C
      5 READ(di,90)a,b,c,d,e,f
        WRITE(do,92)a,b,c,d,e,f
        STØP
     90 FØRMAT (3I5,3F5.1)
     92 FØRMAT ('b',3I5,3F7.1)
        END
```

d_i = your input device number
d_0 = your output device number

INPUT

Keypunch data card as follows:

52132	2	32	2.3	50.	138.
12345	6789 10	12345	6789 20	12345	6789 30
Stu No.	Class Code	Cr Hr	GPA	Ht.	Wt.

12 34 ...

4 FORTRAN

4.1 ... state the use and purpose of the arithmetic statement; . . . write its general form and the definition of each of its elements.

4.2 ... write valid arithmetic statements in accordance with the FORTRAN rules.

4.3 ... use arithmetic statements to convert numbers and variables from one type (integer or real) into another.

4.4 ... identify how data can be entered into a program by the arithmetic statement.

4.5 ... identify function subprograms and . . . use the following system-supplied functions:

SQRT (Argument)
EXP (Argument)
SIN (Argument)
COS (Argument)
TAN (Argument)

4.6 ... convert basic scientific and engineering equations into valid FORTRAN statements.

4.7 ... use the STOP and CALL EXIT statements.

4.8 ... state the use and placement of the END statement.

4.9 ... recognize the general form of the DO and CONTINUE statements and . . . use them in simple applications.

4.10 ... identify execution errors and . . . locate and correct execution errors in the problems in this book.

4.11 ... change the implied type of a variable using system-supplied subprograms.

4.1

OBJECTIVE: . . . state the use and purpose of the arithmetic statement; . . . write its general form and the definition of each of its elements.

One type of FORTRAN statement, the assignment statement does not have a keyword. It is used to assign a value to a FORTRAN variable. The arithmetic statement is an assignment statement which assigns a numerical value to a FORTRAN variable name whose type is integer or real. The arithmetic statement provides the means for performing calculations and evaluating formulas.

GENERAL FORM

```
12345|6|789...
nnnnn| |v=e
```

COMPONENTS

```
nnnnn is the statement number (optional)
v     is a variable name or array element
=     is an assignment character
e     is an arithmetic expression
```

EXAMPLES

```
12345|6|789...
     | |A=5.32
     | |B=A+28.57
     | |C=(A+B)**2
```

The arithmetic statement is interpreted to mean: evaluate the expression on the right-hand side of the symbol '=' and assign the resulting numerical value to the location specified by the variable name on the left-hand side. For example, A=B/C-2. means evaluate the expression B/C-2. and assign the result to the memory location assigned to A.

The assignment character, =, in the arithmetic statement does not have the same meaning of 'equals' that it does in an algebraic equation. Thus,

I=I+1

which is invalid algebraically, is a valid FORTRAN statement meaning: add 1 to the current value of I and store this result back into I, as shown below:

Before Execution of I=I+1		After Execution of I=I+1	
I	5	I	6

The values of all variables on the right side remain unchanged. This is illustrated below.

Before Execution of I=J-K+1		After Execution of I=J-K+1	
I	5	I	2
J	4	J	4
K	3	K	3

4.2

OBJECTIVE: . . . write valid arithmetic statements in accordance with the FORTRAN rules.

The following rules apply to writing arithmetic statements:

1. The left side of the '=' must be a valid FORTRAN variable name. It may be a real or an integer variable. It may not contain any operators.

VALID	INVALID
A=B+C+1.	A+B=C+1
I=X+1.	-B=B

2. The right side of the '=' must be a valid FORTRAN arithmetic expression. The expression may have a real or integer value.

VALID	INVALID
AREA=PI*R**2	AREA= *R**2
A=B*H/2	A=/C=2
Y=I/J	B=((C+D)-2
I=B/A	R**2*PI

3. The value of the variable on the left side of the '=' before execution of an arithmetic statement is destroyed upon the execution of the statement.

Further examples of valid arithmetic statements and their meaning are given in Table 4.2-1.

Table 4.2-1
Examples of Valid Arithmetic Statements

STATEMENT	MEANING
123456789···	
`I=X`	Assign the integer portion of X to I.
`X=I`	Convert the integer value of I to a real variable and assign to X.
`J=J-1`	Replace the current value of J with this value minus one.
`M=N*(N+1)/2`	$M = \frac{N(N+1)}{2}$
`Z=(3*X-4*Y)/(6*W-S)`	$Z = \frac{3X-4Y}{6W-S}$
`X = A**(-B)`	$X = A^{-B}$
`Z = X*Y/(S+R)`	$Z = \frac{XY}{S+R}$

Table 4.2-2 gives examples of invalid arithmetic statements.

Table 4.2-2
Examples of Invalid Arithmetic Statements

STATEMENT	REASON WHY INVALID
1 2 3 4 5 6 7 8 9 • • •	
X+1=Y	Left hand side must be a single variable
X=Y=Z	Only 1 "=" is permitted
A =B+C	Statement must be contained in columns 7-72
R=((S+T)	Mismatched parentheses
X=(Y+Z)/-2	Two operations in a row
Y=2(A+B)/H	Implied multiplication is illegal

Table 4.2-3 gives the values assigned for some FORTRAN arithmetic statements. In the examples, A=6.0, B=2.0, C=4.0, D=.4, I=1, J=-2, and K=3.

Table 4.2-3
Evaluation of Arithmetic Statements

FORTRAN STATEMENT	VALUE ASSIGNED
1 2 3 4 5 6 7 8 9 • • •	
H=A/B*C	H=12.0
H=A/(B*C)	H=.75
H=A+B/C	H=6.5
H=A*B/C+D	H=3.4
K=I-J**3	K=9
J=I/K	J=0
J=I/K*K	J=0

EXERCISE

1. **Indicate which of the following statements are valid (V) and which are invalid (I). If invalid, indicate the reason.**

```
12345 6 789...
        A=B+C          ________  ______________________
        T=(A+B)/C+D)   ________  ______________________
       X=2*Y           ________  ______________________
        Y=X*X          ________  ______________________
        A=(A+B)/-C     ________  ______________________
        Y=AX+CZ        ________  ______________________
        A=2(B+C)       ________  ______________________
```

2. **Write valid FORTRAN arithmetic statements for the following mathematical equations:**

	12345 6 789...
$y=ax^2+b$	
$f=ma$	
$KE=1/2mv^2$	
$a = \frac{b}{c+d}$	

3. **Indicate the value assigned for each statement.**
A = 10.0 B = 2.0 C = 4.0

```
12345 6 789...
        H=A/B+C        ______________________
        H=A/(B+C)      ______________________
        H=A+B/C        ______________________
```

4.3

OBJECTIVE: . . . use arithmetic statements to convert numbers and variables from one type (integer or real) into another.

Some compilers do not permit mixing modes of variables in an expression. However, it is always permissible to mix modes of arithmetic on opposite sides of the assignment character in an arithmetic statement. The computer will evaluate the expression on the right-hand side and then convert it to the mode of arithmetic of the variable on the left before assigning it to the variable.

If the result of the expression is a real number and the variable on the left is an integer, the real number will have the fractional part dropped or truncated, and only the integer portion will be assigned to the integer variable. Rounding does not occur.

For example, after the following two statements are executed,

```
12345 6 789...
        A=1.7
        I=A
```

I will have a value of 1; the value of A is unchanged.

If rounding is desired, the following statement can be used:

```
12345 6 789...
        I=A+.5
```

EXERCISE

1. Indicate the value assigned in each case.

```
12345|6|789...
      |A=15/2        ____________
      |A=16.2/4      ____________
      |N=15/2        ____________
      |N=9./2        ____________
```

2. Indicate the value assigned if A=8. B=2. I=8 J=2

```
12345|6|789...
      |X=I/(I+J)     ____________
      |N=B**2/A      ____________
      |X=A+I/J       ____________
```

4.4

OBJECTIVE: . . . identify how data can be entered into a program by the arithmetic statement.

Before an arithmetic statement can be evaluated meaningfully, all the variables in the expression must have defined values. Variables that represent program constants, such as π, are frequently assigned names, i.e., PI, and defined in a DATA statement or set by means of arithmetic statements. This permits changing the value in one statement only, for example, to give more precision to π . Other variables may have their values set in arithmetic statements if the program is to be run only one time.

Figure 4.4-1 shows a program in which the values for the variables are set in arithmetic statements instead of being read in.

```
12345 6 789...

        A=10.
        B=4.
        C=2.
      5 R1=(-B+(B*B-4.*A*C)**.5)/(2.*A)
        R2=(-B-(B*B-4.*A*C)**.5)/(2.*A)
        WRITE(3,10)R1,R2
     10 FØRMAT('bRØØTS ARE',3F10.1)
        STØP
        END
```

Figure 4.4-1. Variables set by arithmetic statements.

To execute the above program for a different set of values, the three arithmetic statements would have to be changed to the new values and the program re-run. Therefore, a more general approach to the solution of the problem would be to read in these three program variables during program execution from data cards by means of the READ statement which is discussed in Chapter 5.

EXERCISE

1. The values of π (3.1416), radian to degree conversion (57.296), and nautical mile to feet (6076.2) are to be used a number of times in a given program. Write three arithmetic statements to define these constants. Use FORTRAN names PI for π, CR for radian conversion and CM for miles conversion.

```
12345 6 789...
```

> *PT
>
> As an aid for keeping track of units, the variable name may be ended with letters indicating units.
> i.e., CR = radian conversion
> CM = mile conversion
> HTFT = height (ft.)
> HTM = height (miles)
>
> *Pragmatic Tip

2. Write arithmetic statements to assign the following: 2.38,6.49,16.,32. to variables X, Y, ABAR, and BBAR, respectively.

```
12345 6 789...
```

3. Write two DATA statements to provide the same assignments as required by Problem 1 and by Problem 2, respectively.

1 2 3 4 5	6	7 8 9 . . .

4.5

OBJECTIVE: . . . identify FUNCTION subprograms and use the following system-supplied FUNCTIONS:

SQRT(Argument)
EXP(Argument)
SIN(Argument)
COS(Argument)
TAN(Argument)

There are many operations frequently encountered in programming which involve commonly used mathematical functions. Some examples of these are square root, exponential, trigometric functions and logarithms. Although it would be possible for a programmer to write FORTRAN algorithms to perform each of these functions, the task would be beyond the scope of the beginner and needlessly time-consuming for the experienced programmer. Since they are so commonly used, the FORTRAN system has a set of subprograms which can be called and used. A subprogram is a set of FORTRAN statements which solve a portion of a problem or perform a special process and which is used as a part of another program, called the main program. The subprogram is written and compiled separately from the main program, but it cannot be used by itself. Instead, it is joined together with the main program that calls it to perform a particular task. There are several types of subprograms which will be discussed in Chapters 12 and 13. Presently, only one type, namely, the system-supplied FUNCTION subprogram will be discussed.

> *PT
>
> The FUNCTION SQRT (X) is especially written to evaluate square root. Hence, SQRT (X) is likely to be more accurate than X**.5 since the latter is evaluated by a general logarithmic routine.
>
> *Precision Tip

The system-supplied FUNCTION subprogram is a subprogram usually supplied as a part of a library of subprograms accompanying a computer system, although members of a local staff may write a part or all of these subprograms. Each of the FUNCTION subprograms has a unique name and performs a specific task. For example, SQRT is a FUNCTION which takes the square root of a non-negative real number.

FUNCTIONS are used within arithmetic expressions by mentioning the name of the FUNCTION followed by a quantity in parentheses, called the argument, on which the FUNCTION is to be performed. A FUNCTION must have at least one argument of a specified type, and it returns one value of a specified type, which is substituted in the expression in place of the FUNCTION name and argument.

EXAMPLE 1

The following statement takes the square root of X and stores the non-negative real number result in Y. The argument X for SQRT must be a non-negative real number.

```
123456789...
      Y=SQRT(X)
```

EXAMPLE 2

The following statement computes the exponential of X, that is e^X, and stores the result in Z. Both X and the result EXP(X) are real numbers.

```
123456789...
      Z=EXP(X)
```

EXAMPLE 3

The three basic trigometric functions, sine, cosine, and tangent are shown below:

```
123456789...
      A=SIN(B)
      C=CØS(D)
      X=TAN(Y)
```

In each case the argument must be a real number in radian measure.

FUNCTIONS can be used as a part of other expression. FUNCTIONS are evaluated before any arithmetic operations other than those in the FUNCTION'S argument. For example, statement 5 in Figure 4.4-1 could be written as follows:

```
123456789...
    5 R1=(-B+SQRT(B*B-4.*A*C))/(2.*A)
```

The argument may be any valid FORTRAN expression whose type is real. The statement below computes the formula y=2sin1/2(a+b).

```
12345|6|789...
     | |Y=2.*SIN(.5*(A+B))
```

The argument may convert degrees to radians before executing the SIN function as in the following statement:

```
12345|6|789...
     | |Y=SIN(30./57.296)
```

EXERCISE

1. Write statements for each of the following equations:

equation	FORTRAN statement
	12345 6 789...
$e = Ae^{at}$	
$s = \sqrt{y^3}$	
$v = \sin(x) + \cos(x)$	
$e = E_m \sin(wt+p)$	

4.6

OBJECTIVE: . . . convert basic scientific and engineering equations into valid FORTRAN statements.

A number of formulas are given below for practice in writing FORTRAN statements. The rules for writing valid arithmetic expressions (Section 3.9) and arithmetic statements (Section 4.2) as well as rules for naming FORTRAN variables (Section 3.6) should be reviewed at this point.

EXERCISE

Valid FORTRAN statements are given following the practice set. The naming conventions used in writing these statements are given to help you follow the answers.

1. All small letters in the formulas, such as t, are replaced by capital letters, such as T.
2. In cases where the letter would result in the wrong type, an R precedes the letter, such as RI for i.
3. Subscripted letters such as P_1 use the letter followed by the subscript, such as P1.
4. The following names are used for the given symbols.

PI	for	π
XBAR	for	$\bar{X}$
SIGMA	for	σ
RMU	for	μ
THETA	for	θ

1. $A = 2rh\sin\left(\frac{\pi}{p}\right)$ ____________________

2. $ARC = 2\sqrt{y^2 + \frac{4x^2}{3}}$ ____________________

3. $F = 2\pi rS\cos\theta$ ____________________

4. $y = \frac{2S\cos\theta}{pg}$ ____________________

5. $B = \frac{\mu}{4\pi}\frac{2i}{a}$ ____________________

ANSWERS

It should be noted that there are possible correct variations. For example, X can be written using either SQRT (X) or X**.5.

```
1.  A = 2.*R*H*SIN(PI/P)

2.  ARC = 2.*SQRT(Y**2+4.*X**2/3.)

3.  F = 2.*PI*R*S*CØS(THETA)

4.  Y = 2.*S*CØS(THETA)/(P*G)

5.  B = RMU*2.*RI/(4.*PI*A)
```

EXERCISE

Write valid FORTRAN statements for the following equations:

1. $v = 4t^3 - 18t^2 + 24t - 10$

____

2. $V = \dfrac{64\pi(y+8)^2}{3(y-8)}$

____

3. $T = Ae^{-x\sqrt{W/2p}}$

____

4. $CL = P_1 - P_2 + Z\sqrt{\dfrac{P_1(1-P_1)}{N_1} + \dfrac{P_2(1-P_2)}{N_2}}$

____

5. $Z = \dfrac{-1}{\sqrt{x^2 - A^2}} - \dfrac{2A^2}{3\sqrt{(X^2 - A^2)^3}}$

____

4.7

OBJECTIVE: . . . use the **STOP** and **CALL EXIT** statements.

The programmer must provide for a means of termination during program execution after the desired operations have been performed. The STOP and CALL EXIT control statements provide this feature. The STOP statement is written as shown below.

GENERAL FORM	
12345 6 789···	
nnnnn	STØP
COMPONENTS	
nnnnn	is the statement number (optional)
STØP	is the keyword

The statement number consists of one to five digits and is optional. It is required only if the statement is referenced by another FORTRAN statement.

At some installations, the CALL EXIT statement is used instead of the STOP statement for program termination. It instructs the computer to remain in a state ready to continue batch processing without any operator action, if there is a program deck for the next job in the hopper of the card reader. The form of CALL EXIT is as follows:

GENERAL FORM	
12345 6 789···	
nnnnn	CALL EXIT
COMPONENTS	
nnnnn	is the statement number(optional)
CALL	is the keyword
EXIT	is the name of a subprogram

The termination symbol used to code the STOP (or CALL EXIT) statement in the flow diagram is given in Figure 4.7-1.

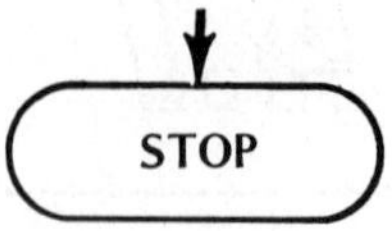

Figure 4.7-1. Termination Symbol

4.8

OBJECTIVE: . . . state the use and placement of the END statement.

The END statement is a non-executable statement that defines the end of a main program or subprogram.

GENERAL FORM		
1 2 3 4 5	6	7 8 9 • • •
		END
COMPONENTS		
END is the keyword		

Physically, it must be the last statement of each program or subprogram. It should not have a statement number as it cannot be branched to, and it may not be continued. The END does not terminate program execution, but rather it is a signal to the compiler that it has reached the end of a program unit. To terminate program execution, the STOP statement is used.

4.9

OBJECTIVE: . . . recognize the general form of the DO and CONTINUE statements and use them in simple applications.

<u>Looping</u> is the process of repeating a sequence of instructions a specific number of times with a different assigned value for at least one variable within the instructions. Some means must be provided to control the number of times this process is repeated. The DO statement provides one means of controlling the looping process. Chapter 10 provides additional means for program looping.

GENERAL FORM

```
12345 6 789...

nnnnn  DØ n i = m1,m2,m3
```

COMPONENTS

nnnnn	is an optional statement number
DØ	is the keyword
n	is the number of an executable statement appearing after the DØ statement in the program
i	is an integer variable (not an array element) called the <u>index variable</u> of the DØ
m_1, m_2, m_3	are unsigned integer constants greater than zero or unsigned integer variables whose value is greater than zero. They may not be array elements.

EXAMPLES

```
12345 6 789...

        DØ 10 J=1,8
        DØ 15 K=I,J,L
```

1. The value of m_1 should not exceed m_2. (FORTRAN 66 says <u>must</u> not. FORTRAN 77 allows for it but bypasses the range of the DO.)
2. m_3 is optional; if it is omitted its value is assumed to be 1. If omitted, the comma after m_2 is also omitted.

EXAMPLE

Write a DO statement to execute ten times a sequence of statements down to and including statement 30.

```
12345 6 789...
        DØ 30 I=1,10,1
```

The meaning of the statement is: perform (DO) all program steps following this one down to, and including, the statement numbered 30, with an initial value of 1 for the DO index variable named I. When statement 30 is executed, increase the index variable by 1. Repeatedly perform all steps between the DO statement and statement 30 for successive values of the index until the index exceeds 10. When the index exceeds 10, go on with the program steps following statement 30.

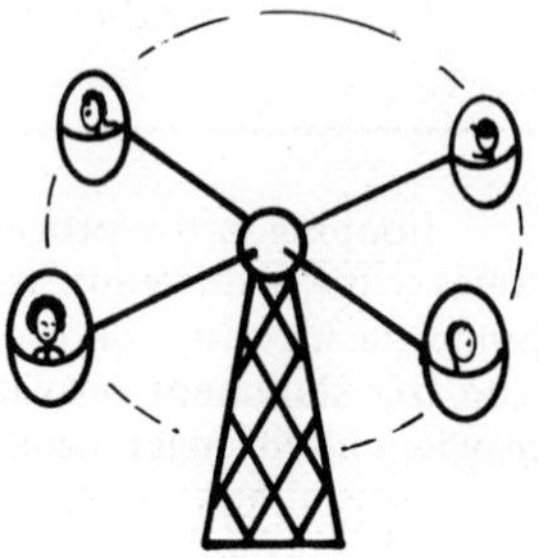

Looping

The CONTINUE statement is often used with the DO statement to identify the last statement in the DO loop.

GENERAL FORM	
12345 6 789...	
nnnnn CØNTINUE	
COMPONENTS	
nnnnn	is the statement number
CØNTINUE	is the keyword

This statement does not instruct the computer to do anything. It is simply inserted as a 'landmark' for the DO statement. Do not try to interpret it as meaning 'go on to the next step'. It is inserted because the STOP, CALL EXIT, END, DO, and FORMAT statements cannot be used as the last statement of a DO loop. A numbered CONTINUE statement is inserted in such cases immediately following the last instruction to be executed, and its number is used as a reference number by the DO statement.

EXAMPLE

The program segment

```
123456789...
      DØ 55 NVAL=1,18,2
         S  }
         S  }
         S  }  block of statements
         S  }          or
         S  }  range of the DO
         S  }
      ...
   55 CØNTINUE
```

executes repeatedly the block of statements beginning with the first statement after the DO statement down to the CONTINUE statement.

FORTRAN 66 specifies that the incrementing of the index and the test for the end-of-loop be done after the execution of the terminal statement of the DO. FORTRAN 77 performs the test ($m_1 > m_2$) before executing the statements within the range of the DO. Both methods are diagrammed in Figure 4.9-1.

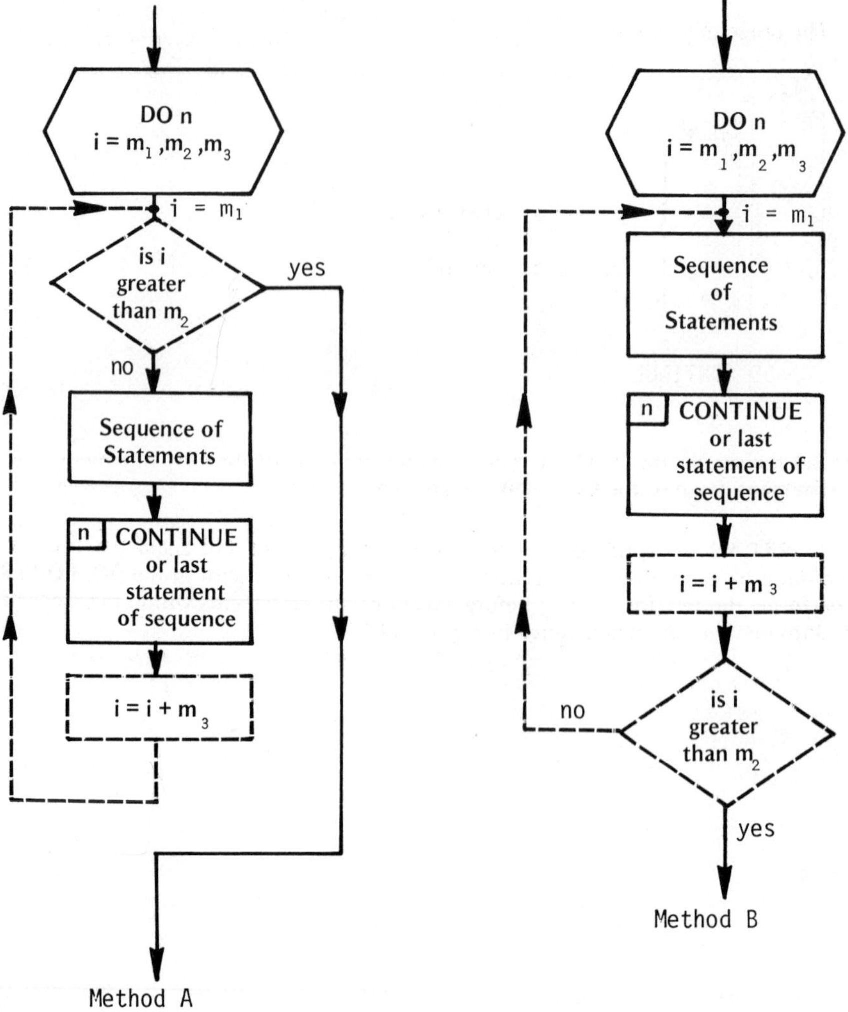

Figure 4.9-1. Detailed Flow Diagram for the DO Loop.

In Method A the test is made before the sequence of statements, and in Method B the test is made after the sequence. While many compilers use Method B, Method A is specified in the new FORTRAN 77 Standard.

My computer uses	Method A ☐	Method B ☐

If m_1 is greater than m_2 Method A will provide a bypass of the specified sequence. Method B will make one pass through the sequence for this condition. Although FORTRAN 66 specified that m_1 must not exceed m_2, some compilers permit it and execute the loop one time; others do not. The following example shows the results in each case.

EXAMPLE

```
123456789...
      M=0
      J=1
      K=0
      DØ 5 I=J,K
         M=M+1
    5 CØNTINUE
    6 ...
```

If test is done first, M=0 at statement 6.

If test is done last, M=1 at statement 6.

> When the above statements are executed on my computer, the value of M at statement 6 is__________.

It would be very tedious to draw out the detailed flow diagrams of Figure 4.9-1 every time a DO loop is to be specified. Simplified flow diagrams can be used to specify this process if the internal operation of the DO loop is kept in mind in writing corresponding FORTRAN statements, they can be used for both methods discussed above and the incrementing and testing is implied in the loop diagram.

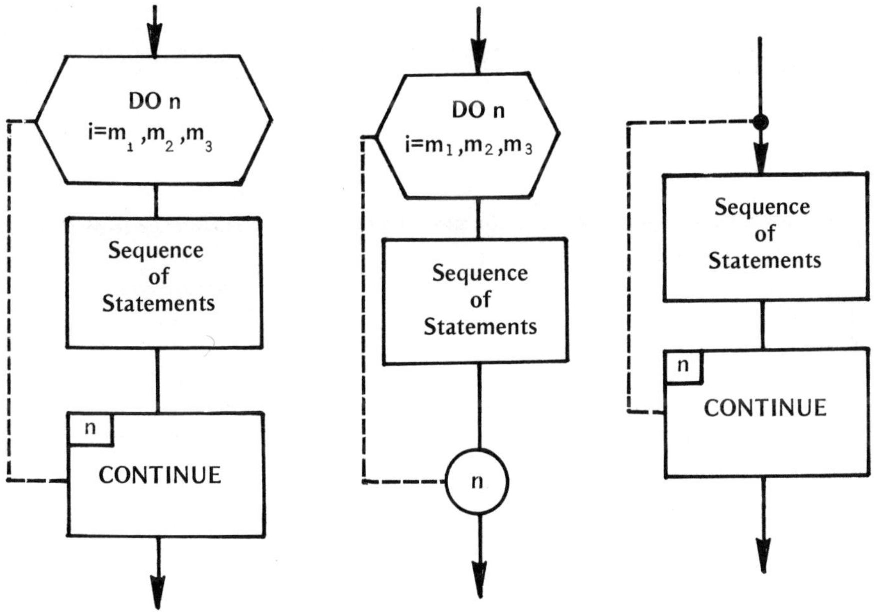

Figure 4.9-2. Practical DO Loop Flow Diagrams.

EXAMPLE

Write a program to sum all even numbers from 50 to and including 60.

```
12345|6|789···
     | |INTEGER SUM
     | |SUM=0
     | |DØ 45 N=50,60,2
     | |  SUM=SUM+N
   45| |CØNTINUE
     | |...
```

The first time through the loop N=50 and N proceeds as follows:

loop	N
1	50
2	52
3	54
4	56
5	58
6	60

The value of the index variable can be used within the loop. The effect of each pass through the loop is to add the increased value of N to the previous accumulated value of SUM. The final value for SUM will then be

SUM=50+52+54+56+58+60

Note: In this book, the block of statements within the DO loop is indented for purposes of clarity. Although indenting is not necessary for the execution of a DO loop, it helps to visualize the DO loop. Some newer processors indent for you.

EXERCISE

Write a program segment to find the sum of all odd numbers from 29 to and including 67.

```
12345|6|789···
     | |
     | |
     | |
     | |
     | |
```

How many times will the loop be executed? Number of time through the loop =______.

4.10

OBJECTIVE: . . . identify execution errors and . . . locate and correct execution errors in your programs written for the problems in this book.

By the time you have reached this section, you may have experienced running several computer programs. No doubt you will have discovered that the odds are against a program running completely and correctly the first time it is submitted. Instead, a program must usually be run several times with errors corrected after each run. Section 2.5 discussed the first kind of error that is usually made, a compilation error. In this section, a second kind of error, an execution error, will be discussed.

After a program has been compiled successfully, the object program is ready to be executed. First, recall what is meant by program execution. During program execution, the set of machine instructions that comprise your object program is executed, starting with the first statement, and continuing sequentially down the statements as they appear from top to bottom on the listing until a statement is encountered that alters this order, such as a DO or STOP statement.

Execution Error

A class of errors, referred to as execution errors, occur during the execution stage. These are errors caused by instructions to the computer to perform tasks which it cannot perform.

Although too numerous to list, a few examples of execution errors are listed below to give you an idea of what to look for:

1. input/output errors, such as forgetting to include the data or improperly specifying it.
2. illegal arithmetic operations, such as division by 0 or taking the square root of a negative number.
3. undefined variable.

Errors can be introduced long before they show up as an execution error. For example, if a variable is undefined, the computer picks up a 'garbage' value and executes on it. This may not show up as an execution error until many steps later, if ever, and it may just result in erroneous results with no execution error ever noted.

Another common way to introduce errors is in using 'integer' arithmetic. For example, if I=0 and J=1 and AVE=(I+J)/2, then AVE=0. not .5. Hence, Y=X/AVE would be a division by 0!

Most but not all execution errors are fatal, that is, they cause execution to halt. It should be noted that execution errors are a bit more tricky to find than compiler errors! One reason for this is that the statement causing the error is not 'flagged' as in compilation.

A second reason for more 'tricky' debugging during execution is that even though we can pinpoint the errant statement, it is not necessarily the 'cause' of the problem. For example, 'bad' data read in may not show up until later on in the program.

Some steps and aids that can be used to debug an execution error are given below.

1. The nature of any diagnostic error message printed when an executive error occurs varies with the computer system. Familiarize yourself with the diagnostic aids of your system.
2. If a specific type of error is mentioned, such as division by 0, scan your program listing to see at which statements such an error could occur.
3. Be sure your input data is correct. After you learn to write output statements, always print out all data that is read in during program testing.
4. When you have learned to write WRITE statements, insert WRITE statements to print out intermediate values to help determine where the incorrect values appear. Hand calculate to see if these values are correct.
5. Check for undefined variables, such as can be caused by misspelling a name.
6. Check initialization of all variables used in DO statements if they are used to calculate sums or products.

Even though your program runs without any error noted, it still does not mean that no errors were made. One must next determine if the answers are correct!

4.11

OBJECTIVE: . . . change the implied type of a variable using subprograms.

NOTE: IF your compiler permits mixed - mode expressions, you may elect to skip this section.

My computer (does / does not) permit mixed-mode expression.

The type specification of a variable name can be modified on a single use basis without changing the designation in other parts of a program. This is done with two subprograms FLOAT(e) and IFIX(e); 'e' is an arithmetic expression of type INTEGER and REAL, respectively.

Some examples of the FLOAT and IFIX are shown below:

```
123456789...
      R=E/FLØAT(I)
      AVE=(A+B+C)/FLØAT(NA+NB+NC)
      NBØX=NCØUNT*IFIX(STACK)
```

FORTRAN 77 permits two additional names which perform the same functions. These names are:

INT is the same as IFIX
REAL is the same as FLOAT

The following examples show REAL and INT used instead of FLOAT and IFIX.

```
123456789...
      R=E/REAL(I)
      AVE=(A+B+C)/REAL(NA+NB+NC)
      NBØX=NCØUNT*INT(STACK)
```

Which names are used on your computer?

Complete the following:

To change an integer to real, use ____________________.
To change a real to an integer, use ____________________.

CHAPTER EXERCISES

1. Which of the following statements are valid (V) and which are invalid (I)?

a) `I = I + 1` ________

b) `R = 2R + 3R` ________

c) `X = 2.* - Y` ________

d) `X = F * (A + (B + C * (D + E))` ________

e) `S = SØ + VØ * T` ________

f) `A = B + C2` ________

g) `A + B = C` ________

h) `Y = X ** 1.5` ________

i) `V = 3.4 E2 + 753.2` ________

j) `VØ = HIGHBALL - H2Ø` ________

2. Write a corresponding FORTRAN expression for each of the following:

a) $\frac{a}{b} + \frac{c}{d}$ ____________________

b) $\frac{a}{b + c}$ ____________________

c) $\frac{1}{2} X^{\frac{1}{2}}$ ____________________

d) $5x^2 + 3x-18$ ____________________

e) $a(b+c)$ ____________________

3. Write a FORTRAN statement for the following equation :

$$y = \frac{X^2}{X+5}$$

1 2 3 4 5	6	7 8 9 · · ·

4. **What value will be stored for A and N?**

```
12345 6 789...
        A=9/2
        N=9./2.
```

A=________

N=________

5. **Indicate the value stored if A=9., B=4.**

```
12345 6 789...
        N=A/B
```

N=________

6. **Write arithmetic statements to assign 8, 6.32, and 23.58 to N, X, and Y, respectively.**

12345	6	789...

7. **What is the purpose of a statement, such as PI=3.1416?**

____

____

8. **Write a DATA statement to accomplish the same requirement as Problem 6.**

12345	6	789...

9. **Write statements for each of the equations.**

$y = (A\cos x_1 + B\sin x_2)e^{at}$ ____________________

$c = \sqrt{a^2 + b^2}$ ____________________

10. Locate several scientific or engineering formulas in your physics, chemistry, or technical textbooks and write FORTRAN statements for each.

equation	FORTRAN statement
______________	______________________________
______________	______________________________
______________	______________________________
______________	______________________________
______________	______________________________

11. What is the purpose of the STOP or CALL EXIT statement?

____

____

12. What is the purpose of the END statement?

____

____

13. What will be the value of IS after this segment of code is executed?

```
123456789...
      IS=1
      DØ 10 K=3,8,2
        IS=IS*K
   10 CØNTINUE
```

IS = __________

CHAPTER PROGRAMMING PROBLEMS

TOPIC APPLICATION
a) Arithmetic statements b) Entering data using arithmetic statements c) Introduction to flow diagram d) Introduction to DO and CONTINUE statements

STATEMENTS SUPPLIED
Flow diagram with the following statements are supplied: a) READ b) WRITE

Problem 4.1

PROBLEM STATEMENT

Compute a table of the altitude of a projectile shot vertically upward after elapsed times of 1 second, 2 seconds, 3 seconds . . . . 10 seconds.

The equation for altitude, s, of a moving object under the influence of gravity is

$$s = s_0 + v_0 t - 1/2\, a t^2$$

where

s = altitude at any instant, t

v_0 = initial velocity at t=0 (160.0 ft/sec)

a = acceleration of gravity (32.2 ft/sec^2)

s_0 = initial altitude at t=0 (10.0 feet)

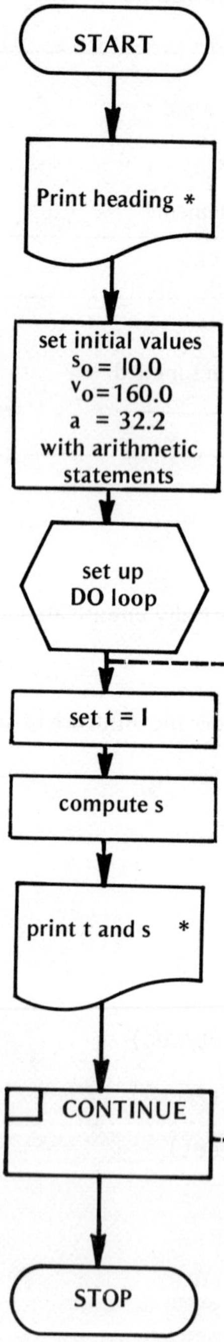
START
Print heading *
set initial values
s_o = 10.0
v_o = 160.0
a = 32.2
with arithmetic
statements
set up
DO loop
set t = I
compute s
print t and s *
CONTINUE
STOP

Notes

1 The START block does not require a statement.

2 All blocks shown in solid lines require one or more statements.

3 Put statements in a sequence corresponding to the flow diagram.

*necessary statements given on next page

Flow Diagram for Problem 4.1

PROCEDURE

Make a Data Table to include (real variable) names for each of the problem variables. Follow the flow diagram, i.e., write necessary arithmetic statements to set the fixed variables to their initial values and to compute the altitudes.

INPUT

No data cards are required for this problem.

OUTPUT

The necessary statements for printing a heading for the table and printing the table are given below. Insert these statements in the program to agree with the given flow diagram.

Statements required to write heading

replace 'd' by your output device number

```
                  1
1 2 3 4 5 6 7 8 9 0 1 2 3 4 5 · · ·
      WRITE(d,10)
   10 FØRMAT('1',34X,'TRAJECTØRY NEGLECTING DRAG'//
     +42X,'TIME    HEIGHT'/)
```

Statements required to write t and s

replace 'd' by your output device number

```
                  1
1 2 3 4 5 6 7 8 9 0 1 2 3 4 5 · · ·

      WRITE(d,20)t,s
   20 FØRMAT(42X,F5.1,3X,F7.1)
```

You must supply valid FORTRAN names for t and s

RESULT

Your solution should show a table of time and height ending with a height of 0.0 at a time of 10 seconds.

Problem 4.2

PROBLEM STATEMENT

Write a program that computes the area of a triangle given the three sides; a, b, and c. The formulas needed are given below. Read in the lengths a, b, and c.

EXERCISE

a) Define a, b, and c with valid FORTRAN names in the FORTRAN Data Table.

b) Code your program on a coding form as outlined on the next page, replacing a, b, and c with your FORTRAN names.

c) Complete the formulas needed to compute the area, A, in the program using the following formulas:

$$s = \frac{a + b + c}{2}$$

$$A = \sqrt{s(s-a)(s-b)(s-c)}$$

d) Code the two control statements needed to terminate the program after the FORMAT statements.

FORTRAN DATA TABLE

PROBLEM NO. ________ PROGRAMMER ________________

DATA ITEM	DEFINITION	UNIT	DATA TYPE[1]	USE[2]	FORTRAN NAME
a	length of side a				
b	length of side b				
c	length of side c				

[1]DATA TYPE: I = Integer, R = Real
[2]USE: I = Input, Ø = Output, T = Temporary, C = Constant

PROGRAM

```
123456789...
C  CØMPUTE THE AREA OF A TRIANGLE GIVEN 3 SIDES
      READ(di,90)a,b,c
      S=
      A=
      WRITE(do,95)a,b,c,A
   90 FØRMAT(3F5.1)
   95 FØRMAT('b',4F10.1)
```

d_i = input device no.
d_o = output device no.

INPUT

Keypunch data card as follows:

```
 18.3 25.6 30.7
123456789012345
  a    b    c
```

Problem 4.3

PROBLEM STATEMENT

Write a program to reverse the digits of any four digit number n. Assign a value to n using a DATA statement. Use the following WRITE statement to print out the original and reverse digits:

For the orginal set of digits   Note: d is your output device number

```
123456789...
      WRITE(d,10)N
   10 FØRMAT('1'//T6,'THE ØRIGINAL NUMBER IS bbb',I4)
```

For the reversed set of digits

```
      WRITE(d,20)N
   20 FØRMAT(//T6,'THE NEW NUMBER IS bbbbbbbb',I4)
```

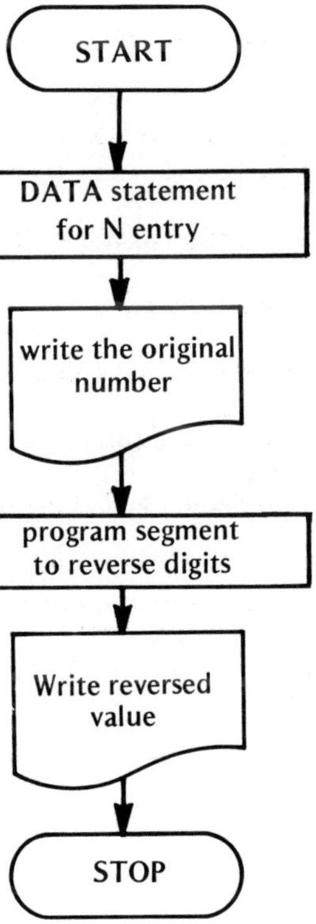
START
DATA statement for N entry
write the original number
program segment to reverse digits
Write reversed value
STOP

FLOW DIAGRAM FOR PROBLEM 4.3

FORTRAN 5

5.1 . . . indicate the function of input/output statements.

5.2 . . . define a record and a data set.

5.3 . . . identify the general form and components and . . . input information using the format-free statement.

5.4 . . . state the general form of the formatted READ statement, and the function of each of its components.

5.5 . . . code for the END-OF-FILE condition.

5.6 . . . indicate the function and general form of the FORMAT statement as it applies to a corresponding READ and . . . state the functions of each of its parts.

5.7 . . . state the nature of format codes and . . . identify the use of I, F, E, T, X, and A format codes.

5.8 . . . read data in I format and indicate which format code goes with each variable . . . specify repetitions of the code using the form aIw.

5.9 . . . select records through the action of the FORMAT statement.

5.10 . . . use the slash (/) in selecting records.

5.11 . . . read real variables using the F format code.

5.12 . . . read in data in E or D exponential form.

5.13 . . . use the tab format control code, T, and the space control format, X, in reading data.

5.14 . . . use parentheses in specifying repetitions of a set of format codes.

5.15 . . . indicate how data is assigned using the A format code and . . . read in character data using the A format.

5.16 . . . read unformatted records.

5.1

OBJECTIVE: . . . indicate the function of input/output statements.

Input and output (I/O) statements are used by the programmer to instruct the computer to select information from a specified input device or provide information to a designated output device. These statements are positioned in the program to input or output information at the proper time.

The basic input statement is the READ statement and the basic output statement is the WRITE statement. Both statements specify the I/O device to be selected and may reference a corresponding FORMAT statement . The FORMAT statement, when used, specifies in detail how to input or output information.

The READ and WRITE with corresponding FORMAT statements operate in a similar manner. This chapter covers the general nature of the READ statement. Much of the information presented, however, will transfer directly to Chapter 6 on WRITE statements.

5.2

OBJECTIVE: . . . define a record and a data set.

A <u>record</u> is a specified subdivision of a <u>data set</u>, which is a collection of similar or related data. Each record is, in turn, divided into fields, whose length is the number of columns it contains, each column representing one character. The data set may be stored on punched cards, disk, paper or magnetic tape or any other permanent storage device. Punched cards will be used to illustrate data input in this text. Each punched card represents a record of 80 card columns.

5.3

OBJECTIVE: . . . identify the general form and components and . . . input information using the format-free READ statement.

The format-free READ statement provides an easy way to input values and assign them to corresponding symbolic names. Some compilers (WATFIV) provide for this statement.

My computer allows the format-free READ.
Yes ☐   No ☐

The general form of the format-free READ statement is:

GENERAL FORM

```
123456789...
      READ, list
```

COMPONENTS

READ is the keyword

list is an input list

EXAMPLE

```
123456789...
      READ,I,N
      READ,A,B,C,J,K
```

Data is keypunched on cards with each data value matching a corresponding name in the list. Data values and corresponding variable names must be of the same type. Data values are separated by one or more blanks or a comma.

EXAMPLE

With the data card

```
23b672b79.8
123456789012345...
```

and the statement

```
12345|6|789···
     | |READ,I,J,X
```

23 will be assigned to I, 672 to J, and 79.8 to X.

EXERCISE

What values of LOT and SIZE will be assigned by the statement

```
12345|6|789···
     | |READ, LOT, SIZE
```

and the data card

```
bb27bb5.32
123456789012345···
```

LOT = 27 SIZE = 5.32

FORTRAN 77 allows free-format READ statements but calls for an asterisk (*) to be used. The above example would be written as

```
12345|6|789···
     | |READ*,LOT,SIZE
```

5.4

OBJECTIVE: . . . state the general form of the formatted READ statement, and the function of each of its components.

The general form of the READ statement is given below. This statement causes one or more records to be read from a data set.

GENERAL FORM	
1 2 3 4 5 | 6 | 7 8 9 ···	
nnnnn	READ(i,n)vn1,vn2,vn3,... (list)

COMPONENTS	
nnnnn	is the statement number
READ	is the keyword that identifies the statement
i	is the data set reference number
n	is the statement number of corresponding FORMAT statement
list	is the set of variable names (vn1,vn2,vn3,...)to be assigned data values.

EXAMPLES

```
123456789...

   10 READ(1,8)X
  200 READ(1,10)ITEM,XRAY
```

The statement number is required only if this statement is referenced by another statement. The data set reference number specifies the input device from which data is to be read. Each computer installation will have designated specific numbers for this purpose. Table 5.4-1 is provided to record the assignment and maximum record length for your computer installation.

Table 5.4-1
Input Device Assignment

DEVICE	DEVICE NUMBER	MAXIMUM COLUMNS
Card Reader		
Disk		
Teletype		
Paper Tape Reader		
Magnetic Tape		

The READ statement identifies the device containing the data to be read, but it does not specify how the data is to be read. The FORMAT statement identified by 'n' describes the exact form and location of the data being read.

The 'list' identifies one or more variable names, separated by commas. Data read from a data set (located by reference number i) is transferred and assigned to locations identified by the list. The statement

```
123456789...
    10 READ(1,8)X
```

will locate a value for X from a punched data card and assign this value to a memory location identified with the variable name 'X'. Internally, the computer assigns a specific address for each such memory location.

5.5

OBJECTIVE: ... code for the END-OF-FILE condition.

A problem occurs when the number of records is not sufficient to satisfy the number of records specified by program READ statements. Various computers behave differently in this situation. FORTRAN 77 provides an option to detect this condition.

GENERAL FORM

```
123456789...
       READ(i,n,END=nt)list
```

The action of the optional END=n_t is to transfer to statement n_t if the number of data cards specified is exceeded. For example, the program

```
123456789...
       ...
    20 READ(1,30,END=99)A
       READ(1,30,END=99)B
       ...
    99 STØP
       END
```

will transfer to statement 99 if only one card or no card is provided in the data set.

When a number of data cards are to be read in, some means must be given to tell when all the values have been read. Some compilers do not have an end-of-data condition check built into the READ statements.

If this is not available, some means must be provided to specify how many input data records are to be read. One way to do this is to specify the number of values, n, on one data card, and then read the data values in using a DO loop as follows:

End of File

```
123456789...
      READ(1,90)N
      DØ 10 I=1,N
        READ(1,92)X,Y
C   PRØCESS RECORD
      ...
   10 CØNTINUE
      ...
```

Note: As each READ statement destroys the previous value of X and Y, the processing statements using X and Y must be in the loop; and the value of X and Y must not be needed any more when the loop is repeated.

An alternative and better method of testing for the end-of-data will be presented in Chapter 10.

EXERCISE

Given the data cards

```
983
123456789...                                      card one
```

```
 44
123456789...                                      card two
```

indicate from which card the values for NOA and NOB will be read by the READ statements:

```
123456789...
    5 READ(1,6)NØA
   10 READ(1,6)NØB
    6 FØRMAT(I4)
```

NØA will be read from card ______________

NØB will be read from card ______________

5.6

OBJECTIVE: . . . indicate the function and general form of the FORMAT statement as it applies to a corresponding READ and . . . state the functions of each of its parts.

The FORMAT statement is used to specify the structure of the records being read and to identify data fields and their locations within the record.

GENERAL FORM

```
123456789...
nnnnn FØRMAT(c1,c2,c3,...,cn)
```

COMPONENTS

nnnnn	is the statement number referenced by a READ statement.
FØRMAT	is the keyword that specifies this type of statement.
$c_1,\ldots,c_n$	are format codes that specify data fields, data type, and data field locations.

EXAMPLES

```
123456789...
   10 FØRMAT(I3)
   20 FØRMAT(3F6.2,T20,I3,3X,3I6)
```

MAT statements are non-executable and may be placed anywhere within the main ıe program.

FORMAT statement may not define a record longer than the maximum allow- ıe input/output device utilized. For the standard card input, it should not define a record longer than 80 characters.

Format codes are used in order from left to right, each code specifying a data field or the beginning of a data field. The first data field begins in column one unless preceded by a positional format code that specifies a different column or that specifies skipping columns.

5.7

OBJECTIVE: . . . state the nature of format codes and . . . identify the use of I, F, E, T, X, and A format codes.

The set of format codes provides a means of defining the number of record columns (field width), type of data, and location of data on each record. The type and use is summarized in the table below:

Table 5.7-1
Types and Use of FORMAT Codes

CODE (C_n)	USED IN SPECIFYING	USED FOR
I	data type/field width	integer data field
F	data type/field width	real data field
E	data type/field width	real data in E notation
A	data type/field width	character data fields
T	location	specifying the position on a record where the next data field starts
X	location	skipping columns within a record

5.8

OBJECTIVE: . . . read data in I format and indicate which format code goes with each variable . . . specify repetitions of the code using the form aIw.

The I format code is used to specify an integer type of data transfer, and the field width of the data in the record. The general form for this code is given below:

GENERAL FORM
`123456789...` `nnnnn FØRMAT(...,aIw,...)`
COMPONENTS

`nnnnn is the statement number`
`a     is the number of times the code is to be repeated`
`I     is the code type`
`w     is the field width`

EXAMPLES

`123456789...`
`    5 FØRMAT(2I4)`
`    6 FØRMAT(I3,I5)`

All blanks within the data field are converted to zeroes by the I format code.

Using the data card

```
4872012763925
123456789 0123456789···
```

the statements

```
123456789···

     READ(1,10)NA,NB,NC
   10 FØRMAT(I1,I3,I2)
```

will assign the following:

Variable	Format Code	No. of Col. in Field	Value Stored
NA	I1	1	4
NB	I3	3	872
NC	I2	2	1

Note that both the variable names in the list and format codes are used from left to right so that

NA is matched with I1

NB is matched with I3

NC is matched with I2

on a one-to-one correspondence. The first field starts in the first column of the data card. Each succeeding field starts in the next column following the last column of the preceding field. In this example, with the format code string I1, I3, I2, the fields can be marked off as follows:

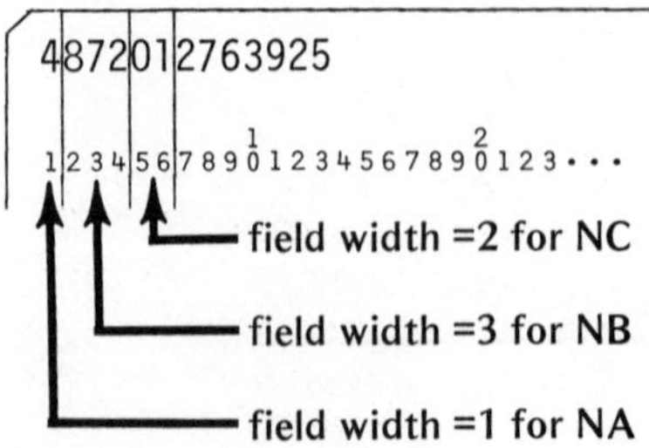

The I format code defines the transfer of data into integer form for storage. The storage format is established by the type of specification defined implicitly by the variable name corresponding to that format code. Since this combination must be compatible, the I FORMAT CODE MUST BE USED WHEN THE CORRESPONDING VARIABLE NAME REPRESENTS AN INTEGER NUMBER.

A repeat number, a, is used to repeat a set of format codes. It multiplies the specification of a given format code.

CODE	EQUIVALENT CODE
aIw 2I3	Iw,Iw,... (repeated "a" times) I3,I3
I1,3I2,2I3	I1,I2,I2,I2,I3,I3

EXAMPLES

1. With the following data cards

1)

```
52713751
123456789...
```

2)

```
16180339
123456789...
```

the values assigned for I and J using the statements

```
12345|6|789...
     |  READ(1,10)I,J
   10|  FØRMAT(I2,I4)
```

will be I = 52, J = 7137;

and with the statements

```
12345678 9...
      READ(1,12)I,J
   12 FØRMAT(2I3)
```

the values assigned for I and J, will be I=527, J=137

2. The values stored for I, J, K, L, M, N using statements

```
123456789...
      READ(1,13) I,J,K
      READ(1,13) L,M,N
   13 FØRMAT(3I2)
```

will be I=52, J=7l, K=37, L=16, M=18, and N=3

EXERCISE

What values of ID1, ID2, and ID3 will be assigned with the data card:

```
56937284
123456789...
```

and statements

```
123456789...
      READ(1,5)ID1,ID2,ID3
    5 FØRMAT(I3,2I2)
```

ID1 = ________________ ID2 = ________________ ID3 = ________________

Each time a "new" READ statement is reached a "new" record is selected. The sequence of statements

```
123456789...
      READ(1,10)X
      READ(1,10)Y
      READ(1,10)Z
   10 FØRMAT(F10.1)
```

would obtain the value of X from one data card and values for Y and Z from the following two data cards, respectively.

Given the data set composed of the three records:

1)
```
23
123456789···
```

2)
```
98
123456789···
```

3)
```
16
123456789···
```

The statement

```
123456789···
      READ(1,10)IX
   10 FØRMAT(I2)
```

would assign a value of 23 to IX.

The statements

```
123456789···
      READ(1,20)M
      READ(1,20)J
      READ(1,20)K
   20 FØRMAT(I2)
```

would assign values of

23 to M
98 to J
16 to K

5.9

OBJECTIVE . . . select records through the action of the FORMAT statement.

A new record is selected each time a READ statement is reached. The corresponding FORMAT statement supplies a string of format codes in order from left to right as written, to satisfy each variable name in the READ list. If the string of format codes is exhausted before the list is satisfied, the action of the FORMAT statement causes termination of that record and the selection of a new one. Reading continues on the new record starting again in column 1.

The means of supplying format codes after the right-hand parenthesis is reached is somewhat complex and is discussed in Section 5.13. In each case, a continuing string of format codes will be supplied until the list is satisfied.

EXAMPLE

I,J, and K will be read from one card using the statements

```
123456789...
      READ(1,10)I,J,K
   10 FØRMAT(3I3)
```

I and J will be read from the first card, and K from the second using the statements

```
123456789...
      READ(1,10)I,J,K
   10 FØRMAT(2I3)
```

5.10

OBJECTIVE: . . . use the slash (/) in selecting records.

The slash is used with the parentheses of a FORMAT statement to indicate the end of a record and the beginning of a new record. Using this means, data can be selected on individual cards within a data deck. Each slash causes a new record to be selected. For card input, the slash causes a new card to be selected.

The slash has the effect of providing multiple records with one FORMAT statement. The statement

$$\text{FORMAT } (c_1, c_2, c_3, \ldots c_n)$$

specifies FORMAT codes for and defines one record. The statement

$$\text{FORMAT } (\underbrace{c_1, c_2, c_3, \ldots}_{\text{record 1}} / \underbrace{c_1, c_2, c_3, \ldots}_{\text{record 2}} / \underbrace{c_1, c_2, c_3, \ldots}_{\text{record 3}})$$

specifies FORMAT codes for three records.

EXAMPLE

Using the statements

```
123456789...
      READ(1,5)I,J,K
    5 FØRMAT(//I3//I2/I5)
```

with the data deck

```
1 239862
2 629906
3 277832
```

4 127899

5 230436

6 189325

will assign the following values

VARIABLE	READ CARD FROM	NO. OF SLASHES	CARDS SKIPPED	VALUE ASSIGNED
		2	2	
I	3			277
		2	1	
J	5			23
		1	0	
K	6			18932

Note that the effect of the slash is to terminate reading on a card and cannot be equated directly to skipping records. Whenever slashes are written at the beginning of a sequence of codes they do have this effect. Thereafter, (n-1) cards are skipped with (n) slashes.

5.11

OBJECTIVE: . . . read real variables using the F format code.

The F format code is used to transfer and convert data to the real form, i.e., as a combination of a fractional part and an exponent. Since the format specification for each variable establishes the conversion made, the correct format code must be used for the type of variable used.

The F code is used for real variables. "F" is used because real numbers were originally called floating point numbers. The F code has the form

GENERAL FORM		
12345	6	789···
nnnnn		FØRMAT(...,aFw.d,...)

COMPONENTS

nnnnn	is the statement number
a	is the number of times the code is to be repeated
F	is the code type
w	is the field width
d	is the number of digits to the right of the decimal place. If a decimal is present in the data, d is ignored.

EXAMPLE		
12345	6	789···
3		FØRMAT(2F6.1,F5.2,F4.0)

The F format code is used in a similar manner as the I code and the field width has the same meaning.

EXAMPLE

Using the data card

```
4872012763925
         1         2
12345678901234567890123···
```

with statements

```
12345 6 789···
          READ(1,10)XRAY
   10     FØRMAT(F5.2)
```

will assign a value of 487.20 to a memory location set up for real data and identified by XRAY.

The assignment will be in the form

VARIABLE	FORMAT CODE	NO. OF COL. IN FIELD	INTERNAL ASSIGNMENT
XRAY	F5.2	5	+ | 03 | 4872000

EXAMPLE 1

Write a READ and FORMAT statement to read in values for R1, R2, and R3 from the data card shown below if

$$
\begin{aligned}
R1 &= 23.68 \\
R2 &= 8.62 \\
R3 &= 60.08
\end{aligned}
$$

```
2368b8626008
                  1                   2
1 2 3 4 5 6 7 8 9 0 1 2 3 4 5 6 7 8 9 0 1 2 3 . . .
 R1      R2      R3
```

```
1 2 3 4 5|6|7 8 9

         |READ(1,18)R1,R2,R3
       18|FØRMAT(3F4.2)
```

In the preceding example, the decimal point was omitted on the data card, and the format code was used to specify this information. A decimal point included within the specified field will override this action as shown below:

DATA CARD	CODE	VALUE ASSIGNED
365.2 1 2 3 4 5 6 7 8 9 . . .	F5.2	365.2
5.38 1 2 3 4 5 6 7 8 9 . . .	F5.3	5.38
-53.2 1 2 3 4 5 6 7 8 9 . . .	F6.3	-53.2

Real and integer variable types can also be mixed in the READ and FORMAT statements.

Statements

```
12345|6|789···
     | |
     | |READ(1,20)I,X,J,Y
   20| |FØRMAT(I2,F3.1,I3,F3.1)
```

with data card

```
63|693|258|621|532278
           1          2
12|345|678|901|234567890123···
 I| X | J | Y |
```

> **PT's***
>
> If the decimal is included in the data field and the fields are separated by blanks, you can visually check your data easier and will have fewer data errors.
>
> *Prescriptive tenet

will yield

I = 63 X = 69.3

J = 258 Y = 62.1

EXERCISE

With data card

```
681208937
123456789···
```

and statements

```
12345|6|789···
     | |
     | |READ(1,50)ITEM,CØST
   50| |FØRMAT(I2,F4.2)
```

what value of ITEM and COST will be assigned?

ITEM ________ COST________

5.12

OBJECTIVE: . . . read in data in E or D exponential form.

The E or D format codes are used to read data as real numbers with E or D exponents.

GENERAL FORM
1 2 3 4 5 6 7 8 9 ...
nnnnn FØRMAT(...,aEw.d,...)
nnnnn FØRMAT(...,aDw.d,...)
COMPONENTS
a is the number of times the code is repeated
E is the code for single precision real numbers
D is the code for double precision real numbers
w is the field width
d is the number of decimal places in the data if no decimal point is present. If a decimal point is present in the data, d is ignored.

Single and double precision real numbers were presented in Section 3.2 and should be reviewed before proceeding. Other than differing in data form, the E and D codes operate in the same manner as the F format code. Table 5.11-1 illustrates the action of these codes.

Table 5.11-1
Valid Forms of E and D Format Codes

Example	Data/field	Format Code	Value
	123456789 ...		
1	48+08	E5.1	4.8E+08
2	163246+09	D9.3	163.246D+09
3	6235-1	E7.2	62.35E-10
4	9872E+02	E9.0	9872.E+20
5	-323E-5	E7.2	-3.23E-05
6	62.3E+0	E7.2	62.3E+00

Note: In Example 4, the field width is from Column 1 through Column 9. This places a blank in Column 9 which is read as a zero in transferring the exponent into storage. The result is an exponent of 20 rather than 2. The exponent in the E-format code must be right-justified in the field.

5.13

OBJECTIVE: . . . Use the tab format control code, T, and the space control format, X, in reading data.

The tab "T" and space "X" codes are used for locating data fields which are not in sequential form. The T code is not available on compilers meeting the minimum standards of FORTRAN '66

The T code is available in FORTRAN at my computer installation.
Yes ☐ No ☐

The T code is used to specify the column in which reading begins and has the form

GENERAL FORM

```
12345 6 789...
nnnnn   FØRMAT(...,Tc,...)
```

COMPONENTS

```
nnnnn is the statement number

T     is the tab format code

c     is the first column of the following field speci-
        fication
```

EXAMPLES

```
12345 6 789...
   23   FØRMAT(T10,F3.1,T20,I3)
```

The use of FORMAT (T18, I6) places the beginning of the field specified by I6 in column 18.

EXAMPLE 1

Read data for variables ID1, ID2, ID3, and ID4 in I3 format from fields starting in columns 1, 11, 21 and 31.

```
123456789...
      READ(1,10)ID1,ID2,ID3,ID4
   10 FØRMAT(I3,T11,I3,T21,I3,T31,I3)
```

EXERCISE

What values will be read by the statements

```
123456789...
      READ(1,20)IN1,IN2,IN3
   20 FØRMAT(T5,I2,T10,I2,T14,I3)
```

and the data card

```
89265478320013278
         1         2
12345678901234567890123456789...
```

IN1 = ________ IN2 = ________ IN3 = ________

The X code is used to skip columns. This format code has the form:

GENERAL FORM

```
123456789...
nnnnn FØRMAT(...,nX,...)
```

COMPONENTS

nnnnn	is statement number
n	is an integer number of columns to be skipped
X	is skip format code

EXAMPLES

```
123456789...
    5 FØRMAT (F5.1,2X,F6.2)
    6 FØRMAT (I2,5X,I3)
```

EXAMPLE 2

Rewrite the FORTRAN statement of the previous Example 1 using the X format code.

```
12345|6|789...
     | |READ(1,10)ID1,ID2,ID3,ID4
   10| |FØRMAT(I3,7X,I3,7X,I3,7X,I3)
```

It should be noted that for the case where one column is to be skipped, n must be specified as 1 and is not implied as in mathematical usage.

EXERCISE

What values will be read by the statements

```
12345|6|789...
     | |READ(1,5)A,B
    5| |FØRMAT(4X,F6.2,2X,F2.1)
```

and the data card

```
18324677783264901 62
         1         2
12345678901234567890123...
```

A = ________ B = ________

5.14

OBJECTIVE: . . . use parentheses in specifying repetitions of a set of format codes.

The group repeat specification is used to repeat a set of format codes. The group repeat count is the same as the repeat number which can be placed in front of other format codes. An example of using the group format specification is as follows:

```
12345 6 789...
   10 FØRMAT(I2,2(I3,I4,I5),I6)
```

This format is the same as the following:

```
12345 6 789...
   10 FØRMAT(I2,(I3,I4,I5,I3,I4,I5),I6)
```

When format control reaches the last (outer) right parenthesis of the format specification, a test is made to determine if another element is specified in the list. If not, control terminates. However, if another list element is specified, the format control demands that a new record start. Control, therefore, reverts to that group repeat specification terminated by the last preceding right parenthesis, or if none exists, then to the first left parenthesis of the format specification. If the group repeat count is omitted, a count of one is assumed.

EXAMPLE

Match the variable in the READ list with the format code specified by the FORMAT statement as specified by

```
12345 6 789...
        READ(1,15)N,A,B,C,D,E
   15 FØRMAT(I2,(F6.1,F9.2))
```

The first record is read for N, A, and B, according to I2, F6.1, F9.2, respectively. Then because the list is not exhausted, control returns to the last group repeat specification. The next record is read and values are transmitted to C and D according to F6.1 and F9.2, respectively, with the F6.1 code starting in column 1. Since there are still items in the list, another record is read and a value for E is transmitted by F6.1. As the list is now exhausted, the remaining format code F9.2, is not now used.

The previous example illustrates the nesting of group format specifications.

((   ))

The degree of nesting permitted varies with the computer and compiler. Some allow two degrees of nesting, such as:

((( ))   )

> PT's*
>
> The simplest FORMAT is the easiest for the beginner. This will mean writing additional READ statements to avoid long and complicated FORMAT statements, which require nested parentheses.
>
> *Preventing Trouble

> My computer allows ______ degrees of nesting.

EXAMPLES

Examples of the compactness obtained by nesting is shown by the following:

NESTED SPECIFICATION	EQUIVALENT
(I3,2(I2,F6.1))	(I3,(I2,F6.1,I2,F6.1))
(2(I2,2(I4,I5),I3))	(I2,I4,I5,I4,I5,I3,I2,I4,I5,I4,I5,I3)
(2(I2,F3.1))	(I2,F3.1,I2,F3.1)

However, a recommended practice is to avoid complicated FORMAT specifications with nested parentheses as much as possible. One way to do this is to use uniform FORMAT codes for data items of the same type, chosing a field width large enough to accomodate the largest data item.

Using I5 for each data item, the FORMAT specification

(2(I2,2(I4,I5),I3))

simplifies to (12I5)

5.15

OBJECTIVE: . . . indicate how data is assigned using the A format code and . . . read in character data using the A format.

A portion of the data processed by the computer consists of character data or literal data that is used to identify output and provide titles and headings. All members of the FORTRAN character set may be used as character data. Character data may be entered into memory by means of a READ statement with FORMAT specification of A, meaning alphanumeric data. As character data is not numeric data, it may not be used for computation, but it may be used in decision making. A-field data may be assigned to FORTRAN variables with integer or real variable names. Once character data is assigned in a memory location by a given name, it may be moved to other locations of the same name type by means of an assignment statement, but it may not be moved to a variable having a name of a different type.

The A format code is used to read in character data and has the general form:

```
GENERAL FORM
123456789...
nnnnn FØRMAT(...,aAw,...)

COMPONENTS
nnnnn   is the statement number
a       is the number of times the code is to be repeated
A       is the alphanumeric format code.
w       is the field width
```

The number of characters that can be assigned in one memory location depends on the number of bits per memory location. Table 5-15.1 gives the number of characters of alphanumeric data that can be assigned for different computers.

Fill in the table for your computer.

Table 5.15-1
Characters/Cell for Several Computers

Computer	No. Bits/ Cell	No. Alphanumeric Characters/Cell
IBM 1130	16	2
IBM 360/370	32	4
UNIVAC 1108 UNIVAC 1100/42	36	6
CDC 6000/7000	60	10
Your Computer		

For example, in a 32-bit word computer, a field width (w) of four assigns the maximum number of characters that can be assigned under one variable name. For example, if it is desired to read names from columns 1 through 15 from a card, such as

```
JØHNbHANCØCKbbb
        1
1234|5678|9012|345|678...
NM1   NM2  NM3 NM4
```

Figure 5.15-1. Sample Data Card.

then four variable names will be required. In Figure 5.15-1, groups of four columns have been marked off with the exception of the last group which will have three columns to complete the field through column 15. Each group is assigned a different variable name. The required READ statement is then

```
12345|6|789···
     | |READ(1,10)NM1,NM2,NM3,NM4
```

Since NM1, NM2, and NM3 have field widths (w) of 4, the required format code for each is A4. NM4 has a field width of 3 requiring a format code of A3. The required FORMAT statement is then.

```
12345|6|789···
   10| |FØRMAT(3A4,A3)
```

EXAMPLE

The identity (in alphanumeric form) of an experimental test is punched into columns 43 through 60. Write the necessary READ and FORMAT to read this information into a computer which uses four characters per location. Use the integer variable names ID1, ID2, . . . IDn.

Determine the number of columns.

$$\begin{array}{r} 60 \\ -43 \\ \hline 17 \\ +1 \\ \hline 18 \end{array}$$

Determine the number of names required.

$$\frac{18}{4} = 4 + \frac{2}{4}$$

Therefore, 5 names are required using

4A4
1A2

The required READ/FORMAT statement set is then

```
12345|6|789···
     | |READ(1,10)ID1,ID2,ID3,ID4,ID5
   10| |FØRMAT(T43,4A4,A2)
```

If your computer stores other than four characters per location, do the following exercise.

EXERCISE

Write the READ and FORMAT statements for the example on the preceding page.

12345	6	789···

Standard codes have been established so that all peripheral devices, such as keypunches, card readers, and printers, can communicate with the computer. Appendix C explains the Hollerith code that is used to store data by means of punched holes on a card. It also explains the Extended Binary Codes Decimal Interchange Code (EBCDIC) which is used for representing data in memory.

5.16

OBJECTIVE: ... read unformattted records.

In this chapter, two forms of the READ statement (formatted and format-free) were presented. Both of these read formatted records. A formatted record consists of a sequence of characters represented in a standard coded form acceptable for printing whereas an unformatted record is a sequence of values in a computer-dependent form. This form is a direct transfer of the internal data representation without being converted to a standard code. It is a more compact form and is frequently used for storing large quantities of data on disk or magnetic tape. It is considerably faster since conversion to standard code is not required; however, it is computer dependent and should not be used when portability is a factor. Since it is not in readable character form, it is not suitable for a punched card or printed output.

The form of the READ statement to read unformatted records (which must have been written by a unformatted write statement) is as follows:

GENERAL FORM

```
123456789···
nnnnn READ(i)list
```

COMPONENTS

```
nnnnn is an optional statement number

READ  is the keyword

i     is the data set reference number

list  is the list of data items to be read
```

EXAMPLES

```
123456789···
      READ(9) A,B,C,D,E,F
```

CHAPTER EXERCISES

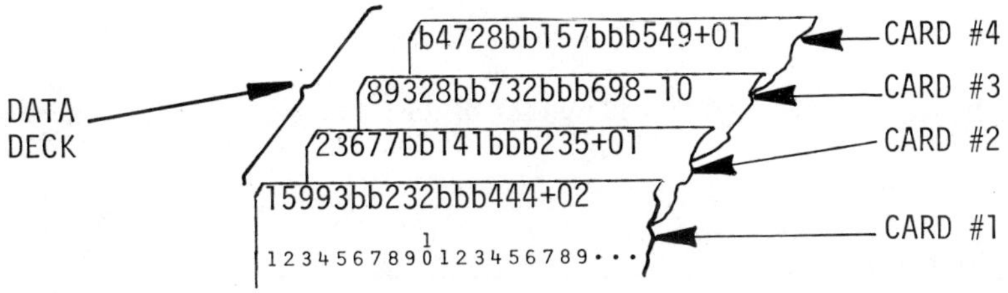

Questions 1 through 4 should be answered assuming that the complete data deck above is used for each problem.

1. What values of IX and IY will be assigned using the following statements:

```
      READ(1,3)IX,IY
    3 FØRMAT(I2,I3)
```

IX = ______
IY = ______

2. What values of ITEM and XRAY will be assigned using the following statements:

```
      READ(1,8)ITEM,XRAY
    8 FØRMAT (//T2,I2,T8,F3.0)
```

ITEM = ______
XRAY = ______

3. What values of I1, I2, I3, and I4 will be assigned by the following statements:

```
      READ (1,12)I1,I2,I3,I4
   12 FØRMAT (2I2)
```

I1 = ______
I2 = ______
I3 = ______
I4 = ______

4. What value of MASS and FORCE will be assigned by the following statements:

```
      REAL MASS
      READ(1,14)MASS,FORCE
   14 FØRMAT(///2X,F3.2,T14,E6.2)
```

MASS = ____________

FØRCE = ____________

5. Given the following:

```
      READ(1,10)ALPHA, BETA, GAMA
   10 FØRMAT(F6.2,F4.2,F10.3)
```

How many card columns would be read?

Answer ____________

6. How many cards would be required to complete the list of the READ with FORMAT statements below?

```
      READ(1,100) A, B, C, D, E, F, G
  100 FØRMAT(3F10.3)
```

Answer ____________

7. Given the following data card:

```
530435678922100579 23
         1         2
12345678901234567890...
```

Indicate the values(s) "read" by each of the following FORMAT statements

a) FORMAT(I3) ____________

b) FORMAT(F7.2) ____________

c) FORMAT(T3,I4) ____________

d) FORMAT(5X,I2) ____________

e) FORMAT (T10,I2,2X,F3.0) ____________

CHAPTER PROGRAMMING PROBLEMS

TOPIC APPLICATION

a) Arithmetic statements
b) READ statement with corresponding FORMAT statements
c) Type specification statements

STATEMENTS SUPPLIED

a) WRITE statements with corresponding FORMAT statements

Problem 5.1

PROBLEM STATEMENT

In the various fields of Engineering and Science it sometimes is necessary to perform a sequence of arithmetic calculations. In this problem, three short calculations from the electrical field are specified. The programmer need not be knowledgeable about electric circuits since the necessary equations are specified along with given variables and their values.

Three values are to be calculated: X_L (inductive reactance of inductor L), X_c (capacitive reactance of capacitor C) and f_R (the resonant frequency of the L-C combination). The necessary equations are:

for inductive reactance $X_L = 2\pi f L$

for capacitive reactance $X_C = \frac{1}{2\pi f C}$

for resonant frequency $f_R = \frac{1}{2\pi\sqrt{LC}}$

where
L = inductance
C = capacitance
f = frequency
π = constant

INPUT

Test this program using the following values:

L = 0.382
f = 60.
C = $139. \times 10^{-9}$
π = 3.1416

Complete the Data Table below:

DATA ITEM	DEFINITION	UNIT	DATA TYPE	USE	FORTRAN NAME
L					L
f					
C					
π					
X_L					XL
X_C					XC
f_R					FR

[1] DATA TYPE: I = Integer, R = Real, A = Alphanumeric,
[2] USE: I = Input, Ø = Output, T = Temporary, C = Constant

Use the following flow diagram as a guide in writing the required statements:

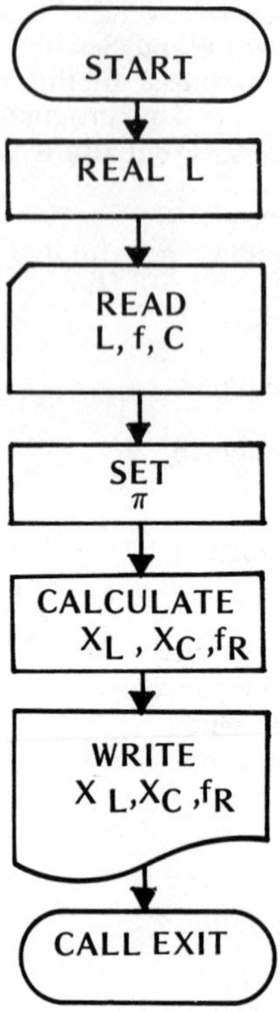
START
REAL L
READ
L, f, C
SET
π
CALCULATE
XL , XC ,fR
WRITE
X L,XC ,fR
CALL EXIT

Flow Diagram for Problem 5.1

Using one READ and corresponding FORMAT statement, read data from the following card:

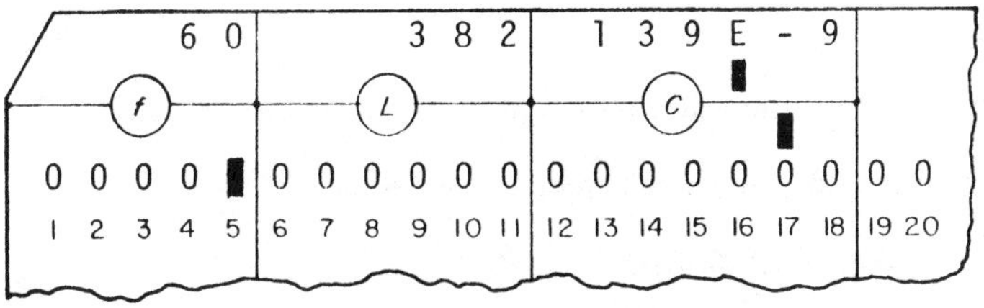

Use a type specification statement to override the implicit definition of L as an integer variable.

The type specification statement should precede all other program cards.

Use the following statements to readout values of X_L, X_C, and f_R

```
123456789...
      WRITE(do,10)XL
   10 FØRMAT(//T10,'XL=',F11.2)
      WRITE(do,15)XC
   15 FØRMAT(T10,'XC=',F11.2)
      WRITE(do,20)FR
   20 FØRMAT(T10,'FR=',F11.2)
```

NOTE: d_o is your output device number

NOTE: The algebraic notations, X_L, X_C, f_R, when written in your FORTRAN program should use the following FORTRAN names: XL, XC, FR

Problem 5.2

PROBLEM STATEMENT

The velocity and acceleration of a body moving about the center of a circle of radius, r, and taking time, t, for a complete revolution is given by the following formulas: (Assume the magnitude of the velocity is constant.)

$$v = \frac{2\pi r}{t}$$

$$a = \frac{v^2}{r}$$

EXERCISE

Write a program to compute the velocity of the moon and the acceleration of the moon toward the earth. Choose appropriate fields on a data card for your input data and write the READ and FORMAT statements that will read your data. Include the WRITE and FORMAT statements provided below to print your input data and results. Begin your program by completing the data table and flow diagram below. Test your program with the following input values:

INPUT DATA

$r = 12.6 \times 10^8$ ft (radius of rotation of the moon about the earth)

$t = 23.4 \times 10^5$ sec (time of a complete revolution)

OUTPUT WRITE AND FORMATS

```
123456789...                          Note: do = output device number
      WRITE(do,92)r,t
   92 FØRMAT('1RAD=b',E12.3,3X,'bTIME=',E12.3/)
      WRITE(do,94)v,a
   94 FØRMAT('bVELØCITYbØFbMØØNb',1X,E13.3,'bFT/SEC.'/
     1'bACCEL.bØFbMØØNbTØWARDbEARTH',E13.3,'bFT/SEC**2')
```

DATA TABLE

DATA ITEM	DEFINITION	UNIT	DATA TYPE[1]	USE[2]	FORTRAN NAME

[1]DATA TYPE: I = Integer R = Real, A = Alphanumeric
[2]USE: I = Input, O = Output, T = Temporary, C = Constant

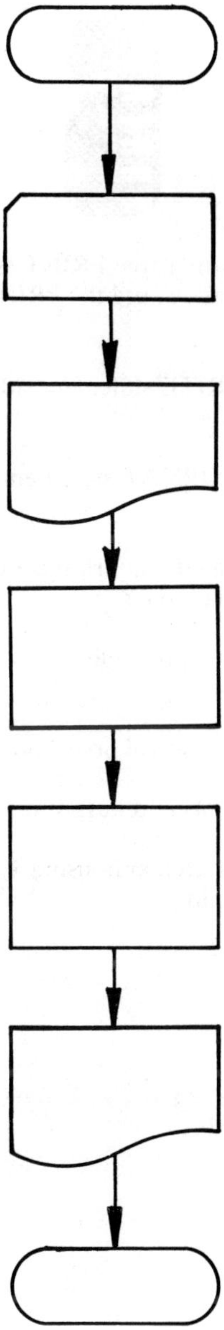

FLOW DIAGRAM

Problem 5.2

FORTRAN 6

6.1 ... specify the use of the format-free PRINT statement, identify its general form, and define each of its parts ... use the PRINT statement to output information in a printed form.

6.2 ... specify the use of the WRITE statement, identify the general form, and define each of its parts.

6.3 ... specify the use of the FORMAT statement that is used with a corresponding WRITE statment.

6.4 ... identify a record as defined for printed output and . . . use parentheses to specify repetition of format codes.

6.5 ... write character data using apostrophes and the H code ... use the slash to provide spacing.

6.6 ... specify means for carriage control on output to a line printer.

6.7 ... use the slash for selecting printed output records.

6.8 ... construct valid WRITE statements using I, F, E, T, X, and A format codes with repetitions and grouping.

6.9 ... write unformatted records.

6.1

OBJECTIVE: . . . specify the use of the format-free PRINT statement, identify its general form, and define each of its parts . . . use the PRINT statement to output in a printed form.

The format-free PRINT statement is an easy way to print data values. However, not all compilers have this format-free capability.

> My computer [does / does not] have the format-free statement.

The PRINT statement allows the programmer to provide an output of desired values on a printed page. The general form for the PRINT statement is

GENERAL FORM

```
12345 6 789...
        PRINT list
```

COMPONENTS

```
PRINT  is the keyword

list   is a list of variable names whose values are to
          be printed
```

EXAMPLES

```
12345 6 789...
        PRINT X,Y
        PRINT I,J,K
        PRINT A,B,ID
```

Integer values will be printed as integer numbers. The maximum number of digits and number of values per line depend on the computer and compiler used.

> My computer system allows up to ___ digits with up to ___ values per line.

Integer values will be right-justified or shifted to the right-most column of the allocated field.

Real values will be printed in exponential form and will have several parts: leading blanks, sign "–" for negative and "b" for positive, a leading zero, a decimal point, digits representing the number, "E", the sign of the exponent, and an exponent. A real number is printed in a form such as:

```
bbbs0.nnnnnnnEsnn
 |  |    |    ||
 |  |    |    |└─exponent
 |  |    |    └─sign of the exponent
 |  |    └─number
 |  └─sign of the number
 └─leading blanks
```

> The real output form for my computer is
>
> __________________________________
>
> with up to __________ values per line.

This method provides a simple form to print out values but is restricted to the specific format provided by the compiler.

6.2

OBJECTIVE: . . . specify the use of the WRITE statement, identify the general form, and define each of its parts.

The general form of the WRITE statement is shown below. This statement causes one or more records to be written to a specified output device.

GENERAL FORM	
12345 6 7 8 9 . . .	
nnnnn	WRITE(i,n) $\underbrace{vn_1, vn_2, vn_3}_{\text{list}}, \ldots$

COMPONENTS	
nnnnn	is the statement number (optional)
WRITE	is the keyword that identifies the statement
i	is the data set reference number
n	is the statement number of the corresponding FORMAT statement
list	is the set of variable names (vn_1, vn_2, vn_3, . . .) for which the data values are to be transferred to the output device referenced.

EXAMPLES

```
12345 6 789...

       WRITE(3,25)
       WRITE(3,10)X,Y,Z
  300  WRITE(N,100)I,J
```

The statement number is required only if this statement is referenced by another statement. The data set reference number specifies the output device to which the data values of the list items are to be transferred. Each computer installation will have designated specific numbers to the output devices that they use. Table 6.2-1 shows examples of typical output devices. Complete the table to record the assignments for your installation .

Table 6.2-1
Output Device Assignments

DEVICE	UNIT NUMBER	MAX. LENGTH OF RECORD
Printer	______	__________
Card Punch	______	__________
Disk	______	__________
Tape	______	__________
Other ________	______	__________

The statement number 'n' references a FORMAT statement. Just as with a READ statement, the WRITE statement identifies the device and list elements but it does not specify the form the data is to have. The FORMAT statement specified by the n describes the exact form and placement that the data will have on the output medium.

The list may be blank or contain one or more variable names, separated by commas. A WRITE statement with no list is used to write character data and is discussed in Section 6.5.

If the list contains one or more variable names, the data values of these variables are transferred from memory to the output device in the form and location given in the FORMAT. The following statements would cause the values for XR, XC, and QR to be printed.

```
123456789...

      WRITE (3,30) XR,XC,QR
   30 FØRMAT (3F10.1)
```

6.3

OBJECTIVE: . . . specify the use of the FORMAT statement that is used with a corresponding WRITE statement.

The FORMAT statement referenced by a WRITE statement is used to specify the form and location of the data values specified in the WRITE list.

GENERAL FORM	
1 2 3 4 5 6 7 8 9 · · ·	
nnnnn	FØRMAT (c_1,c_2,c_3,...c_n)

COMPONENTS	
nnnnn	is the statement number referenced by a WRITE statement
FØRMAT	is the keyword
c_1,c_2,c_3...	are the format codes that specify data fields, data types, and data field locations

EXAMPLES

```
123456789...

   10 FØRMAT('b',I3,I2)
   30 FØRMAT(//1X,3F10.1,I2,3F8.2)
   40 FØRMAT(2X,F3.1,T30,F4.1)
```

The rules for FORMAT statements referenced by WRITE statements are similar to those for READ statements; namely,

1. FORMAT statements are non-executable statements and may be placed anywhere before the END statement in the program unit.

2. The FORMAT statement may not define a record longer than the maximum allowable size for the output device used. If a record is to be printed, it should not exceed the printer's line length. If the record were to be punched, it could not exceed the 80 punched columns on a card.

3. FORMAT codes are used in order left to right, each code specifying the data field of the list element whose order corresponds to it.

4. If there are more FORMAT codes than list items, unused codes are ignored.

5. If there are more list items than format codes, the format codes are repeated from the last parentheses group. This is illustrated in Section 6.4.

6. Each c_i represents a format code. These codes are discussed in Section 6.8.

6.4

OBJECTIVE: ... identify a record as defined for printed output and ... use parentheses to specify repetition of format codes.

When specified by the program, data is gathered from the diverse memory locations of the list elements and placed into a record which is transferred to the output device. If the output device is a printer, a record corresponds to the number of print positions on a printed line. This number varies with different printers. Two frequent printer line lengths are 121 or 133 characters, all except the first being used for data.

The line length for my computer is 132 characters.

For printed output, the first character of a record is a carriage control character which is explained in Section 6.6.

The parentheses of the FORMAT statement define one record. When the right parenthesis is reached, the record is terminated. If the number of variable names in the list of the WRITE statements is less than or equal to the number of format codes within the parentheses of the FORMAT, the write operation is complete for the WRITE statement.

EXAMPLE 1

In this example, the number of list elements is equal to the number of format codes. Upon reaching the right parenthesis, the record is terminated and one output line containing three values is written.

```
123456789...
C    EXAMPLE 1
      WRITE (3,100)N,X,Y
  100 FØRMAT(I5,F10.1,F12.2)
```

EXAMPLE 2

In this example, the number of list elements is less than the number of format codes. When all list element values have been printed, the remaining field specifications are ignored and the record is terminated. One output line which contains two values is printed.

```
123456789...
C    EXAMPLE 2
      WRITE(3,50)A,B
   50 FØRMAT(F10.1,F12.3,F15.1)
```

EXAMPLE 3

In this example, the number of variables in the output list is greater than the number of format codes. When the computer is executing this write operation, upon reaching the last right parenthesis, the current record is terminated. Then a search is made from right to left until the next right parenthesis is found. If no right parenthesis is found before encountering the left parenthesis, the entire FORMAT will be repeated. Each time the right parenthesis is reached, another record is terminated. This process is continued until all list items have been exhausted.

The following WRITE causes three lines to be printed, two values per line.

```
123456789...
C  EXAMPLE 3
      WRITE(3,5)A,B,C,D,E,F
    5 FØRMAT(F10.1,F12.2)
```

OUTPUT

```
         1         2
1234567890123456789012345...
1   A(F10.1)   B(F12.2)
2   C(F10.1)   D(F12.2)
3   E(F10.1)   F(F12.2)
```

EXAMPLE 4

If the list is not exhausted when the final right parenthesis is reached, then a backward search from right to left is made until another right parenthesis is found. The parenesis group to which the first right parenthesis found during this search belongs is used for all the remaining list elements.

Each time this inner parentheses group is exhausted, the right-most outer parenthesis is encountered and another record is terminated. The following WRITE statement will print four lines as shown.

```
123456789...
C  EXAMPLE 4
      WRITE(3,7)N,T,A,X1,Y1,X2,Y2,X3,Y3
    7 FØRMAT(I5,(F5.1,F6.1))
```

OUTPUT

	Value of	Code Used	Value of	Code Used	Value of	Code Used
1	N	I5	T	F5.1	A	F6.1
2	X1	F5.1	Y1	F6.1		
3	X2	F5.1	Y2	F6.1		
4	X3	F5.1	Y3	F6.1		

6.5

OBJECTIVE: . . . write character data using apostrophes and the H code . . . use the slash to provide spacing.

Character data is alphanumeric data (i.e., letters, digits, and special characters) used to supply headings, labels and comment information to make printed output meaningful. One way to supply this information is by using a WRITE statement with a blank list.

Since the list is blank, no data values are transferred; however, alphanumeric information, such as titles, labels, and messages contained in the specified FORMAT, would be written. There are two ways of supplying the alphanumeric data with the FORMAT statement.

We use the FORTRAN 77 method in this book, which is to write a string of characters, enclosed in apostrophes.

If your computer does not permit the use of apostrophes, the FORMAT would be written using the H code.

EXAMPLE

```
123456789...
    10 FØRMAT(T50,19HREGRESSIØN ANALYSIS)
```

The count (19) must be equal to the number of characters specified. It must also count any blank which is meaningful in alphanumeric data.

If this is the only method approved for your computer, convert each of the FORMAT statements containing literal data enclosed in apostrophes to the H format code for each example below.

The following WRITE and FORMAT statement would cause the title, REGRESSION ANALYSIS, to be printed:

```
123456789...
       WRITE(3,10)
    10 FØRMAT(T50,'REGRESSIØN ANALYSIS')
```

It is frequently desirous to intersperse character and numerical data as shown in the next example.

```
1 2 3 4 5|6|7 8 9 . . .
          |WRITE(3,5)ITEMP
         5|FØRMAT('bTHE AVE. TEMP WASbbb',I3,
         +|1X,'DEGS.')
```

The printed output would look as follows:

OUTPUT

```
              1                   2                   3
 1 2 3 4 5 6 7 8 9 0 1 2 3 4 5 6 7 8 9 0 1 2 3 4 5 6 7 8 9 0 1 2 3 . . .
1 bTHE AVE. TEMP WAS...nnn.DEGS.
2
3
```

A different way to supply character information without using the FORMAT statement is to read in and write out alphanumeric data by means of an 'A' format. This is discussed in Section 6.8.

6.6

OBJECTIVE: . . . specify means for carriage control on output to a line printer.

For line printer output, the output FORMAT must supply a carriage control character as the first character of each record. The examples in this book use the printer only. The first character of each record is not printed. If the programmer does not supply a carriage control character, whatever character is in the first column of the record will be used by the printer, resulting in unpredictable spacing and paging, and a character of output will be lost. The carriage control characters are given in Table 6.6-1.

Table 6.6-1
Carriage Control Characters

CHARACTER	NUMBER OF LINES ADVANCED BEFORE PRINTING THE RECORD
+	No advance
blank	1 line (single spacing)
0	2 lines (double spacing)
1	Advance to top of a new page before printing

The most straightforward way to supply the carriage control character is as an alphanumeric character. There are two ways of doing this. The first way (FORTRAN 66) is by using an H format code as follows:

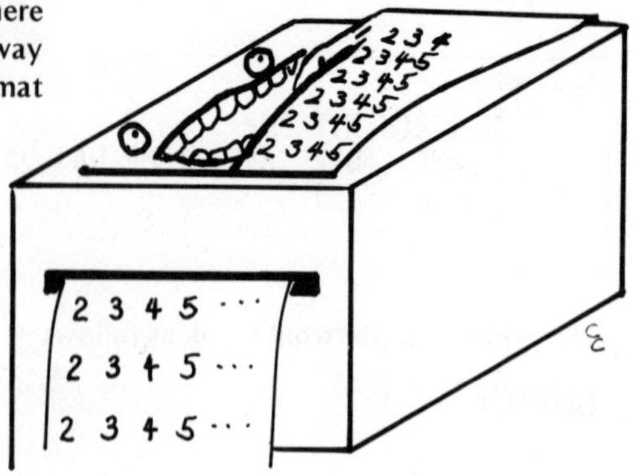

The printer 'eats' the first character.

```
123456789...
    77 FØRMAT(1H1,...)
```

This specifies that the first character of the record is a '1', signifying a new page.

This was a standard method until FORTRAN 77. It is the most universal way to supply the carriage control character. However, many computer systems extended FORTRAN 66 to permit the use of the apostrophe in place of the H format code. This method is now included in the FORTRAN 77 Standard. The previous FORMAT example would be written as follows:

```
123456789...
    77 FØRMAT('1',...)
```

Both methods are presented but the second method will be used in the examples of the text, since it is already available on many computers.

Complete the following:

My computer [does / ~~does not~~] permit use of apostrophes in FORMAT statements in place of the H format code.

The next FORMAT statement specifies double spacing between the printed lines.

```
12345|6|789...
     | |
     | |WRITE(3,13)X1,Y1,X2,Y2,X3,Y3
   13| |FØRMAT('0',F5.1,F8.2)
```

If single spacing is desired, the blank that automatically fills in the record when columns are skipped may be used. The following example would result in a single-spaced column of values each starting in record position 5. The T or tab is used similarly as in input. The T and F format codes are discussed in Section 6.8.

EXAMPLE

```
12345|6|789...
     | |
     | |WRITE(3,12)X,Y,Z
   12| |FØRMAT(T5,F10.1)
```

The field may also be made larger than needed to ensure a leading blank.

```
12345|6|789...
     | |
     | |WRITE(3,12)X,Y,Z
   12| |FØRMAT(F14.1)
```

6.7

OBJECTIVE: . . . use the slash for selecting printed output records.

A slash (/) may be used in a FORMAT specification to indicate the end of a record (that is a printed line). Each slash causes a <u>record</u> to be terminated so several slashes can be used to leave blank lines or space down a page. The slash does not cause an automatic advance to a next line. Instead, the carriage control character of the next record determines the advancement. If two consecutive slashes are used, the first terminates the current record and the second inserts a blank record.

Slashes have the effect of specifying multiple records by one FORMAT statement.

```
FORMAT (__________/__________/__________)
          1st record  2nd record  3rd record
```

If the FORMAT statement is written for a WRITE statement that has referenced a printer, a carriage control character must be specified after each slash (the beginning of a new record). Examples 1 and 2 demonstrate the use of slashes in defining records and the use of the carriage control character.

The following WRITE and FORMAT cause two lines to be printed, one at the top of a page and the next double-spaced below it.

EXAMPLE 1

```
123456789...
      WRITE(3,8)X1,Y1,X2,Y2
    8 FØRMAT('1',F5.1,F9.2//1X,F5.1,F9.2)
              record   record   record
                #1       #2       #3
```

OUTPUT

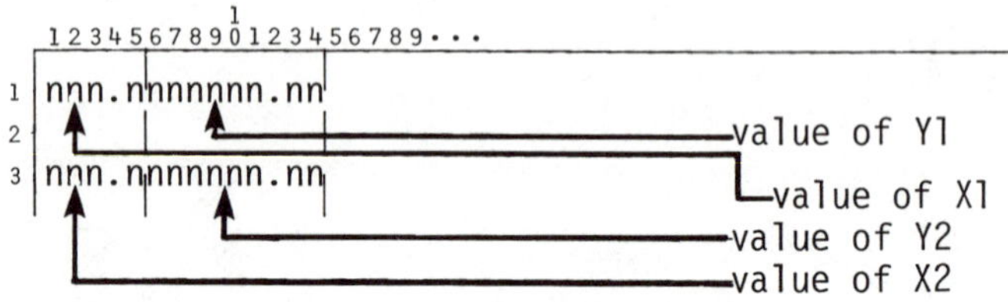

Three records are specified with the following carriage control characters:

RECORD	CARRIAGE CONTROL CODE
1	1
2	b
3	b

FORMAT code F9.2 is larger than needed for the data value of Y1 or Y2 ensuring blanks between the two values on each line.

EXAMPLE 2

The following statements show the use of the slash and group parentheses.

```
12345 6 789···

        WRITE(3,6)N,X1,Y1,X2,Y2,X3,Y3
      6 FØRMAT('1',I5//(1X,F4.1,F6.1))

          record   record    record
            #1       #2        #3
```

OUTPUT

```
 123456789
1value of N
2
3value of X1   value of Y1
4value of X2   value of Y2
5value of X3   value of Y3
```

The values X1, X2, X3 use F4.1 format code and Y1, Y2, Y3 use F6.1.

EXAMPLE 3

The following example shows how to write character headings and the use of the '/' to provide spacing on the output page.

```
12345 6 789···

        WRITE(3,8)
      8 FØRMAT('1'////T61,'SUMMARY'/'+',T61,7('-')/'0',
       1  T51,'TIME',T61,'VELØCITY',T71,'ACCL.'/)
```

OUTPUT

```
       5         6         7
  ···01234567890123456789012345
1
2
3
4
5                 SUMMARY
6                 -------
7       TIME      VELØCITY  ACCL.
8
```

NOTES

1. Slashes (/) are separators and commas are not needed with them.

2. Each record must have a carriage control character. Using T61 inserts a blank in column 1 for this purpose.

3. The T refers to record position and not the print position; hence, it refers to one less in print line.

4. After beginning on line 1 of a new page ('1' for carriage control), 4 records are terminated by the four /'s. The print control character, a blank, supplied by T61 causes the fifth record to be printed single-spaced from the previous; hence, on line 5. Terminating a record does not cause an automatic advance to a new line.

5. The '/' after SUMMARY terminates record 5. The next record is printed with no carriage advance; hence underlining SUMMARY. This record is terminated with a /. The '0' directs the next record to be printed with double spacing from the previous record; hence it is printed on line 7.

   Note: (. . . / '0' , T51 . . .) in the FORMAT could be replaced with (. . . // T51. . .) for the same appearance.

6.8

OBJECTIVE: . . . construct valid WRITE statements using I, F, E, T, X and A format codes with repetitions and grouping.

The format codes used for output are the same as those used for input data. However, there are some differences in their use for output. As in the case of input, each of the format codes specifies a type of data and the code used must agree with the data type of the variable name associated with it.

The general form of the format codes associated with each data type and the external representation of these values on the printed page are given in Table 6.8-1. The Minimum Output Field Width gives the minimum field width that should be used with each type to allow for a sign, a decimal point, and an exponent, depending on the type.

In all cases, the output will be right-justified (located as far right as possible) in the field. Leading zeros are not printed on numeric output.

Table 6.8-1
Format Code Specifications

GENERAL FORMS

Format Code	Data Type	External Representation	Minimum Output Field Width
aIw	Integer	± nnnn	No. of significant digits + 1 for sign
aFw.d	Real number	± nn.nn	d + 3
aEw.d	Real number	± 0.nnnE±nn[1]	d + 7[1]
aDw.d	Real number	± 0.nnnD±nn[1]	d + 7[1]
wX	Skip field	blank field	1
Tw	Tab	blank field	1
aAw	Character	character	1

COMPONENTS

a	repeat number
w	field width (number of columns on printed page)
d	number of digits in the fractional part of the number
n	any digit

EXAMPLES

```
123456789...
     1 FØRMAT(2I5, F10.1)
     2 FØRMAT(2E16.5)
     3 FØRMAT(F7.0,5X,F6.2)
     4 FØRMAT(T5,3A4,A2)
```

[1] d+8 for 3-digit exponents (CDC 6600)

The repeat number 'a' is used in exactly the same manner as in an input FORMAT. The following two FORMAT specifications are equivalent.

```
123456789...

     5 FØRMAT(I2,I2,F6.1,F6.1,F6.1)
     6 FØRMAT(2I2,3F6.1)
```

Integer Format Code (I)

The integer format code is used to write integer variables. Some important points are:

1. The computer will right-justify the output in the field whose width is specified by w. Leading zeros are not printed.

2. A column must be provided for the sign if the number is negative. Positive numbers are written without a sign.

3. When the field width is not wide enough to permit the number to be written out correctly in the field, some computers fill the field with asterisks.

Table 6.8-2 shows how a variable with an internal value of −238 would be written out by different formats.

Table 6.8-2
Output for Different Field Widths

FORMAT	PRINT LINE
123456789···	123456789···
7 FØRMAT('b',I3)	***
8 FØRMAT('b',I4)	-238
9 FØRMAT('b',I6)	-238

Real numbers without exponent (F)

The F-field format code is used to write real numbers without exponents.

Some important points are:

1. Data is right-justified in the field. Leading zeros are not printed except as specified in 4 below.

2. A decimal point is always printed; hence a space must be provided for it.

3. If the sign is negative, a space must be provided for it.

4. If the number is less than 1.0 a space should be provided for a leading zero on most systems. For example, .9 generally appears on output as 0.9. Hence, the suggested minimum size for F-field is the number of digits + 3.

5. If the field is insufficient to correctly output the number, asterisks are written. The number of asterisks will be equal to the field width w.

To use the F-field format code to print real numbers, the relative magnitude of the number should be known. For example, if $-100.0 \leq R \leq +100.0$, a format code of F6.1 would be sufficient; however, if $-0.0001 \leq R \leq 0.001$ and F6.1 were used, the value printed would be 0.0. A better F specification for the second range of R would be F7.4, in order to print out four significant digits, or an E format code might be used.

In printing out real variables, the format code specifies the number of decimal places that are to be printed. In printing the decimal, some computers round the number in the last decimal place. Other computers may truncate or cut off at the specified decimal position without rounding. Table 6.8-3 shows how each of the quantities, whose internal value is shown in column one, would appear if they were rounded off and printed by the given format specification.

> PT's*
>
> - Again, the simpler FORMAT is the easiest for the beginner. Use additional WRITE statements to avoid long, complicated FORMATS.
> - Increasing the field width to allow for spacing frequently simplifies a FORMAT.
>
>   (T5,4(2X,F5.0),2(3X,I2))
>
>   is simpler as
>
>   (T5,4F7.0,2I5)
>
> *Practical Techniques

Table 6.8-3
Examples of F Format Codes

INTERNAL VALUE	SPECIFICATION	PRINTED OUTPUT FIELD COLUMNS
		1 2 3 4 5 6 7 8 9 • • •
4312.345	F6.1	4312.3
-4312.345	F6.1	******
4312.345	F6.2	******
4312.345	F7.2	4312.34
4312.367	F7.1	b4312.4
89.123	F5.0	bb89.
89.183	F5.1	b89.2
-89.123	F5.1	-89.1
.00123	F5.1	bb0.0
.00123	F5.3	0.001
.002	F7.5	0.00200
.999	F5.2	b1.00

<u>Real numbers with exponents (E)</u>

The E format code is used to print real variables in an exponential form. It is useful for printing real numbers whose magnitude is very large or very small or whose magnitude is unknown. Some points to remember are:

1. The computer right-justifies the output in the field whose width is specified by w. Leading zeros are not printed except as specified in 2. below.

2. The output appears in a scientific notation form as follows:

   $\pm$0.nnn...E$\pm$nn

   The number of n's varies with the E-specification. The exponent is always printed with an E, sign, and digits. The sign of the number is omitted on positive numbers. Hence, the minimum w in the specification should be 7 more than the number of significant digits, d, desired (8 more for 3-digit exponents).

3. Although the E-data field has several variations on input data, such as omitting

the E or the sign of the exponent, there is only one output form as given below.

Table 6.8-4 shows how each of the quantities whose internal value is given in column one would appear on the output page if printed by the given specification.

Table 6.8-4
Examples of E Format Code Output

INTERNAL VALUE	SPECIFICATION	PRINTED OUTPUT FIELD COLUMNS 123456789···
384.1122	E8.1	b0.4E+03
384.1123	E9.2	b0.38E+03
385.1123	E11.2	bbb0.39E+03
-384.1000	E11.2	bb-0.38E+03
.006741	E10.3	b0.674E-02
-.00674	E10.3	-0.674E-02
1.23	E12.4	bb0.1230E+01
19.9999	E10.2	bb0.20E+02

Skip Field (X)

X is used to provide spacing in the output. The following example shows its use. (R=1.523,A=4.714)

```
12345 6 789

        WRITE(3,8)R,A
      8 FØRMAT(1X,'R=',F5.1,2X,'A=',1X,F6.1)
```

OUTPUT

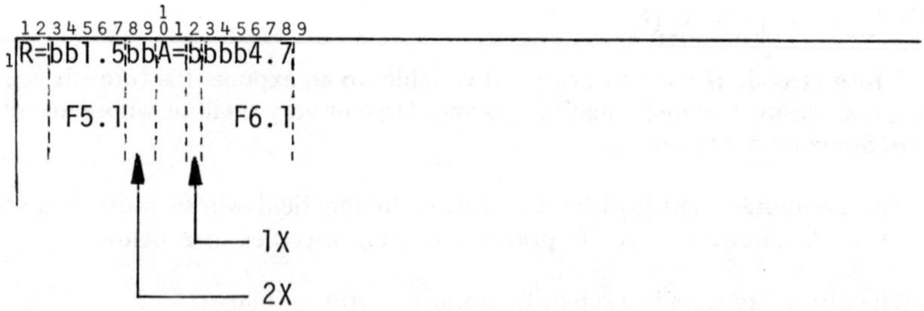

Note: The first X skipped one column causing a blank to fill in. This first column is used for carriage control, causing this line to be printed with single-spacing.

The beginner should avoid writing long, complicated FORMAT statements. One way to do this is to write one FORMAT statement for the heading information, and another for the data list. Another way is to use uniform FORMAT codes for data items of the same type if they are of relatively the same magnitude and precision. For example,

(1X,F6.1,F5.1,F8.1) could be written as (1X,3F8.1). Another way to simplify a FORMAT is to include space between the data items in the field width instead of using the X format code, whenever it is feasible. This is shown in the following example.

EXAMPLE

Write out eight items, each of which is to be of the form nnnn.n; put four items per line with two spaces between each item. Double space the lines. One way to do this is

```
12345|6|789···
     | |WRITE(3,8)X1,X2,X3,X4,X5,X6,X7,X8
    8| |FØRMAT(('0',4(F6.1,2X)))
```

The extra set of parentheses is necessary so that the '0' is included in the parentheses that is used when repeating to print the second set of four items.

However, a much simpler approach is to replace 4(F6.1,2X) with 4F8.1. This eliminates the need for any nested parentheses and the FORMAT simplifies to

```
12345|6|789···
    8| |FØRMAT('0',4F8.1)
```

There is a slight difference in the output of these two FORMAT statements, but it is a difference that seldom matters. The second FORMAT shifts the output two spaces to the right.

Tab Format Code (T)

The T code is available for programming at my computer installation. Yes ☐ No ☐

The T format code is used for output to specify the position in the FORTRAN record where data fields are to begin. For printed output, the first character of the output record is used for carriage control and is not printed. Thus, if T5 is specified in a FORMAT statement, the printed output field will appear in the fourth print position. Since blanks fill areas with no data specification, the first character, a blank, becomes the carriage control giving single-spacing. This is shown in the following example:

```
12345|6|789···
     | |WRITE(3,8)
    8| |FØRMAT(T5,'RADIUS',T14,'AREA')
```

OUTPUT

```
Record position 12345678901234567...
Print position   1234567890123456...
               1 |bbbRADIUSbbbAREA
               2 |
               3 |
```

When a record written by a WRITE statement is terminated by a / or), the placement of the next record depends on the carriage control character for the next written record. In the following example, the two consecutive WRITE statements cause two lines of printout double-spaced (because of the '0' carriage control character) starting at the top of a new page.

```
12345 6 789...
        WRITE(3,7)
        WRITE(3,8)AVE,SIG
    7   FØRMAT('1',T5,'AVERAGE',T15,'SIGMA')
    8   FØRMAT('0',T7,F5.1,T15,F5.1)
```

```
 123456789012345 6789...
1   AVERAGE   SIGMA
2
3     nnn.n   nnn.n
```

Note: T5 causes the output to begin in record position 5 which is print position 4.

The next two FORMAT codes used with the same two WRITE statements would produce the same output lines. Notice the X code is used instead of T and a '/' and single spacing are used instead of double spacing.

```
12345 6 789...
    7   FØRMAT('1',3X,'AVERAGE',3X,'SIGMA'/)
    8   FØRMAT('b',5X,F5.1,3X,F5.1)
```

<u>Alphanumeric Format Code</u> (A)

The alphanumeric or A format code is used to write out character data that was read in by an A format code. Generally, alphanumeric data should be written out using the same A specifications that were used on input. Example 1 shows how one card containing three data fields was read in and printed out on three lines.

INPUT CARD

COLS. 1-10	COLS. 20-22	COLS. 70-75
PART ID (alphanumeric)	CODE OF SUPPLIER (alphanumeric)	NO. IN STOCK (integer)

STATEMENTS

```
12345 6 789···
        READ(1,8)P1,P2,P3,CØD,NS
      8 FØRMAT(2A4,A2,T20,A3,T70,I6)
        WRITE(3,9)P1,P2,P3,CØD,NS
      9 FØRMAT('1','PARTbID',T16,2A4,A2/
     + 'bCØDE',T23,A3/'bNØ.bINbSTØCK',
     + T20,I6)
```

OUTPUT

```
          1         2
12345678901234567890123456789···
1 PARTbIDbbbbbbbXXXXXXXXXX
2 CØDEbbbbbbbbbbbbbbbbbXXX
3 NØ.bINbSTØCKbbbbbbdddddd
```

Note: X is an alphabetic character
d is digit
b is blank

If an A field greater than four is specified, the data field is right-justified, preceded by blanks. If P8 contained the data, PART, and were printed out with an A7, it would appear as follows:

OUTPUT

```
123456789···
1 bbPART
2
3
```

If data is read with an A format code with a field width less than 4, the word is filled with blanks. The next example shows how a name read in one character per word (A1) would appear if printed out with A4.

INPUT CARD

```
JØHN DØE

123456789···
```

STATEMENTS

```
12345 6 789···
        READ(1,5)N1,N2,N3,N4,N5,N6,N7,N8
      5 FØRMAT(8A1)
```

HOW STORED

N1	J	b	b	b
N2	Ø	b	b	b
N3	H	b	b	b
N4	N	b	b	b

N5	b	b	b	b
N6	D	b	b	b
N7	Ø	b	b	b
N8	E	b	b	b

OUTPUT STATEMENTS

```
123456789...
      WRITE(3,8)N1,N2,N3,N4,N5,N6,N7,N8
    8 FØRMAT (T21,8A4)
```

OUTPUT

```
                    2         3         4         5
12      8901234567890123456789012345678901234567890123
1                   JbbbØbbbHbbbNbbbbbbbDbbbØbbbEbbb
2
3
```

6.9

OBJECTIVE: . . . write unformatted records.

An unformatted record is written by the unformatted WRITE statement. The general form of this statement is as follows:

GENERAL FORM

```
123456789...
nnnnn WRITE(i)list
```

COMPONENTS

```
nnnnn   is an optional statement number
WRITE   is the keyword
  i     is the data set reference number
list    is a list of data items to be transferred in their
           internal form
```

EXAMPLE

```
123456789...
      WRITE(9)A,B,C,D,E,F
```

The action of this statement is similar to that presented in Section 5.16.

CHAPTER EXERCISES

1. The internal values of A = 23.42, B = −15.984, C = .000826, J = 892. If these variables were written out by the following WRITE statement, show how the output line would appear if each of the FORMAT statements were used.

```
123456789...
      WRITE(3,-)A,B,C,J
    1 FØRMAT('b',3F5.1,2X,I3)
    2 FØRMAT('b',2F5.0,E10.3,I5)
    3 FØRMAT('b',F4.2,2F5.2,T16,I3)
    4 FØRMAT('b',3E10.3,2X,I2)
```

OUTPUT

```
         1         2         3
12345678901234567890123456789012345...
1
2
3
4
```

2. Write a WRITE and FORMAT statement to write the value of ANG with one decimal place and with the labeling as follows:

```
         1         2         3
12345678901234567890123456789012345...
THEbLIFTbANGLEbISbnnn.nbDEGREES
```

```
123456789...


```

3. What is wrong in the following FORMATS?

```
123456789...
   10 FØRMAT(///'1',F10.1)
   20 FØRMAT('1',F10.1/F5.1)
```

4. Write WRITE and FORMAT statements to write I1, I3, and I5 using 6 columns for each. Start I1 on the first line of a new page, I3 on the third and I5 on fifth line.

```
|12345|6|789...
|     | |
|     | |
|     | |
```

5. Write a WRITE and FORMAT statement that together will:
   a) go to the top of a new page
   b) begin printing on the third line and print two lines as shown below.

   Values of XV and IN are printed on the third line, and YV and JN on the fifth line.

```
           1
 1234567890123456...
1|
2|
3|  nnn.nn   nnn
4|
5|  nnn.nn   nnn
```

```
|12345|6|789...
|     | |WRITE
|     | |FØRMAT
```

6. Write a FORMAT statement that causes the printer to skip to the top of a new page, then print as shown below.

```
          1         2         3         4
 1234567890123456789012345678901234567890...
1|         nnn.n IS nn.n PERCENT ØF nnn.n
2|
```

where the characters nnn.n, nn.n and nnn.n are the values of real variables.

```
|12345|6|789...
|     | |WRITE(3,8)A,B,C
|     | |FØRMAT
```

7. Describe on the line below what will be printed by the following two statements, assuming the variable N has the value 7 and DOT is 47.12389

```
12345|6|789···
     | |WRITE(3,6)N,DOT
    6| |FØRMAT('bØN HANDb',I2,2X,F8.5)
```

```
         1         2         3         4
1234567890123456789012345678901234567890123···
1|
2|
```

8. Describe on the line below what will be printed by the following two statements, assuming the variable N has the value 382 and DESCR is .4712389

```
12345|6|789···
     | |WRITE(3,6)N,DESCR
    6| |FØRMAT('bØN HANDb',I2,2X,F8.5)
```

```
         1         2         3         4
1234567890123456789012345678901234567890123···
1|
2|
```

9. Write a WRITE and corresponding FORMAT statement to write out the heading shown below along with values for E, I, and P. I has been designated as a real variable. Start at the top of a new sheet for printing.

```
         1         2         3
123456789012345678901234567890123···
1|      VØLTAGE    CURRENT     PØWER
2|
3|       nnn.n      nnn.n      nnn.n
4|
```

```
            1
12345|6|7890123
     | |
     | |
     | |
     | |
```

10. Match column A with the proper action in column B.

First Character in Record		Paper Advance Before Printing Record
Blank	______	a.) No advance
0	______	b.) Two
1	______	c.) New page
+	______	d.) One

11. Write a WRITE statement and a FORMAT statement that together will
    a) produce three blank print lines, then
    b) print a line containing four variables.

The variables to be printed are, in order, I, AA, JU, B. Each variable should be allotted 10 print columns. The real variables should be printed in F format with three digits to the right of the decimal point.

1 2 3 4 5	6	7 8 9 • • •

12. Write a FORMAT statement that causes the printer to skip to the top of a new page, then print a page header which says

THIS IS PAGE nnn OF nnn

where the characters nnn are the values of integer variables. The line should be centered on the page. (There are 135 print positions across the page on the CDC printer, and the print line above contains 23 characters total, including spaces.)

1 2 3 4 5	6	7 8 9 • • •
		WRITE(3,18)IPN,ITP

CHAPTER PROGRAMMING PROBLEMS

TOPIC APPLICATION

a) Set up data card
b) READ Statement
c) Read FORMAT Statement
d) Arithmetic Statement
e) WRITE Statement
f) Write FORMAT Statement
g) T and X Format Codes

STATEMENTS SUPPLIED

a) None

Problem 6.1

PROBLEM STATEMENT

A series electrical circuit is shown below along with values of the impressed voltage, E, and resistances, R_1, R_2, and R_3.

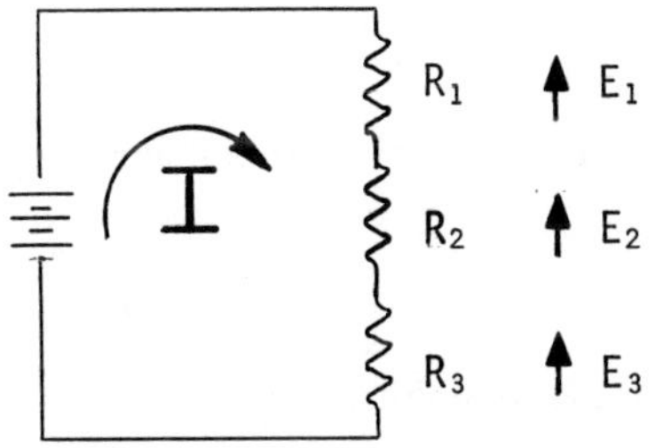

$$E = 11.50 \text{ volts}$$
$$R_1 = 22.1 \text{ ohms}$$
$$R_2 = 15.7 \text{ ohms}$$
$$R_3 = 8.2 \text{ ohms}$$

E_1, E_2, and E_3 are voltages across R_1, R_2, and R_3 respectively. Each resistor R_1, R_2 and R_3 absorbs power P_1, P_2, and P_3 respectively.

Write a program to read data E, R_1, R_2, and R_3 in on one card and to calculate values of E_1, E_2, E_3, P_1, P_2, P_3, and I using the following equations:

$$E_1 = IR_1 \text{ volts}$$
$$E_2 = IR_2 \text{ volts}$$
$$E_3 = IR_3 \text{ volts}$$

$$P_1 = I^2R_1 \text{ watts}$$
$$P_2 = I^2R_2 \text{ watts}$$
$$P_3 = I^2R_3 \text{ watts}$$

$$I = \frac{E}{R_1+R_2+R_3}$$

I/O REQUIREMENTS

Write FORTRAN statements to print values of I, E_1, E_2, E_3, P_1, P_2, and P_3, starting at the top of a new page. Arrange for a printout in the following format:

```
   1         2         3         4         5         6         7
...0123456789012345678901234567890123456789012345678901234567890123456789012...
--------------------------------------------------------------------------------
                      3 blank lines
I(AMPS) E1(VØLTS) E2(VØLTS) E3(VØLTS) P1(WATTS) P2(WATTS) P3(WATTS)
                      1 blank line
nn.nn   nnn.nn    nnn.nn    nnn.nn    nnn.nn    nnn.nn    nnn.nn
```

Note: Draw a data table and flow diagram before coding the program on a FORTRAN coding form. Provide for two decimal places in each answer.

Problem 6.2

PROBLEM STATEMENT

The distance between two points P_1 and P_2 on a two-dimension plane is given by

$$d = \sqrt{(x_2-x_1)^2 + (y_2-y_1)^2}$$

where (x_1, y_1), (x_2, y_2) are the coordinates of two points, P_1 and P_2.

The coordinates of the mid-point of the time segment $P_1 P_2$ are given by

$$x_m = \frac{x_1 + x_2}{2} \qquad y_m = \frac{y_1 + y_2}{2}$$

EXERCISE

Write a complete program which will read in values for x_1, y_1, x_2, y_2 and compute d and x_m, y_m.

Keypunch the number of point sets on the first card in the data deck. Write the appropriate READ and FORMAT statements to read in and store this value.

Choose a card format for the coordinates and write the appropriate READ and FORMAT statements for one pair of points on each card. Place the WRITE statement that prints out your input data immediately following your READ statement to detect any input errors before processing.

Print the input data and results in the following form:

```
             1         2         3
    1234567890123456789012345678901234567890123...
   ------------------------------------------------
 1 |P1=bbnn.n,bnn.n    P2=bbnn.n,bnn.n
 2 |DISTANCE FRØM P1 TO P2 = bbnn.n
 3 |CØØRDINATES ØF MIDPØINT ØF P1P2=nn.n,bnn.n
 4 |
 5 }
 6 }lines 1-3 repeated
 7 }
 8 |
 9 }
10 }lines 1-3 repeated
11 }
12 |
...|          etc.
```

Test your program with the following input data. Select your own data fields. DO NOT put parentheses on data card.

P_1 = (1.,2.) P_2 = (3.,-4.)
P_1 = (3.,4.) P_2 = (-3.,-4.5)
P_1 = (-1.,2.) P_2 = (3.5,-4.5)

Problem 6.3

PROBLEM STATEMENT

The harmonic mean H of a set of numbers, x_1, $x_2 \ldots x_n$ is the reciprocal of the arithmetic mean of the reciprocals of the numbers:

$$\text{Arithmetic mean} = \frac{\Sigma X}{N} \quad \text{or} \quad \frac{X_1 + X_2 + \ldots X_n}{N}$$

$$H = \frac{N}{\Sigma \frac{1}{X}} \quad \text{or} \quad \frac{N}{\frac{1}{X_1} + \frac{1}{X_2} + \ldots \frac{1}{X_n}}$$

EXERCISE

Write a program that reads in N cards, 1 number per card in F4.0 format code. Compute the arithmetic mean and the harmonic mean of these numbers. Test your program with the following numbers: N = 5 and data

1., 5., 9., 20., 32.

Print out should consist of the input data, printed immediately after it is read in, and the arithmetic and harmonic mean printed with appropriate labeling.

Problem 6.4

PROBLEM STATEMENT

The formulas for computing the amounts of money on deposit in a savings account at simple interest and at compound interest for N years are as follows:

For simple interest, the amount $S = P(1 + RN)$

For compound interest, the amount $C = P(1 + R)^N$

where P = principal
R = rate
N = number of years

EXERCISE

Write a program that will read in values for P, R and N and compute the simple interest and compound interest for N years at a rate R. Print out P, R, N, S, and C as shown below. Recycle so any number of values for P, R, and N could be read in by using a DO loop and first reading in the number of sets of data. A flow diagram is given below. Make a data table before coding.

Test your program with the following data and print the output as shown below.

INPUT

```
 N     P        R
           1
1234567890123456789...
 5    1000     .06
10    1000     .06
10    1000     .065
15    1000     .06
15    1000     .065
```

OUTPUT

```
         1         2         3         4         5
123456789012345678901234567890123456789012345678901234
1 PRINCIPALbbbRATEbbbbNØ.YRS.bbSIMPLEbINT.bbCØMPØUNDbINT.
2
3   nnnn.nn    n.nnn      nn       nnnn.nn        nnnn.nn
4
```

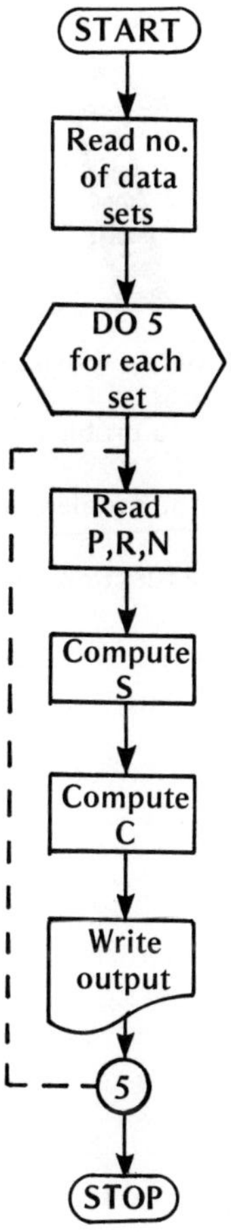

Flow Diagram for Problem 6.4

7 FORTRAN

7.1 ... state the five-step approach to top-down program design.

7.2 ... understand the steps in solving a problem.

7.3 ... list the data requirements of the problem in a data table.

7.4 ... draw a hierarchy chart of the functions to be done in order to solve a problem.

7.5 ... make a detailed flow diagram.

7.1

OBJECTIVE: ... state the five-step approach to top-down program design.

Up to this point, you have been writing a part of each program. Let us now look at a step-by-step approach to designing the complete program. We call our five-step approach to writing a program top down program design because we begin at the top or most general overview of the solution and work down in stages until we arrive at a detailed solution. You have been introduced to some of the tools that are used in this step-by-step approach, namely, the data table and flow diagram. The five steps which will guide you in the design of any program are listed below. Steps one through four are discussed in the next four sections.

STEP 1. Understand the problem.

STEP 2. Make a Data Table.

STEP 3. Make a Hierarchy Chart.

STEP 4. Make a detailed flow diagram of the algorithm for solving the problem.

STEP 5. Code the program in FORTRAN.

TOP DOWN DESIGN

7.2

OBJECTIVE ... understand the steps in solving a problem.

The problem we will consider here is simple enough that it could easily be solved by using a calculator (or by arithmetic, if anyone remembers how to divide anymore!). What we are interested in is the logical process that one must go through in solving any problem. Here is a problem:

> Suppose you are in a tennis league and you wish to write down a step-by-step procedure that should be followed by each member of the league each week in updating his/her average. The average is to be computed as the percentage of games won that are played.

WHERE DO YOU BEGIN?

Step 1. Understand the problem.

Where do you begin in solving the problem? First, it is essential to understand the problem in your own words, perhaps adding some information as to 'how to' do it? ..... Your statement might read like this. 'I want to compute the percentage of games won, which is equal to the total number of games won divided by the number of games played.'

Where do you begin?

The problem here is a simple one so no further time needs to be spent on understanding it. However, some problems may take several readings before you are ready to proceed toward the solution. And it is most important that you understand WHAT you are to do BEFORE attempting to do it.

7.3

OBJECTIVE: . . . list the data requirements of the problem in a data table.

At Step 2, each data item that is needed in the program is listed in a table which gives the pertinent facts about the data item. This table was introduced in Chapter 2, and you should be familiar with its usefulness by this time. The data table for our tennis problem is given in Table 7.3-1.

Table 7.3-1
Tennis Average Data Table

DATA ITEM	DEFINITION	UNIT	DATA TYPE	USE	FORTRAN NAME
	No. of games played prior				
	to this week		I	I	NPLAY
	No. of games won prior to				
	this week		I	I	NWØN
	No. of games played this week		I	I	NPWK
	No. of games won this week		I	I	NWWK
	Percent of games won		R	Ø	PCWØN

[1] DATA TYPE: I = Integer, R = Real, A = Alphanumeric,
[2] USE: I = Input, Ø = Output, T = Temporary, C = Constant

The data item and unit columns are left blank as there are no DATA ITEM symbolic designations or UNIT terms for any entry in this example. An additional data type has been added to the possible choices for the Data Type column, namely, A, for alphanumeric. Any data item read in under an A format code or set in a DATA statement as alphanumeric would have an A designation.

For example, the following statement

```
12345|6|789...
     | |DATA FEET/'FT.'/
```

stores alphanumeric data into FEET, so FEET is data type A.

The next example shows a temporary data item.

```
12345|6|789...
     | |TEMP=A
     | |A=B
     | |B=TEMP
```

The contents of the memory locations of A and B are exchanged using arithmetic statements. In order to do this, it is necessary to temporarily save the contents of one of them in a storage location, TEMP. TEMP would be listed in the data table with type T.

Careful planning should make this table as complete as possible. However, it is likely that revisions will need to be made as Step 3 and Step 4 are done. The data list should be reviewed during these steps and revised as necessary. In particular, many of the temporary locations that are needed will not be defined until Step 4, the detailed flow diagram, is done.

7.4

OBJECTIVE: . . . draw a hierarchy chart of the functions to be done in order to solve a problem.

Step 4. Make a Hierarchy Chart.

After the data requirements have been listed, the next step is to make a list of the tasks or functions that need to be accomplished in order to do the problem. In order to do this in an orderly manner, a hierarchy chart is made. To understand what is meant by a hierarchy chart, consider again an overly simplified diagram of any problem solution on the computer.

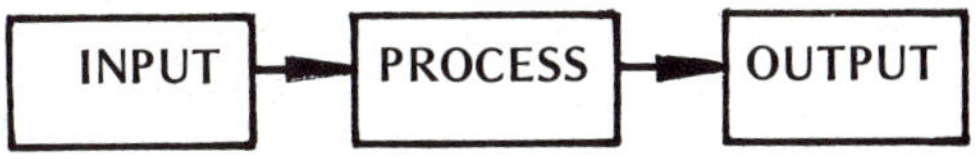

Figure 7.4-1. General Hierarchy Chart

Figure 7.4-1 shows a general hierarchy chart of almost all problems we encounter for solution by computer; namely, INPUT-PROCESS-OUTPUT in some hierarchial order. For this reason, this chart or any refinement will be referred to as a hierarchy chart, or simply, a HIPO chart, for 'hierarchy-input-process-output'.

A hierarchy chart can be compared to a company's organizational chart in that it is functionally oriented and shows the flow of control, which is from top to bottom. An example of an organizational chart for a small business is seen in Figure 7.4-2.

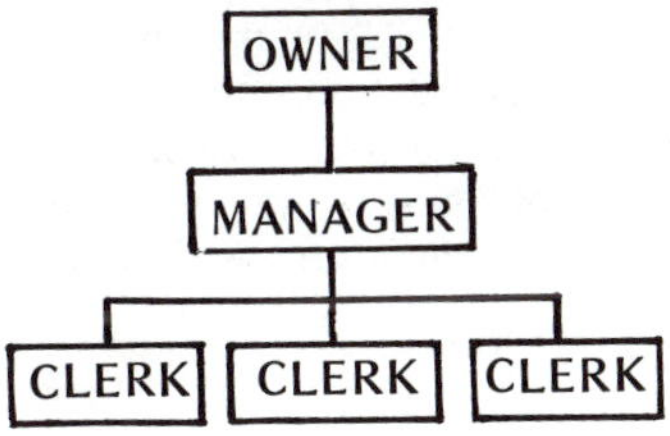

Figure 7.4-2. Organizational Chart.

A top-level hierarchy chart focuses on what needs to be done before deciding on how to do it. It differs from the detailed flow diagram discussed in the next section in that it contains no decision making or flow of execution. For example, the organizational chart in Figure 7.4-2 does not show who is the manager if the manager is gone.

The top-level hierarchy chart gets you started and gives an overview of what needs to be done. Once this has been done, successive refinements of the blocks in the chart aid one's thinking so that the details can be worked out. Too often, a beginner cannot get started due to focusing on a small portion of the problem which is totally out of perspective to the rest. This bottom-up approach results in small pieces of the program being written which when put together without prior top-down over-all planning do not result in a carefully designed program. Therefore, begin the design of a program by drawing the input-process-output blocks of the general HIPO chart.

Next, replace each of these three major boxes with the functions and tasks of a particular problem. Put each of the functions in a separate box with connecting lines showing the order of doing them. The boxes are written here in a horizontal fashion as a space-saving convenience. However, the order of performing the functions is shown by the direction of the arrows.

After the input and output requirements have been listed in the data table, and as an aid in breaking down the PROCESS box, ask yourself, "What must I do to the input data in order to arrive at the output data?" This will aid you in specifying the processing tasks.

Let us return to our tennis problem and modify our general HIPO chart to reflect this problem, as in Figure 7.4-3.

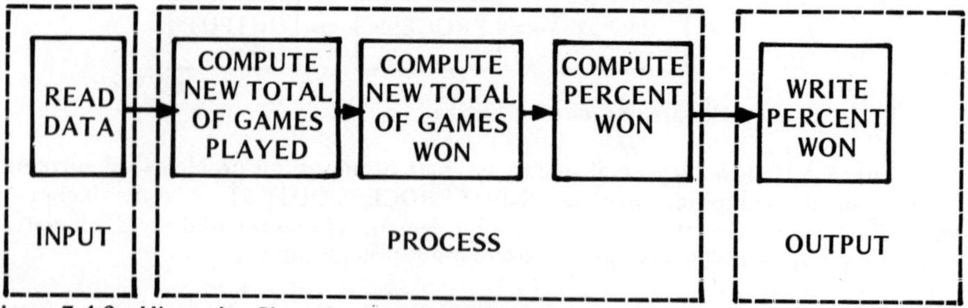

Figure 7.4-3. Hierarchy Chart for Tennis Program

As we get familiar with making hierarchy charts, the outside lines of the general HIPO chart can be omitted.

Continue to break down functions into the smaller, simpler functions needed to do your specific problem. Depending upon the complexity of the problem, several refinements of the HIPO chart may be necessary until you arrive at one which states all the functions simply enough that you are ready to detail the complete logic of your program. Our tennis program is complete on the first try. Now let us use this approach in another problem.

EXAMPLE

PROBLEM STATEMENT

Prepare successive hierarchy charts for a program which computes the payroll of a small business.

A top-level hierarchy chart for computing the payroll of a company is shown in Figure 7.4-4.

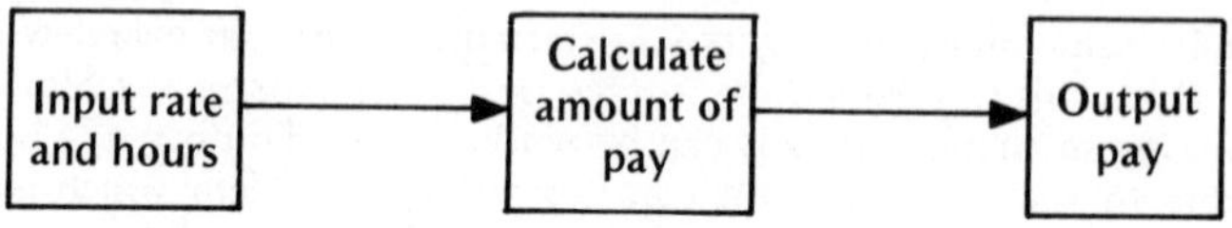

Figure 7.4-4. Top-level Hierarchy Chart for Company Payroll

A refinement of this top-level HIPO chart is shown is Figure 7.4-5.

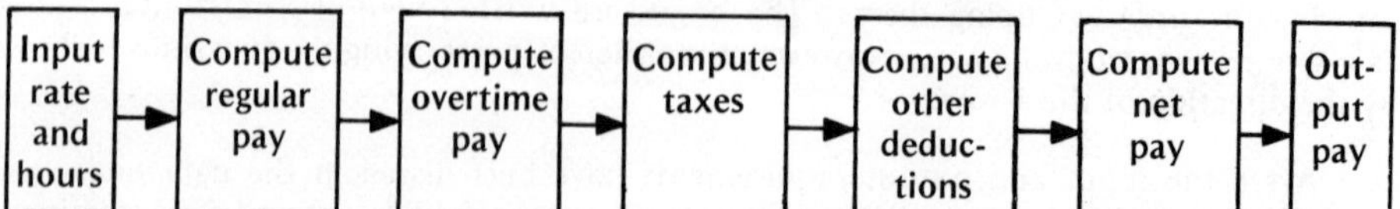

Figure 7.4-5. Revised Hierarchy Chart for Company Payroll Program.

EXERCISE

For the problems below, design a computer program to implement each of the problems by doing the following:

a) Determine the data requirements and list them in a data table.

b) Draw a top-level hierarchy chart.

c) Refine your hierarchy chart until you feel you have arrived at one which expresses all the functions to be performed and shows the flow from one to the other. (The hierarchy chart does not show logical decisions and is not yet codable.)

d) In class, have a 'walk-through' where one member presents a data table and hierarchy charts for class discussion to look for omissions and error in either.

Note: Management (the instructor) does not participate actively in the "walk-through" nor is it a basis for a performance rating (grade).

PROBLEMS

1. Mr. Unreal, an eccentric rich ex-programmer, in a humanitarian effort to spread computer programming, proposes to pay all the students in your class according to the number of hours spent weekly on the class. The weekly rate is also a variable dependent on the Dow Jones Stock Average and it is read in each week.

2. Draw a hierarchy chart of your career goal. Decide your overall goal for the top box. List the tasks that must be done to meet your goal below, subdividing these tasks until they are simple enough to be met.

3. Do the above for any of the problems given at the end of this chapter.

7.5

OBJECTIVE: . . . make a detailed flow diagram.

At Step 4, the overview is refined to show the detailed steps of exactly how to do each task. The series of detailed steps that perform a particular task is an algorithm. A diagram of the algorithm is called the detailed flow diagram and would show any decisions that need to be made. The FORTRAN names are used, and equations are written that show how the functions are to be done. The flow diagram symbols were given in Section 2.6. A vertical representation is used to accommodate a longer diagram, with connectors (small, labeled circles) connecting the bottom of one column to the top of another column. A detailed flow diagram for our tennis problem is given in Figure 7.5-1.

An alternate and acceptable way of drawing the detailed flow diagram is to use the mathematical symbols or verbal descriptions and indicate each computation to be made. This flow diagram is accompanied by the Data Table and list of all equations used. Figure 7.5-2 shows an example of this for the tennis problem. FORTRAN names are used as there are no mathematical symbols.

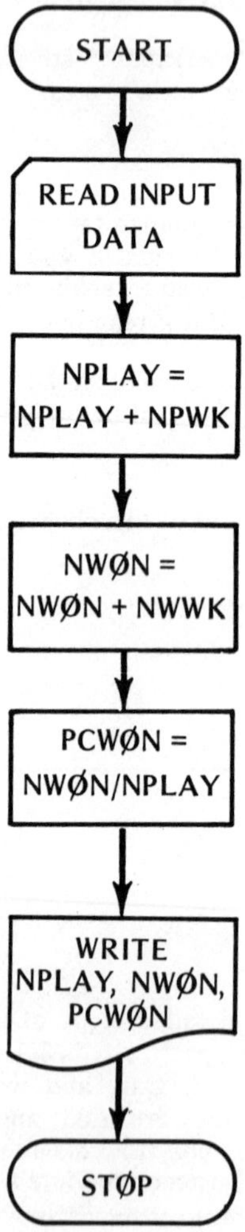
START
READ INPUT DATA
NPLAY = NPLAY + NPWK
NWØN = NWØN + NWWK
PCWØN = NWØN/NPLAY
WRITE NPLAY, NWØN, PCWØN
STØP

Figure 7.5-1. Detailed Flow Diagram - Tennis Problem

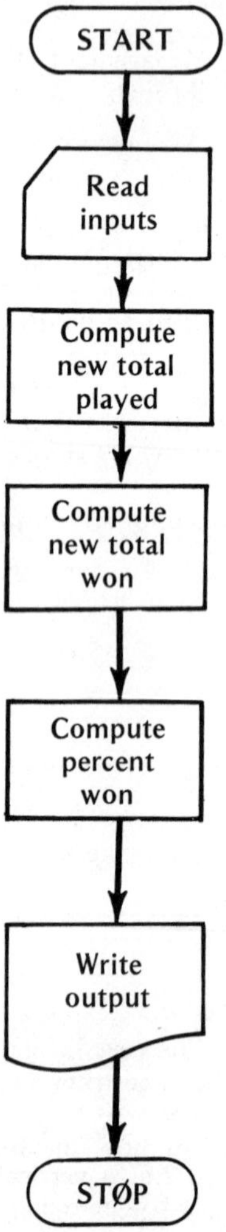
START
Read inputs
Compute new total played
Compute new total won
Compute percent won
Write output
STØP

Figure 7.5-2. Alternate Method - Detailed Flow Diagram

CHAPTER PROGRAMMING PROBLEMS

TOPIC APPLICATION

a) READ, WRITE, and FORMAT statements
b) Arithmetic Statements
c) FORTRAN - supplied function subprograms
d) Five-Step Approach to Program Design

Problem 7.1

Using the five-step approach to program design, write a program to compute the present position (latitude and longitude) of an aircraft flying in the St. Louis area given the following:

h_a = altitude of aircraft above sea level

R_{slant} = line-of-sight distance from the aircraft to a specified ground radio station*

Ψ = Bearing (compass direction) of the aircraft from the radio station

h_s = altitude of the radio station above sea level

λ_s = latitude of the ground station*

γ_s = longitude of the ground station*

INPUT

h_a = 2122 feet

R_{slant} = 4.16 nautical miles

Ψ = 66.850 degrees

h_s = 572 feet

λ_s = 38.754 degrees

γ_s = 90.365 degrees

*Note: The station position data given are those of the approach radar at Lambert St. Louis Municipal Airport.

The data card should be arranged as follows:

F7.3	F7.3	F6.0	F6.0	F7.3	F7.3
λ_s	γ_s	h_s	h_a	R_{slant}	Ψ

REQUIRED EQUATIONS

$$R_{true} = \sqrt{R^2_{slant} - (h_a - h_s)^2} \text{ nautical miles}$$

a) Correct the-line-of-sight (slanted) distance between the radio station and the aircraft to a true distance by use of the Pythagorean theorem.

(R_{slant}, h_a, and h_s must be in nautical miles.)

b) Find the latitude of the aircraft (λ_a) from the equation

$$\lambda_a = \lambda_s + \frac{R_{true} \cos(\Psi)}{h_a + a} \text{ radians}$$

where λ_s and Ψ are in radians

R_{true}, h_a, and a are in nautical miles

The radius of the earth, a, is about 3440.0 nautical miles in the St. Louis area. Do not read 'a' on a data card; substitute directly into your arithmetic statement.

c) Find the longitude of the aircraft(γ_a) from the equation

$$\gamma_a = \gamma_s + \frac{R_{true}\sin(\Psi)}{h_a + a\cos\left(\frac{\lambda a+\lambda s}{2}\right)}$$

where γ_s, Ψ, λa, and λ_s are in radians

R_{true}, h_a, and a are in nautical miles.

You will need the following conversion factors:

One radian equals 57.296 degrees
One nautical mile equals 6076.2 feet

OUTPUT

Write FORTRAN statements to write the output, starting at the top of a new page in the following form:

```
         1         2         3
1234567890123456789012345678901234...

        PRESENT PØSITION CALCULATIØN

PARAMETER NAME            VALUE

AIRCRAFT LATITUDE    nnn.nnn DEGREES
AIRCRAFT LØNGITUDE   nnn.nnn DEGREES
```

Answer

$\lambda_a = 38.781$

$\gamma_a = 90.283$

Problem 7.2

PROBLEM STATEMENT

A missile is shot at a target (d) miles away as shown below

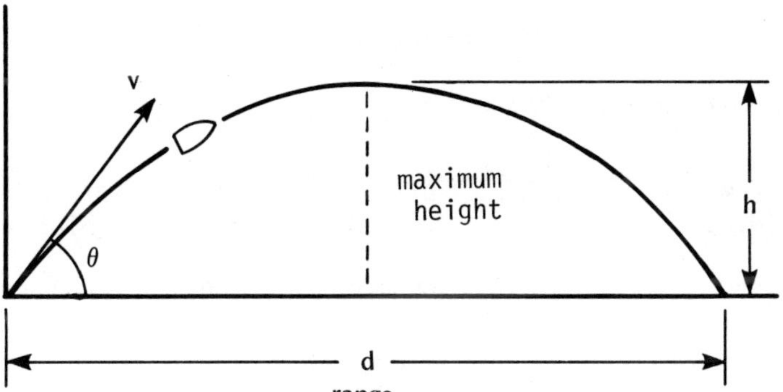

Ballistic Curve

The following ballistics equations can be used to calculate approximations for the following:

1) the distance (d) along the earth's surface the missile will travel if it is shot at an initial velocity of V_0 mph and at launching angle of θ degrees.

$$d = \frac{v^2 \sin 2\theta}{g}$$

2) the time (t) in hours it will take the missile to reach the target

$$t = \frac{d}{v\cos\theta}$$

3) the maximum altitude achieved during the flight

$$h_{max} = \frac{(v\sin\theta)^2}{2g}$$

where g, acceleration due to gravity, =

$$32\ \frac{ft}{sec^2} = 7.855*10^4\ \frac{miles}{hour^2}$$

EXERCISE

Follow the five-step approach in the design of a program that will calculate d, t, and h_{max} described above.

Test your program with the following sets of values of v and θ which are input on cards. Set the value for g, a constant, in the program.

(1) V = 16500 m.p.h. $\theta = 30$ degrees

(2) V = 15350 m.p.h. $\theta = 45$ degrees

(3) V = 15500 m.p.h. $\theta = 50$ degrees

Output should be as follows:

```
                   1                   2                   3                   4                   5
  1234567890123456789012345678901234567890123456789012345
1 VELØCITY     THETA     DISTANCE     TIME      MAX. ALT.
2 (M.P.H.)   (DEGREES)   (MILES)     (HØURS)     (MILES)
3
4 nnnnn.        nn.n      nnnn.n        .nn        nnn.n
5
```

Problem 7.3

PROBLEM STATEMENT

The "We'll Floor U" Carpet Company gives free estimates of the cost of carpeting several rooms of a house, based on the room sizes and cost of carpet selected. The installation charge is \$3. per square yard, plus \$1. for each yard of carpet edging around the perimeter of the room. Currently, they are offering 15% off the cost of the carpet but not the labor. State tax of 4% is figured on the cost of the carpeting after the discount, but not on the installation fee.

EXERCISE

Write a program that prepares a cost estimate for a house. The program should read in the number of rooms, followed by the length and width (in feet) of each room, and the cost per square yard of carpeting. The output should be a cost estimate of your input data test case, choosing your own card formats.

OUTPUT

```
                COØST ESTIMATE

THE NUMBER ØF RØØMS IS 3

LENGTH    WIDTH      CØST OF CARPET    CØST ØF CARPET
  FT.       FT.        PER SQ. YD.         THIS RØØM

   9        12            9.55              nnn.nn
  10        13            8.50              nnn.nn
   8         9           12.25              nnn.nn



                        TOTAL CØST               nnnn.nn
                        AMOUNT ØF DISCØUNT       nnnn.nn
                        CØST AFTER DISCØUNT      nnnn.nn
                        AMOUNT ØF TAX            nnnn.nn
                        INSTALLATION FEE         nnnn.nn
                        YØUR CØST                nnnn.nn
```

Problem 7.4

PROBLEM STATEMENT

A student's final grades in Mathematics, Physics, English, and Music are 82, 86, 90, and 70, respectively. If the respective credits received for these courses are 3, 5, 3, and 1, determine an appropriate average grade. To do this, find a weighted arithmetic mean using the formula below, in which the weights that are indicated by w are the credits associated with each grade, x.

$$X = \frac{\Sigma wx}{\Sigma w} \qquad \Sigma wx = w_1x_1 + w_2x_2 + \ldots$$

EXERCISE

Write a general program that will read in N, the number of grades, and then read in the grades and the associated credits. Compute and print out the weighted mean and the input data, as shown. Use the data given in the output sample as your input test case.

OUTPUT

```
CLASS                        CREDIT HRS.              GRADE

MATH                                3                   82

PHYSICS                             5                   86

ENGLISH                             3                   90

MUSIC                               1                   70

THE AVERAGE GRADE IS                                    nn.n
```

Problem 7.5

PROBLEM STATEMENT

If a body falls through the atmosphere and the air resistance is proportional to the square of the velocity, the distance fallen is given by the following formulas:

$$S_c = \frac{w}{2c} \log_e \left(\frac{wg - cv_0^2}{wg - cv^2} \right) \qquad S_n = \frac{v^2}{2g}$$

where

S_c = distance when considering air resistance
S_n = distance when neglecting air resistance
w = weight in pounds (lb.)
g = gravity (32 ft/sec.^{2})
c = constant of air resistance (lb./ft.)
v_0 = initial velocity (ft/sec.)
v = final velocity (ft/sec.)

EXERCISE

Write a program that will determine the distance a body falls using the above formulas. Read in the values for w, c, v_0, and v. Use your program to find out how far a 10 pound object falls, if it starts at rest and reaches a final velocity of 60 ft./sec. Use c = .05.

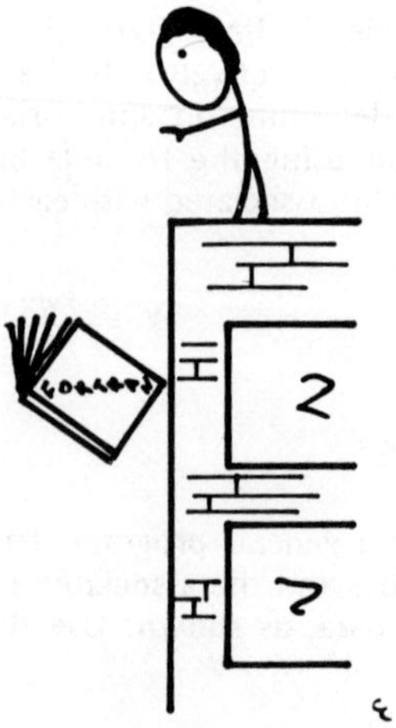

Compute the distances fallen considering air resistance, and the distances fallen neglecting air resistance for velocities from 1.0 FT/SEC to 60.0 FT/SEC at intervals of 1. Print out your input data with proper labeling, and output your results in the following form:

OUTPUT

```
123456789...
SC IN FT     V FT/SEC     SN IN FT

  .016          1.          .016

  .062          2.          .062

  .140          3.          .140

               ...

81.873         60.        55.901
```

Problem 7.6

PROBLEM STATEMENT

The current flowing through an A–C circuit can be determined using the following formula:

$$I = \frac{E}{\sqrt{R^2 + \left(2\pi FL - \frac{1}{2\pi FC}\right)^2}}$$

where I = current, L = inductance, E = voltage, C = capacitance, R = resistance, F = frequency

EXERCISE

Write a program that will compute the currents for voltages ranging from 1.0 volts to 5.0 volts, in increments of .5 volts, using the following values which are read in on a data card:

R = 100. C = .001

L = .005 F = 60.

OUTPUT

Print out the information in the following form:

```
123456789...
RESISTANCE = nnn.n   INDUCTANCE = .nnn   CAPACITANCE = .nnn

FREQUENCY = nn.n

          VØLTAGE          CURRENT

            1.0              .010
            1.5              .015

            ...              ...
```

FORTRAN 8

8.1 . . . define and write one-dimensional arrays.

8.2 . . . show how one-dimensional arrays may be used to efficiently specify many variables.

8.3 . . . establish arrays with DIMENSION and type specification statements.

8.4 . . . write subscripts as arithmetic expressions.

8.5 . . . transfer values into and from one-dimensional arrays.

8.6 . . . calculate values of subscripted variables using arrays within DO loops.

8.7 . . . write the FORMAT statements used to input one-dimensional arrays.

8.8 . . . write the FORMAT statements used to print one-dimensional arrays.

8.9 . . . use DO loops with arrays and . . . use nested DO loops.

8.1

OBJECTIVE . . . define and write one-dimensional arrays.

DEFINITION: Array
An array is a sequence of data with common characteristics identified by the same name, called the array name. An array element is one item in the sequence.

A particular element in an array is identified by the array name and its position in the array: that is, first, second, or tenth. A number written in parentheses following the array name and called a subscript is used to indicate the position in the array. An array element with its subscript is called a subscripted variable. Variables may have one, two or three subscripts. An array with only one subscript is called a one-dimensional array. Examples of one-dimensional array elements are: ARY(3), TEMP(4), and ROW(8).

Assume that a programmer has collected 125 temperature readings and wishes to compile statistics on them. Instead of assigning a different name to each temperature, say, TEM1, TEM2, . . . TEM125, one name is assigned to the set and each separate element of the set is identified by a different subscript, that is, TEMP(1), TEMP(2), . . . TEMP(125). The array element, TEMP(I), refers to the 'Ith' element in the array, where I is an integer from 1 to 125.

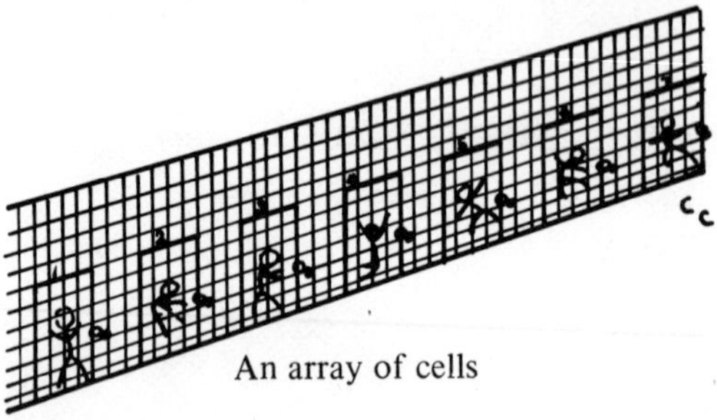

An array of cells

EXERCISE

1. Write an array to identify the weights of 20 registered Texas bulls. ____________

2. A(8) is an element of an array. What is the array name? ______

   What element is specified? ______

3. Specify the first elements of two corresponding single dimensional arrays: the first identifying each employee by employee number, and the second his/her corresponding base pay.

____

____

8.2

OBJECTIVE: ... show how one-dimensional arrays may be used to efficiently specify many variables.

Arrays are used for more efficient handling of quantities of data when assigning individual names would be tedious and inefficient. Collections of data are very common in scientific problems, such as the 125 temperature readings; and in non-scientific applications, such as the grade averages of all the college freshmen.

Consider the problem of entering the 125 temperature readings into the computer for processing. Without arrays, 125 different names would have to be used and the READ statement would look as follows:

```
12345|6|789...
      READ(1,10)TEMP1,TEMP2,TEMP3,...,TEMP125
```

An easier way to write the above statement and a more efficient method for computer processing is to establish TEMP as an array name, and the 125 values can then be entered by the following READ statement:

```
12345|6|789...
      READ(1,10)TEMP
```

When the array, TEMP, is established, 125 memory locations are set aside. The READ statement reads the input data and assigns the first temperature into TEMP(1), the second into TEMP(2) and so forth with the last reading going into TEMP(125). Array names are constructed using the same rules specified for non-subscripted real and integer variable names.

EXERCISE

Specify array names for the following:

a) loading at each of 50 stations along a bridge truss

____

b) daily receipts of the XYC Retail Sales Corp. for one month of operation

____

c) voltages at 200 test points in an electronic circuit

____

d) number of defects in each of 25 specified samples of 6mm bolts

____

8.3

OBJECTIVE: ... establish arrays with DIMENSION and type specification statements.

Arrays are established using the DIMENSION statement.

GENERAL FORM

```
123456789···

      DIMENSIØN name1(subscript1),name2(subscript2),
     +... namen,(subscriptn)
```

COMPONENTS

namen — are array names

subscriptn — are dimensions of corresponding arrays

EXAMPLES

```
123456789···

      DIMENSIØN X(100)
      DIMENSIØN I(50),NØN(50),BR(75)
```

If an array is to be used in a program, a DIMENSION statement, which declares the number of elements in the array, may be used to request memory for the array. The following DIMENSION statement will reserve 10 memory locations for JOY, 20 for IDEA, and 30 for TIME.

```
123456789...
      DIMENSIØN JØY(10),IDEA(20),TIME(30)
```

The DIMENSION statement is a specification statement and must be located before all executable statements. The only statements which may precede a DIMENSION statement are another specification statement, a FORMAT statement or a subprogram statement. It is essential that subscripted variables be dimensioned because without dimension information the computer will not be able to distinguish between a subscripted variable and a subprogram.

If the variable name used in the array is defined as a specific type by means of an explicit type specification statement, the variable may be dimensioned in the type statement and a DIMENSION statement will not be required. The type statements,

```
123456789...
      REAL JØY(10),IDEA(20)
      INTEGER TIME(30)
```

explicitly define JOY as a real variable array with 10 elements, IDEA as a real variable array with 20 elements, and TIME as an integer array with 30 elements. The number used in the DIMENSION statement to define the size of the array must be an integer constant. A variable cannot be used to define array size because memory is reserved during compilation but values are not assigned until execution of the program. The DIMENSION and type statements may dimension any number of arrays.

It is important to dimension arrays to the maximum size needed since attempting to assign more values to an array than the DIMENSION provides will cause an error. Care should be exercised so that arrays are not considerably larger than needed since extra memory may increase the cost and decrease the efficiency of running your program.

Too many may be costly

Too few is chaotic

EXERCISE

Write DIMENSION statements to define the arrays in the practice question of Section 8.2

	12345	6	789···
a)			
b)			
c)			
d)			

8.4

OBJECTIVE: . . . write subscripts as arithmetic expressions.

A subscript is an integer quantity that is used to identify a particular element in the array. The dimensions of the array, as specified in the DIMENSION statement, give the number of subscripted quantities the array has and the maximum number each quantity can be.

There are definite rules to be followed in writing subscripts. FORTRAN '77 specifies the following:

1. Subscript quantities may contain arithmetic expressions that use any of the arithmetic operators: +, -, *, /, ** ,i.e., `SM(J+4)`

2. Subscript quantities may contain function references ,i.e., `XZ(SIN(TH))`

3. Subscript quantities may contain subscripted names ,i.e., `XR(MX(I,J))`

4. Mixed-mode expressions (integer and real only) may be used and they are evaluated the same as other FORTRAN expressions. If the evaluated expression is real, it is converted to an integer, since a subscript must be an integer.

5. The evaluated result of a subscripted quantity should always be greater than zero and less than or equal to the size of the corresponding dimension.

6. The number of subscript quantities in a subscript must be the same as the number of dimensions of the array as given in the DIMENSION statement.

EXAMPLES

VALID	INVALID	
A (IX)	A (-6)	(negative)
B (100)	N (0)	(zero)
M (J + 3)	J (A=2)	(statement, not expression)
NROW (2*I)		
COL (2*J-1)		
X (I(2))		

FORTRAN 66 is more restrictive. This standard requires the subscript to be one of these forms, where c and k are integer constants, and v is an integer variable reference:

FORM	EXAMPLE
c*v+k	A(2*I+3)
c*v-k	A(2*I-3)
c*v	A(3*M)
v+k	A(M+5)
v-k	A(M-8)

> My computer [is / is not] restricted to the FORTRAN 66

EXERCISE

Indicate which of the following are valid (V) and which are invalid (I):

a) ARY(IX) ____________________

b) ARY(A) ____________________

c) ARY (Z) ____________________

d) ARY (0) ____________________

e) ARY(-2) ____________________

f) ARY(I-2) ____________________

8.5

OBJECTIVE: . . . transfer values into and from one-dimensional arrays.

Subscripted variables are used in arithmetic statements just as other variables are and the values assigned to the various elements of the array may be changed within the program by means of an arithmetic statement. The statement

```
12345|6|789···
     | |ITEM(4)=ITEM(4)*2
```

will double the value assigned to the element ITEM (4) and replace the value assigned to ITEM (4) with this new value.

In all the examples in this section, READ could be replaced with WRITE to print out the data in the order explained for the READ.

Values may be assigned randomly to different array elements or they may be assigned sequentially. The entire array or any part of it may be used. The following example shows an entire array first being initialized to -1. sequentially by means of a DO loop, and then values are assigned randomly by computing an index based upon an input number.

EXAMPLE

Assume the part numbers of a certain machine are 4-digit numbers ranging from 1000 to 1999. These part numbers are used to compute indices from 1 to 1000 and the prices of the parts are then stored in array, PRICE, indexed by the shifted part numbers.
NOTE: Assume a valid FORMAT statement is present in each example in this section.

```
12345|6|789···
     | |DIMENSIØN PRICE(1000)
     | |DØ 5 I=1,1000                NOTE:
     | |  PRICE(I)= -1.0             NØPT  is the 4-digit
    5| |CØNTINUE                           part number
    6| |READ(1,10,END=20)NØPT,PR     PR is the price of this
   10| |FØRMAT(I4,F6.2)                    part
     | |IDX=NØPT-999
     | |PRICE(IDX)=PR
     | |GØ TØ 6
   20| |CØNTINUE
```

In the preceding example, each element was initialized to a -1.0, a value that is not a valid price, so that each element could be tested to see if each part number had a price. Any missing part number would have a price of -1.

It is not always necessary to initialize arrays. The important concept to remember is that arrays, like single variables, have undefined values until assigned values by your program. One may not assume that they are set to zero at the start of a program.

Selected sections of an array or specific elements of an array may be read into storage by assigning the appropriate subscript in the READ statement. The following statements will assign the value read from a card to array element A(10).

```
123456789...
      J=10
      READ(1,5)A(J)
```

which is equivalent to writing

```
123456789...
      READ(1,5)A(10)
```

Data to be assigned to a subscripted variable or printed out from memory as a subscripted variable may be read in or printed out by means of a READ/WRITE statement and a DO loop, such as follows:

```
123456789...
      DØ 5 J=1,100
        READ(1,6)UNIT(J)
    5 CØNTINUE
```

which is equivalent to writing 100 READ statements as follows:

```
123456789...
      READ(1,6)UNIT(1)
      READ(1,6)UNIT(2)
      READ(1,6)UNIT(3)
         ...
      READ(1,6)UNIT(100)
```

An implied DO loop can also be used to read in selected arrays.

The general form of the implied DO loop is as follows:

GENERAL FORM

```
123456789...
      ...(v(ix),ix=m1,m2,m3)
```

COMPONENTS

v is the array name

ix is a non-subscripted variable used as the index of the implied loop

m_1 is the inital value of the index; it may be a positive integer constant or non-subscripted integer variable

m_2 is the upper bound of the value of the index; it may be a positive integer constant or non-subscripted integer variable

m_3 is the increment of the index; it may be a positive integer constant or non-subscripted integer variable

EXAMPLES

```
123456789...
      READ(1,6)(UNIT(J),J=1,100)
      WRITE(3,7)(UNIT(J),J=1,100)
      READ(1,8)A,B,(X(I),I=1,20)
```

If 10 is punched on a card as the value of J, the following READ statement will read data from a card and assign the values read to elements A(1) through A(10).

```
123456789...
      READ(1,5)J,(A(K),K=1,J)
```

This has the meaning of one long list as follows:

```
123456789...
      READ(1,5)A(1),A(2),A(3),...A(10)
```

Two rules to note on the implied DO loop are:

1. The implied DO loop is used with the READ and WRITE statements only. (FORTRAN '77 permits an implied DO loop in a DATA statement. This was not permitted by FORTRAN 66.)

2. If m_3 is omitted, it is assumed to be 1.

If all elements of any array are to be read into the array (that is, none of the reserved memory locations are to be left blank), they may be read in or printed out by the following statement:

```
12345|6|789...

       READ(1,6)UNIT
       WRITE(3,6)UNIT
```

Character data, using the A format, may also be assigned to an array and retrieved from memory by calling for the appropriate subscripted variables.

EXAMPLE

Read a name punched in columns 1 to 22 of a card; assign it to array, NAME.

If each word can store 4 alphanumeric characters, then 6 words are needed to store 22 characters. (22÷4 = 5 full words + 2 characters requiring 6 words).

INPUT CARD:

```
RAND|ØLPH|bJØH|NATH|ANbS|.b|
1234|5678|9012|3456|7890|12|34567890...
```

STATEMENTS:

```
12345|6|789...

       DIMENSIØN NAME(6)
       READ(1,10)NAME
   10  FØRMAT(5A4,A2)
```

The data would be stored in NAME as follows:

NAME(1)	R A N D
NAME(2)	Ø L P H
NAME(3)	b J Ø H
NAME(4)	N A T H
NAME(5)	A N b S
NAME(6)	. b b b

If your computer stores a different number of alphanumeric characters than 4, determine the number of words needed to store 22 characters and re-write the three statements above for your computer.

```
12345 6 789...
```

At times it is desired to read in or write out only part of an array. This is done by means of a READ or WRITE and an implied DO loop, as shown in the following program segment:

```
12345 6 789...

        DIMENSIØN ARRAY(100)
        READ(1,15)(ARRAY(I),I=51,100)
```

In the above example only half of the array is read in and stored in ARRAY (51) to ARRAY (100). The implied DO loop parameters have the same <u>order</u> specified as in a DO loop written as follows:

```
12345 6 789...

        DIMENSIØN ARRAY(100)
        DØ 10 I=51,100
          READ(1,15)ARRAY(I)
   10   CØNTINUE
```

However, the number of records read, which depends on the FORMAT statement, may be different.

An optional incremental value may be used on the implied DO loop. The following would read every third value into ARRAY starting with ARRAY(51), that is, ARRAY (51), ARRAY(54), . . . ARRAY(99).

```
12345 6 789...

        DIMENSIØN ARRAY(100)
        READ(1,15)(ARRAY(J),J=51,100,3)
```

Input/output specifications for subscripted variables from different arrays may be defined to read in values from alternate arrays or in sequence all from one array and then from the other. The following would read alternate values from array A and B.

```
12345 6 789...

        DIMENSIØN A(4),B(4)
        READ(1,10)(A(K),B(K),K=1,4)
```

The order read is:

A (1), B (1), A (2), B (2), A (3), B (3), A (4), B (4)

The next statement would read 4 values into A and then 4 values into B when A and B are dimensioned as above.

```
12345|6|789...
     | |READ(1,10)A,B
```

The order read is:

A (1), A (2), A (3), A (4), B (1), B (2), B (3), B (4)

EXERCISE

1. Write a statement that will reserve 500 locations for a variable Y.

```
12345|6|789...
     | |
```

2. List in order the variables which would be read with the following statements.

```
12345|6|789...
     | |DIMENSIØN X(2),Y(2)
     | |READ(1,3) X,Y
```

3. Which variables will be printed by the following statement?

```
12345|6|789...
     | |WRITE(3,20) (JX(I), I=6,9)
```

4. Replace these two statements by one which accomplishes the same purpose.

```
12345|6|789...
     | |DIMENSIØN SCØRE(100)
     | |INTEGER SCØRE
```

8.6

OBJECTIVE: . . . calculate values of subscripted variables using arrays with DO loops.

Arrays are used frequently with DO loops to store the values computed within the DO loop. Assume two arrays A and B each containing N values have been read in as well as a value for N. Compute

$$C_i = \sqrt{A_i^2 + B_i^2} \quad \text{for all } i = 1, \ldots, N$$

The following statements will provide C_i.

```
123456789...
      ...
      DØ 10 I=1,N
        C(I)=SQRT(A(I)**2+B(I)**2)
   10 CØNTINUE
```

8.7

OBJECTIVE: . . . write the FORMAT statements used to input one-dimensional arrays.

In reading arrays, the FORMAT statement referenced in the READ statement supplies the information about the form, width, and location of data fields on the records in exactly the same way that it does for reading single variables. The array elements, in the order specified in the READ statement, are in one-to-one correspondence with the format codes of the specified FORMAT. The rules applied when all the array elements have not been read but the format codes have been exhausted are exactly the same as outlined in Chapter 5 for selecting a new record and repeating format codes. The use of the slash for record selection is also the same. Some applications in reading arrays under FORMAT control follow to aid in writing FORMAT statements for arrays.

EXAMPLE 1

Read all 10 values into array R if the values are given 10 per card using an F8.1 format code for each value.

```
123456789...

C  EXAMPLE 1
      DIMENSIØN R(10)
      READ(1,18) R
   18 FØRMAT(10F8.1)
```

One card is read containing 10 values. The first field in columns 1 to 8 is stored in R (1), the second field in columns 9 to 16 is stored in R (2), and so forth.

EXAMPLE 2

Read all 10 values into array R if the values are given 2 per card using an F8.0 format code for each value.

```
123456789...

C  EXAMPLE 2
      DIMENSIØN R(10)
      READ(1,20)R
   20 FØRMAT(2F8.0)
```

The format code (2F8.0) specifies two values per record. When the right parenthesis is reached terminating record one and there are more list elements to be read, a new record is read and the format code 2F8.0 is repeated and so forth until ten values have been read from five cards.

EXAMPLE 3

Read all 10 values into array R when the values are given one per card in columns 3 to 10 using F8.0 format code.

```
123456789...

C  EXAMPLE 3
      DIMENSIØN R(10)
      READ(1,8)R
    8 FØRMAT(2X,F8.0)
```

Ten cards are read. The value from card 1 is assigned to R(1), the value from card 2 to R(2), and so on.

EXAMPLE 4

The 20 elements of array A are read into A one at a time within a DO loop.

```
123456789...

C  EXAMPLE 4
      DIMENSIØN A(20)
      DØ 10 I=1,20
        READ(1,5)A(I)
   10 CØNTINUE
    5 FØRMAT(10F5.1)
```

The READ specifies only one list item to be read on each pass of the DO loop. Although the FORMAT specifies 10 values per record, only the first FORMAT code is used and the remaining codes are ignored. A total of 20 cards is read and one value in columns 1 through 5 of each card is assigned to the elements of A, from A (1) to A (20).

EXAMPLE 5

Only N values are to be read into array A which is dimensioned to handle 100. The value of N is read in from columns 1 and 2 of the first data card. The array values are read in 10 per card, in fields 5 columns wide.

```
123456789...

C  EXAMPLE 5
      DIMENSIØN A(100)
      READ(1,10)N,(A(I),I=1,N)
   10 FØRMAT(I2 /(10F5.1))
```

A total of 11 cards is read. The first card is read for the value of N by the code I2. The '/' then terminates that record and a new record is selected. A (1) to A (10) are read from card 2 in consecutive fields of 5 columns each. Then, upon reaching the right parenthesis, a new record is selected and the format codes are repeated from the last parentheses group, namely (10F5.1). Hence, the next 10 values are read into A (11) to A (20) from card 3, again from 10 fields each 5 columns long, and so on until all N values have been read.

EXERCISE

1. Answer the questions below given the following statements.

```
123456789...

      DIMENSIØN X(3),Y(3)
      READ(1,11)X,Y
   11 FØRMAT(F8.1)
```

a) List the variables in the order they would be read.

______ ______ ______ ______ ______ ______

b) How many data cards would be read? _______

c) Write a different **FORMAT** that would read in all 6 data values from one card.

1 2 3 4 5 6 7 8 9 · · ·

d) Write a different **READ** and **FORMAT** that would read in the values if they were punched on 3 cards in fields 8 columns wide in the order shown below.

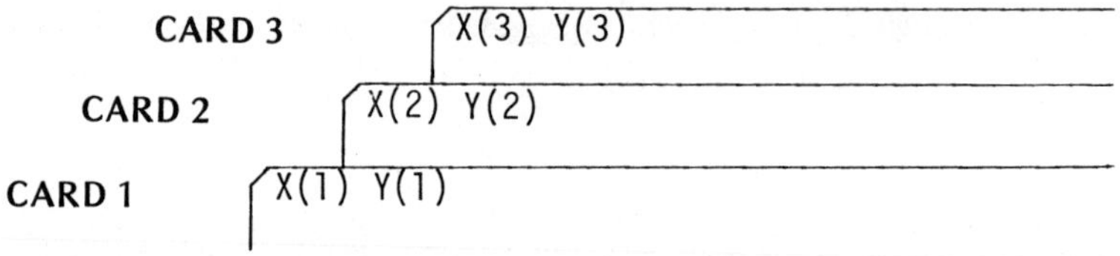

1 2 3 4 5 6 7 8 9

2. Given the following statements:

```
123456789...
      READ(1,40)(X(I),I=1,15,3)
   40 FØRMAT(F5.3,F8.1,F6.1)
```

List the variables in the order that they would be read and give the format code used and state which record was read as shown for X (1).

VARIABLE	FORMAT CODE	RECORD READ
X (1)	F5.3	1

3. Write a DIMENSION, READ and FORMAT statement to read in a title from columns 5 to 30 of a card.

```
12345|6|789...
     | |
-----+-+-------------------------------
     | |
-----+-+-------------------------------
     | |
-----+-+-------------------------------
```

8.8

OBJECTIVE . . . write the FORMAT statements used to print one-dimensional arrays.

Although no new principles are involved in writing one-dimensional arrays under FORMAT control, the following examples are given to aid in writing FORMAT statements for arrays. The rules for writing FORMAT statements given in Chapter 6 for single variables apply to arrays.

EXAMPLE 1

Array A dimensioned at 80 had all 80 values computed in the program. Write the WRITE and FORMAT statements to print out all the values, ten values per line with double spacing. Use F12.2 format code.

```
12345|6|789...
     | |
     | | ...
     | |WRITE(3,10)A
   10| |FØRMAT('0',10F12.2)
```

Eight lines each containing 10 values are printed. Line two contains the values for A (1) through A (10), line four has A (11) through A (20), and so forth, with line 16 containing A (71) through A (80).

Each number is printed with 2 decimal places, right-justified in fields 12 columns long.

EXAMPLE 2

Two arrays X and Y are each dimensioned to handle up to 100 values each. A number N, less than 101, and N values for the N elements of the X array were read in. The N corresponding values for Y were computed in the program where Y was a function of X. Write the WRITE and FORMAT statement to print the N values of X and Y so that corresponding values of X and Y appear on each line. Print headings of X and Y above each column.

```
12345 6 789...
        ...
        WRITE(3,70)
        WRITE(3,60)(X(I),Y(I),I=1,N)
   60   FØRMAT(1X,F10.1,5X,F10.1)
   70   FØRMAT(T6,'X',T20,'Y')
```

the output would appear as follows:

```
            1         2
   1234567890123456789012345678 9...
1      X             Y
2  nnnnnnnn.n    nnnnnnnn.n
3  nnnnnnnn.n    nnnnnnnn.n
4
```

8.9

OBJECTIVE:. . . use DO loops with arrays and . . . use nested DO loops.

DO loops are used extensively with arrays since the DO loop provides a ready means of incrementing an index that can be used for selecting array elements.

EXAMPLES

In Example 1, the 20 elements of array RAY are initialized to 0.0 and the index of the DO is used to reference elements one to twenty, respectively.

```
123456789...

C EXAMPLE 1
      DIMENSIØN RAY(20)
      DØ 7 J=1,20
        RAY(J)=0.0
    7 CØNTINUE
```

In Example 2 five values are assigned to RATE in a DATA statement. A value of TIME is read in and a DO loop is used to calculate the five distances that would be traveled for each RATE.

```
123456789...

C EXAMPLE 2
      DIMENSIØN RATE(5), DIST(5)
      DATA RATE/45.,50.,55.,60.,65./
      READ(1,90)TIME
   90 FØRMAT(F10.2)
      DØ 8 I=1,5
        DIST(I)=RATE(I)*TIME
    8 CØNTINUE
      WRITE(3,92)TIME,(RATE(I),DIST(I),I=1,5)
   92 FØRMAT('bTIME=',F10.2/(2F10.0))
      ...
```

DO loops can be nested as shown in the following diagram.

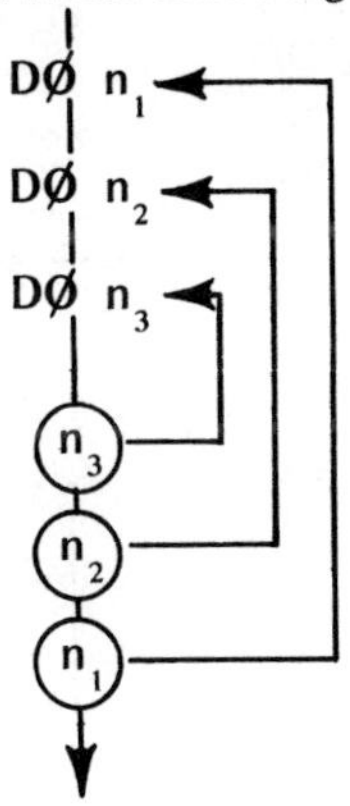

Figure 8.9-1. Nested DO Loops

The nested DO contains an innermost loop and an outermost loop. When a DO loop is contained with another DO loop, no overlap is allowed. The following branch is not permitted.

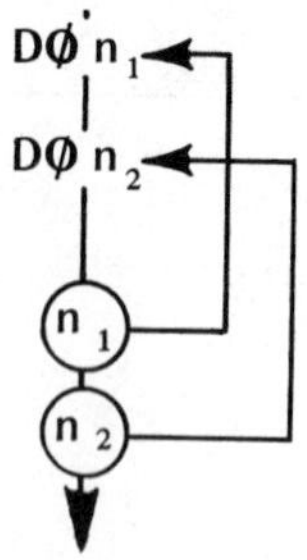

Figure 8.9-2. Overlapping DO Loops.

DO loops may end on the same statement as shown below.

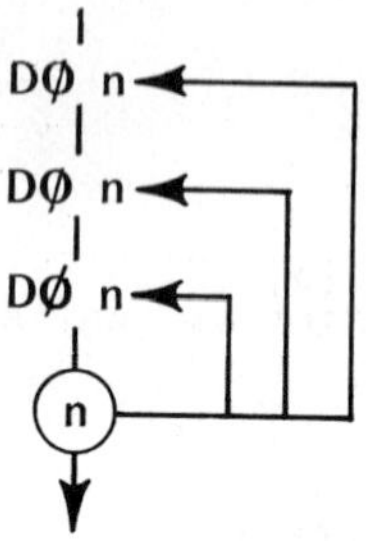

Figure 8.9-3. Nested DO Ending on the Same Statement.

Transfers can be made within any DO loop. Transfers can be made out of a DO loop but not into a DO from outside the DO.

Whereas nested DO's are found throughout the Computer World, the nested DODO is now extinct.

It is visually helpful to indent the statements within the range of the DO loops. Figure 8.9-4 shows three DO loops in a general nested form with each inner loop indented.

```
 12345 6 789012345 6789...
         DØ 10 I=1,NA                                 ┐
           S                                          │
           S                                          │
           DØ 20 J=1,NB              ┐                │
             S                       │                │
             S                       │                │
             S                       │                │  outer DØ
             DØ 30 K=1,NC ┐          │  middle DØ     │    loop
               S          │inner DØ  │    loop        │
               S          │  loop    │                │
               S          │          │                │
   30        CØNTINUE     ┘          │                │
             S                       │                │
             S                       │                │
   20      CØNTINUE                  ┘                │
           S                                          │
           S                                          │
   10    CØNTINUE                                     ┘
```

Figure 8.9-4. Indenting Nested DOs.

EXAMPLES

It may be desired to make computations for combinations of parameters. For example, compute and print the distances traveled for each of the five velocities above but also for different values of TIME. This can be done by using a nested DO loop as illustrated in example 1.

```
12345|6|789···

C EXAMPLE 1
      DIMENSIØN RATE(5),DIST(5)
      DATA RATE/45.,50.,55.,60.,65./
      DØ 4 J=1,6
        TIME=J
    6   DØ 8 I=1,5
          DIST(I)=RATE(I)*TIME
    8   CØNTINUE
        WRITE(3,92)TIME,(RATE(I),DIST(I),I=1,5)
    4 CØNTINUE
   92 FØRMAT('bTIME',F10.0/(2F10.0))
      ...
```

If the values for TIME were not spaced at even increments so that the index of the DO loop could be used, an array could be used and the values initialized in a DATA statement (or read in or computed). Example 2 shows how this would be.

```
12345|6|789···

C EXAMPLE 2
      DIMENSIØN RATE(5),DIST(5),T(6)
      DATA RATE/45.,50.,55.,60.,65./
      DATA T/1.,5.,10.,25.,50.,100./
      DØ 4 J=1,6
        TIME=T(J)
       ... same as example 1 from statement 6 on
```

CHAPTER EXERCISES

1. Write statements which will print all the elements in array R in a column. Single space the output. Allow a maximum of 10 places for each value of R with 1 decimal place. The DIMENSION statement is given.

```
12345|6|789···

      DIMENSIØN R(30)
```

2. Write the statements which will print the value of every even element of the array NRAY. Print the numbers 8 to a line allowing 6 digits for each number with 3 spaces between them. Double space the output. The DIMENSION statement is given.

```
123456789...
      DIMENSIØN NRAY(64)
```

3. Write a program segment which takes N different positive integers, IN_1, IN_2, IN_3, . . . , IN_n and determines the square of each number, the product of all N numbers ($IN_1 \cdot IN_2 \cdots IN_n$) and the product of the squares of all the numbers ($IN_1^2 \cdot IN_2^2 \cdots IN_n^2$). Write each number and its square from 1 to N on a separate line followed by the product of the numbers and the product of their squares.

```
123456789...
```

4. Write the necessary statements to compute an array Y(I) where each element is equal to X**I. Provide values for I from 2 to 8. Read in the value of X used. Write the value of X and a table of values containing each I and X**I.

1 2 3 4 5	6	7 8 9

CHAPTER PROGRAMMING PROBLEMS

TOPIC APPLICATION

a) Dimension statement
b) Reading one dimensional arrays
c) Arithmetic statements with subscripted variables
d) Writing one dimensional arrays
e) Reading and writing alphanumeric data

Problem 8.1

PROBLEM STATEMENT

Write a program to determine the first twenty terms of a Fibonacci series. Starting with the first two terms (n_1 and n_2) given, determine each succeeding term such that it is the sum of the two preceding terms or

$$n_j = n_{j-1} + n_{j-2}$$

For example, if the first two terms given are 2 and 5 the third term, n_3, will be 7 (2+5). The fourth term would be 12, the fifth 19, the sixth 31 and so on, producing the series

$$2,5,7,12,19,31,\ldots,n_j$$

where j for this problem is 20

PROBLEM NOTES

Write an arithmetic statement using subscripted variables to calculate the required terms. Precede this with a DO statement providing a DO variable to index the subscripted variables from 3 to 20, in steps of one.

INPUT

A Data Card with information punched into the indicated fields will be supplied by the instructor.

Card Column 1-21:	Series Name
Card Column 22-34:	Problem No.
Card Column 38 & 39:	Value of First Term n_1
Card Column 41 & 42:	Value of Second Term n_2

Read in data as follows:

Series name:	A format code using real variable names
Problem number:	A format code using integer names
Value of terms:	I2 Format code

OUTPUT

Provide an output of the 20 values by printing 5 lines of 4 values each. Print out as follows starting at the top of a new page.

Skip two lines

Print series name in columns 11 through 31 and problem no. in columns 33 through 45 using A format code.

Skip two lines

Write out series terms in the form shown below starting in column 12.

n_1 n_2 n_3 n_4

n_5 n_6 n_7 n_8

n_9 n_{10} n_{11} n_{12}

n_{13} n_{14} n_{15} n_{16}

n_{17} n_{18} n_{19} n_{20}

Use I10 format for each term. Leave at least two spaces between values.

Problem 8.2

Write a program (using two nested DO loops) to compute an array M(I)=NX**I for I = 2 to 4 for each value of NX from 1 to 5. Write out a table for values calculated in the following form:

```
         1         2
12345678901234567890123456789...
NX    I=2     I=3     I=4

 1  nnnnnnn nnnnnnn nnnnnnn
 2  nnnnnnn nnnnnnn nnnnnnn
 3  nnnnnnn nnnnnnn nnnnnnn
 4  nnnnnnn nnnnnnn nnnnnnn
 5  nnnnnnn nnnnnnn nnnnnnn
```

Problem 8.3

Write a program (using two nested DO loops) to compute the amount of money earned for each year 'IY' from 1 to 10 years and for rates 'i' of .05, .055, .06, .065, .07 and .075. Initialize the rates in a DATA statement. Read in the value for the principal 'P'. Write out the principal, followed by a table of number of years, rates and amounts.

The formula for amount earned at simple interest for t years is

$$A = P + Prt$$

where A = amount
P = principal
r = rate
t = time in years

9 FORTRAN

9.1 . . . define and specify two-dimensional arrays.

9.2 . . . transfer data into and from two-dimensional arrays.

9.3 . . . write FORMAT statements to input two-dimensional arrays.

9.4 . . . write FORMAT statements to output two-dimensional arrays.

9.5 . . . initialize array variables by means of DATA statement.

9.6 . . . define and specify three-dimensional arrays.

9.7 . . . write FORMAT statements to read and write three-dimensional arrays.

9.1

OBJECTIVE: . . . define and specify two-dimensional arrays.

A two-dimensional array is one in which two subscripts are used to refer to an element in the array.

The subscripts are written in parentheses, separated by commas. Examples of two-dimensional array elements are A(3,4) and I(5,4).

Two-dimensional arrays can be visualized as a table of values where the first subscript indicates the number of the row and the second subscript indicates the number of the column. An example is shown in Figure 9.1-1. The total number of storage locations required is the product of the number of rows times the number of columns.

	Column 1	Column 2	Column 3	Column 4
Row 1	10.8 A(1,1)	7.5 A(1,2)	8.4 A(1,3)	6.5 A(1,4)
Row 2	11.2 A(2,1)	-5.4 A(2,2)	6.2 A(2,3)	8.0 A(2,4)
Row 3	1.6 A(3,1)	2.7 A(3,2)	-4.8 A(3,3)	6.5 A(3,4)

Figure 9.1-1. Two-dimensional Array, A(3,4)

The element in Row 2, column 3 would be referred to by the subscripted variable name, A(2,3), and it contains the value 6.2. The FORTRAN subscript notation is similar to the mathematical notation a_{ij}, where i and j refer to the row and column of the item, respectively.

Two dimensional arrays are established in a DIMENSION or type specification statement at the start of the program as was done with one-dimensional arrays. The following DIMENSION statement,

```
123456789...
      DIMENSIØN A(2,4),B(3,5)
```

will reserve 8 memory spaces for A and 15 memory spaces for B. Each of these arrays may just as well have been dimensioned with a single subscript with regard to computer memory considerations. The reason for using double subscripts is to permit the presentation of data in accordance with the programmer's conceptual visualization of data. Data associated with determinants and matrices are always visualized and identified by row and column positions. Consequently, the programmer can handle such data best by double-subscripted notation, using the first subscript to define the row and the second subscript the column in which the element is located. The computer will assign multiple-subscripted data in a specific sequence just as it does single-subscripted data, and the programmer must be aware of the sequence in memory in order to properly assign data to an array and transfer data out of it.

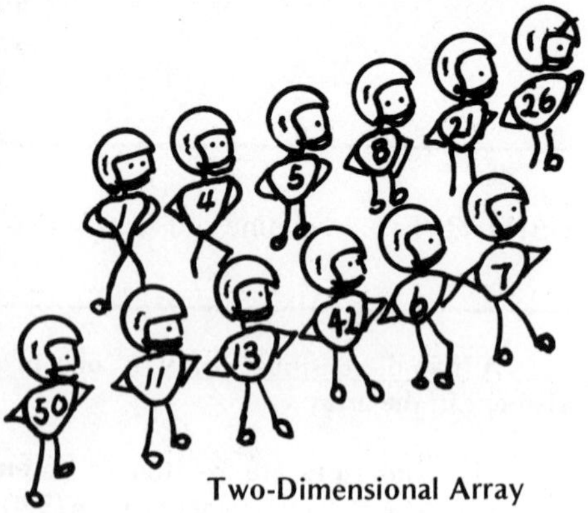

Two-Dimensional Array

The 3 by 4 array, A, in Figure 9.1-1 would be assigned to memory locations in the following order:

A(1,1)	
A(2,1)	Column 1
A(3,1)	
A(1,2)	
A(2,2)	Column 2
A(3,2)	
A(1,3)	
A(2,3)	Column 3
A(3,3)	
A(1,4)	
A(2,4)	Column 4
A(3,4)	

The order in which two-dimensional arrays are assigned is as follows: start with (1,1), and first increase the first subscript up to the maximum, and then the second. Another way of stating this is that the elements are stored by columns, all of column 1, then column 2, and so forth as is indicated above.

EXERCISE

1. Fill in the subscripts for matrix A using row, column notation

```
        (__,__)  (__,__)  (__,__)
A  =    (__,__)  (__,__)  (__,__)
        (__,__)  (__,__)  (__,__)
```

2. How many storage locations does the computer need for A?

answer ______________________

3. Show the order of the subscripted variables as the computer denotes them by filling in the subscripts.

```
(__,__)
(__,__)
(__,__)
(__,__)
(__,__)
(__,__)
(__,__)
(__,__)
(__,__)
```

4. Write a DIMENSION statement to specify A in a program.

1 2 3 4 5	6	7 8 9 • • •

9.2

OBJECTIVE: ... transfer data into and from two-dimensional arrays.

Values are assigned to and transferred from two-dimensional arrays by means of assignment statements and by READ/WRITE statements, just like one-dimensional arrays are. When double subscripted variables are used in a statement, they must be identified by both subscripts, because memory locations are assigned to these variables by their subscript identity. The following statement assigns the square of the value assigned to XROW(3,4) into SQD:

```
123456789...
      SQD=XRØW(3,4)**2
```

Operations can be performed using multiple subscripts supplied by DO index variables as shown in the following example.

EXAMPLE

Write a program segment to multiply two matrices A and B forming a third matrix, C. Assume that matrix A has m rows and n columns, and matrix B has n rows and m columns. The elements of matrix are defined by:

$$C_{i,j} = \sum_{k}^{n} a_{i,k} \cdot b_{k,j} \quad \text{for } i=1,2\ldots m \quad j=1,2\ldots m$$

with the corresponding Flow diagram

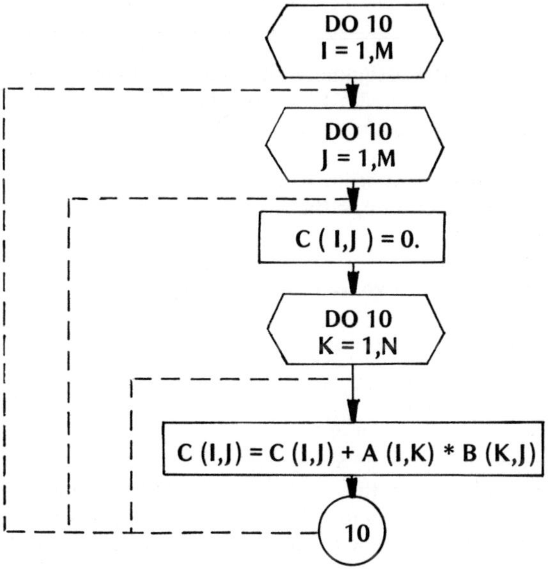

DO 10
I = 1,M
DO 10
J = 1,M
C (I,J) = 0.
DO 10
K = 1,N
C (I,J) = C (I,J) + A (I,K) * B (K,J)
10

The program segment corresponding to the flow diagram is then:

```
12345 6 789...
      DØ 10 I=1,M
         DØ 10 J=1,M
            C(I,J)=0
            DØ 10 K=1,N
               C(I,J)=C(I,J)+A(I,K)*B(K,J)
   10 CØNTINUE
```

EXERCISE

1. Write a program segment to initialize each element of array A to zero, and each element of array B to one. Assume each has m rows and n columns.

```
123456789...
```

In reading data from cards, the assignment of each data item to its proper subscripted array element must be considered. Likewise, the retrieval of subscripted data from memory for printout must fit the desired format of the output page.

The order in which data is read in from cards or printed out from memory can be altered by the use of a double DO loop, either explicit, implied or a combination of both, in a READ or WRITE statement.

The implied DO loop consisting of two loops is as follows:

```
((X(I,J),J=1,N), I = 1,M)
  \______/
   inner
 \_______________________/
          outer
```

The implied DO loop is used with the READ and WRITE statements only.[1] The inner loop is executed first and then the outer, in the same order as if they had been explicitly stated in one explicit and one implied DO loop (EXAMPLE 1) or in two explicit DO loops (EXAMPLE 2).

EXAMPLE 1

```
123456789...
      DØ 10 I=1,M
        READ(1,20)(X(I,J),J=1,N)
   10 CØNTINUE
```

EXAMPLE 2

```
123456789...
      DØ 10 I=1,M
      DØ 10 J=1,N
        READ(1,20)X(I,J)
   10 CØNTINUE
```

[1] Some compilers permit implied DO statements on the DATA statement.

In each case above, I is set to 1 and J ranges from 1 to N, I is incremented to 2 and J ranges from 1 to N, and so forth until I exceeds M. An optional increment can be added to the implied DO loop just as it can be to the explicit DO loop.

In EXAMPLE 1, for a value of M=3, N=2, the READ statement is executed three times. EXAMPLE 1 is equivalent to the following statements written without DO loops.

```
123456789...

      READ(1,20) X(1,1),X(1,2)
      READ(1,20) X(2,1),X(2,2)
      READ(1,20) X(3,1),X(3,2)
```

In EXAMPLE 2, for M=3, N=2, the READ statement is executed six times. EXAMPLE 2 is equivalent to the following statements written without DO loops.

```
123456789...

      READ(1,20) X(1,1)
      READ(1,20) X(1,2)
      READ(1,20) X(2,1)
      READ(1,20) X(2,2)
      READ(1,20) X(3,1)
      READ(1,20) X(3,2)
```

Table 9.2-1 shows variations of a READ statement for implied and explicit DO loops and the order that variables are assigned. In each case, READ could be replaced with WRITE. Note that I and J are interchangeable and could be replaced by any integer variable. Assume M=3 and N=2 for a 3 by 2 array, X.

Table 9.2-1

List Order of Array Elements
for Explicit and Implied DO Loops.

EXPLICIT DO STATEMENT	IMPLIED DO STATEMENT	LIST ORDER
12345 6 789···	789···	
DØ 20 J=1,N DØ 20 I=1,M READ(1,10)X(I,J) 20 CØNTINUE	READ(1,10)X	X(1,1) X(2,1) X(3,1) X(1,2) X(2,2) X(3,2)
DØ 20 J=1,N DØ 20 I=1,M READ(1,10)X(I,J) 20 CØNTINUE	READ(1,10)((X(I,J),I=1,M),J=1,N)	X(1,1) X(2,1) X(3,1) X(1,2) X(2,2) X(3,2)
DØ 20 I=1,N DØ 20 J=1,M READ(1,10) X(J,I) 20 CØNTINUE	READ(1,10)((X(J,I),J=1,M),I=1,N)	X(1,1) X(2,1) X(3,1) X(1,2) X(2,2) X(3,2)
DØ 20 I=1,M DØ 20 J=1,N READ(1,10) X(I,J) 20 CØNTINUE	READ(1,10) ((X(I,J),J=1,N),I=1,M)	X(1,1) X(1,2) X(2,1) X(2,2) X(3,1) X(3,2)
DØ 20 J=1,M DØ 20 I=1,N READ(1,10) X(J,I) 20 CØNTINUE	READ(1,10) ((X(J,I),I=1,N),J=1,M)	X(1,1) X(1,2) X(2,1) X(2,2) X(3,1) X(3,2)

EXERCISE

For questions 1 through 7 the array A is given values and keypunched on one card as shown below:

$$A = \begin{vmatrix} 2.1 & 1.0 & 4.0 \\ 3.1 & 4.0 & 1.2 \\ 6.0 & 2.1 & 7.1 \end{vmatrix}$$

```
   2.1  3.1  6.0  1.0  4.0  2.1  4.0  1.2  7.1

         1         2         3         4         5
12345678901234567890123456789012345678901234567890
```

1. Write a READ statement to read matrix A into core with the data punched as shown above using the array name without subscripts.

```
12345|6|789...
     | |
-----+-+------
     | |
```

2. Write a READ statement to read matrix A into core using an implied DO.

```
12345|6|789...
     | |
```

Answer question 3 if the data is repunched as follows:

```
   2.1  1.0  4.0  3.1  4.0  1.2  6.0  2.1  7.1

         1         2         3         4         5         6
123456789012345678901234567890123456789012345678901234567890
```

3. Write a READ statement to input matrix A if the data is repunched in the form shown.

12345	6	789···

4. Write a DO loop to add the elements in row 1.

12345	6	789···

5. Write a DO loop to add the elements in column 3.

12345	6	789···

6. Write a WRITE statement to printout the elements so they appear in the order read in question 2.

12345	6	789···

7. Write a WRITE statement to print the main diagonal.

```
123456789···


```

9.3

OBJECTIVE: ... write FORMAT statements to input two-dimensional arrays.

In reading two-dimensional arrays, it is important to recall the order that arrays are stored so that the proper association is made between the elements of the arrays and the format codes. The information supplied by the FORMAT is the same as for single variables. The following applications show how to write FORMAT statements for two-dimensional arrays.

EXAMPLE 1

Read the elements of a 3 by 2 array, MTX, into memory if the values use adjacent fields 5 columns wide and are punched on cards using one card for each column, as shown below:

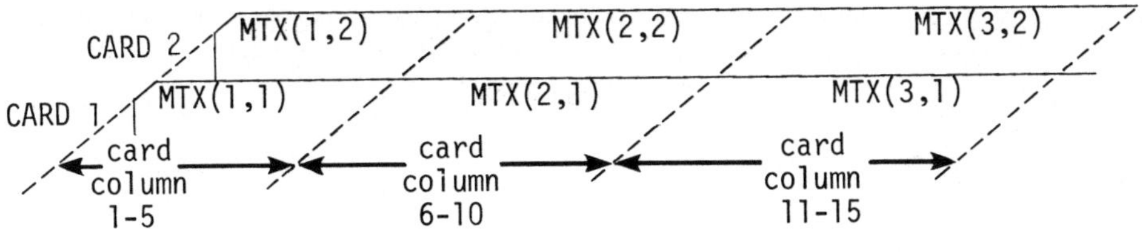

This would be done as follows:

```
123456789···

      DIMENSIØN MTX(3,2)
      READ(1,5)MTX
    5 FORMAT(3I5)
```

As two-dimensional arrays are stored by columns, the array name can be used without subscripts to write them out. Another correct way would use the following READ statement:

```
123456789...
      READ(1,5)((MTX(I,J),I=1,3),J=1,2)
```

EXAMPLE 2

Read the elements of a 3 by 2 array, NTX, if each value uses a field 5 columns wide and if each card contains the elements of a row as shown:

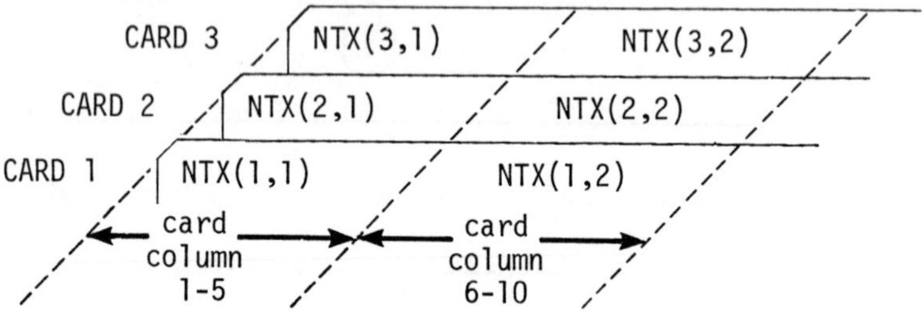

This would be done as follows:

```
123456789...
      DIMENSIØN NTX(3,2)
      READ(1,6)((NTX(I,J),J=1,2),I=1,3)
    6 FØRMAT(2I5)
```

An implied DO loop must be used to override the column order that is used if the array name only is used. The FORMAT specifies two values per card after which a new record is selected for the next two values and so on until the list is exhausted.

EXERCISE

Data for practice problem:

INPUT DECK

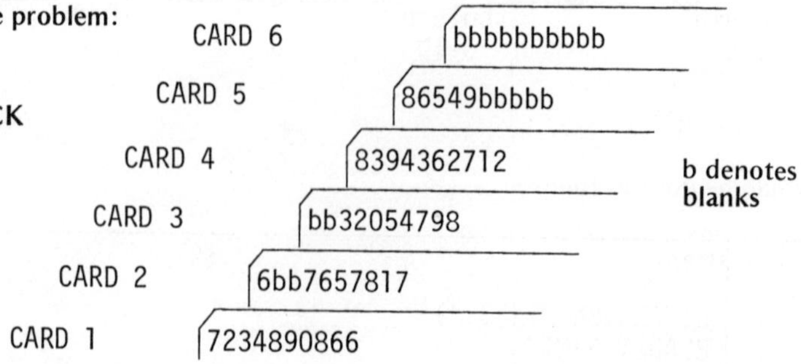

1. Given the following statements, what would be the values for the array elements using the above data deck.

```
123456789...

      DIMENSIØN R(3,2)
      READ(1,10)R
   10 FØRMAT(F3.1)
```

ANSWER

ELEMENT	VALUE
R(1,1)	______
R(2,1)	______
R(3,1)	______
R(1,2)	______
R(2,2)	______
R(3,2)	______

2. Answer using the above input deck and DIMENSION but using the following READ and FORMAT statements.

```
123456789...

      READ(1,7)((R(I,J),I=1,3),J=1,2)
    7 FØRMAT(2F3.1)
```

ELEMENT	VALUE
R(1,1)	______
R(2,1)	______
R(3,1)	______
R(1,2)	______
R(2,2)	______
R(3,2)	______

9.4

OBJECTIVE: . . . write FORMAT statements to output two-dimensional arrays.

The following examples are given to apply the rules for writing FORMAT statements to the printing of arrays.

EXAMPLE 1

The following DIMENSION and READ statements were used to read in matrix MX. The WRITE and FORMAT statements below print MX out, 15 elements per line. The format code I7 includes 2 spaces between elements. Single spacing is used between lines.

```
123456789...

      DIMENSIØN MX(15,8)
      READ(1,5)MX
    5 FØRMAT(15I5)
      WRITE(3,10)MX
   10 FØRMAT('b',15I7)
```

EXAMPLE 2

In order to write out the above array, MX, printing 1 row per line with the same spacing as above, the following statements are used:

```
123456789...

      WRITE(3,15)((MX(I,J),J=1,8),I=1,15)
   15 FØRMAT('b',8I7)
```

EXAMPLE 3

To write out the main diagonal of array, NX (dimensioned 5 by 5) in the following form,

	1-5	6-10	11-15	16-20	21-25
1	NX(1,1)				
2					
3		NX(2,2)			
4					
5			NX(3,3)		
6					
7				NX(4,4)	
8					
9					NX(5,5)
10					

the statements below are used:

```
123456789...
      WRITE(3,40)(NX(I,I),I=1,5)
   40 FØRMAT('b',I5//T7,I5//T12,I5//T17,I5//T22,I5)
```

9.5

OBJECTIVE: . . . initialize array variables by means of a DATA statement.

The DATA statement provides a convenient way to initialize an array. For example, if it is desired to initialize the elements of array, ARY, dimensioned 15 by 10, to 0., the following DATA statement is used:

```
123456789...
      DIMENSIØN ARY(15,10)
      DATA ARY/150*0./
```

In order to initialize ARY without using a DATA statement, the following DO statements would be used:

```
123456789...
      DIMENSIØN ARY(15,10)
      DØ 5 I=1,15
        DØ 6 J=1,10
           ARY(I,J)=0.
    6   CØNTINUE
    5 CØNTINUE
```

When the DO loops are simple as on the previous page, an alternate shorter version of the DO may be used as is shown below.

```
12345 6 789...

        DØ 5 I=1,15
          DØ 5 J=1,10
    5     ARY(I,J)=0.
```

If the CONTINUE is not used, care must be taken that the last statement is executable, but not a branch statement, a termination statement, or another DO statement. Using the CONTINUE to end the DO loop makes it more easily modified.

The DATA statement initializes the variables and arrays only once, at the start of the program. If re-initialization is required in a program, the DO statements would have to be used.

Arrays, like variables, do not need to be initialized if they are going to be read into or have values assigned into them as both operations are destructive of any prior contents. In the following program segment, initialization is not required.

```
12345 6 789...

        DIMENSIØN RAY(5,6)
        READ(1,90)RAY
        ...
```

If, however, the first appearance of the array is on the right-hand side of the "=" in an assignment statement, as in a summing operation, it is essential to assign initial values. In the next example, SUM must be initialized, TEMP need not be.

```
12345 6 789...

        DIMENSIØN SUM(2,7),TEMP(2,7)
        DATA SUM/14*0./
    4   READ(1,3,END=90)TEMP
         DØ 5 I=1,2
           DØ 6 J=1,7
              SUM(I,J)=SUM(I,J)+TEMP(I,J)
    6      CØNTINUE
    5   CØNTINUE
        GØ TØ 4
   90   CØNTINUE
```

The statements above sum up the like elements of array, TEMP, which might store two temperature readings for seven days of the week. Because SUM appears on the right of the "=", it must be assigned a value before it can be used. TEMP does not need initializing because the READ destroys any previous values.

All the elements of the array do not have to be initialized to the same value. The next example shows the first 50 elements of IRY initialized to 0, and the second 50 elements to -1, using a DATA statement.

```
123456789...

      DIMENSIØN IRY(100)
      DATA IRY/50*0,50*-1/
```

The DATA statement can also be used to initialize character data in arrays. Chapter 11 explains how this is done.

9.6

OBJECTIVE: ... define and specify three-dimensional arrays.

Three-dimensional arrays use three subscripts, which represent a three-dimensional table where the subscripts are the row, column, and rank, respectively. For example X(2,3,4) means 2 rows, 3 columns, and 4 ranks.

Three-dimensional arrays are defined similarly to two-dimensional arrays. The following DIMENSION statement establishes X as a three-dimensional array:

```
123456789...

      DIMENSIØN X(2,3,4)
```

The total number of memory locations reserved is 2 times 3 times 4 or 24.

Values can be assigned to array elements by means of the assignment statement. In the next example, a functional value of X is stored in the array element, PLANE (4,6,3). Assume X has a value from previous statements.

```
123456789...

      I=4
      J=I+2
      PLANE(I,J,3)=X**3+2.*X+7.5
```

The three-dimensional array X(2, 3, 2) would be assigned memory locations as follows:

X (1, 1, 1)	Row 1	Column 1	Rank 1
X (2, 1, 1)	Row 2		
X (1, 2, 1)	Row 1	Column 2	
X (2, 2, 1)	Row 2		
X (1, 3, 1)	Row 1	Column 3	
X (2, 3, 1)	Row 2		
X (1, 1, 2)	Row 1	Column 1	Rank 2
X (2, 1, 2)	Row 2		
X (1, 2, 2)	Row 1	Column 2	
X (2, 2, 2)	Row 2		
X (1, 3, 2)	Row 1	Column 3	
X (2, 3, 2)	Row 2		

Again, the first subscript increases most rapidly, then the second and finally the third.

The following example shows when a 3-dimensional array might be used to READ in data.

EXAMPLE 1

A weather station has collected daily average temperature readings for the past five years. They wish to read in the data and compute statistics on it, while preserving the date information so that information could be printed out as follows: "Mar. 3, 1975 had the lowest 5 year average temperature". The data is tabulated for each day of each month for each of the 5 years. The array, TEMP, is used to read in the values. TEMP is dimensioned 31, 12, 5 for a maximum of 31 days per month, 12 months, 5 years. Some months, such as Feb, would not use all 31 values. When the data is used, a separate table giving the days per month is used to allow skipping the unfilled arrays.

Only the temperatures are punched on the cards, but they are arranged by month so that the first 31 values would be for month 1, year 1; the next 31 values for month 2, year 1; and so on. Zeros are read to fill arrays for months with less than 31 days. The following read statement is used:

```
123456789...

C  EXAMPLE 1
      READ(1,20)TEMP
```

This assigns the first 31 values as follows:

TEMP (1, 1, 1), TEMP (2, 1, 1), . . . TEMP (31, 1, 1)

the next 31 values to:

TEMP (1, 2, 1), TEMP (2, 2, 1) . . . TEMP (31, 2, 1)

and so forth, and hence,

TEMP (21, 3, 2) contains the reading for Mar 21 of the second year.

EXAMPLE 2

The example below shows the list order for the array R, dimensioned (3 by 2 by 2) if read in any of the following ways:

STATEMENTS

```
123456789...

C  EXAMPLE 2
      DIMENSIØN R(3,2,2)
      READ(1,8)R
            or
      READ(1,8)(((R(I,J,K),I=1,3),J=1,2),K=1,2)
            or
      DØ    10    K=1,2
      DØ    10    J=1,2
      DØ    10    I=1,3
        READ(1,8) R(I,J,K)
   10 CØNTINUE
```

<u>ORDER READ</u>

R (1, 1, 1)
R (2, 1, 1)
R (3, 1, 1)
R (1, 2, 1)
R (2, 2, 1)
R (3, 2, 1)
R (1, 1, 2)
R (2, 1, 2)
R (3, 1, 2)
R (1, 2, 2)
R (2, 2, 2)
R (3, 2, 2)

The first and second READ statements above are equivalent to one READ statement with a list of 12 items as follows:

```
123456789...

      READ(1,8)R(1,1,1),R(2,1,1),R(3,1,1)...R(3,2,2)
```

The third statement, using three DO loops is equivalent to 12 READ statements, each reading only one item as follows:

```
123456789...

      READ(1,8)R(1,1,1)
      READ(1,8)R(2,1,1)
      READ(1,8)R(3,1,1)
        ...
      READ(1,8)R(3,2,2)
```

This order can be varied by varying the order of the indices in the implied or explicit DO loops, just as was done with two-dimensional arrays.

9.7

OBJECTIVE: ... write FORMAT statements to read and write three-dimensional arrays.

The manner in which three-dimensional arrays are read and written is similar to two-dimensional arrays, as shown in the following examples.

EXAMPLE 1

An airline keeps data on the number of seats sold on each of its flights to 10 cities, 3 flights a day for 7 days of the week. A three-dimensional array NR is used to store the number of seats sold. The first subscript represents the number code of the city, (1 to 10), the second represents the flight (1 to 3) and the third represents the day of the week. Hence, NR (3, 2, 4) = 51 means 51 seats were sold on city number three's second flight on Wednesday. The number of seats sold is punched on cards at the end of each week, arranged as follows:
(c represents city, f the flight, and d the day.)

	1-4	5-8		37-40
CARD 1	$c_1f_1d_1$	$c_2f_1d_1$	. . .	$c_{10}f_1d_1$
CARD 2	$c_1f_2d_1$	$c_2f_2d_1$	. . .	$c_{10}f_2d_1$
CARD 3	$c_1f_3d_1$	$c_2f_3d_1$	. . .	$c_{10}f_3d_1$
	. . .			
CARD 21	$c_1f_3d_7$	$c_2f_3d_7$	. . .	$c_{10}f_3d_7$

The DIMENSION statement and READ and FORMAT statements to read in the above data are as follows:

```
123456789...
C  EXAMPLE 1
      DIMENSIØN NR(10,3,7)
      READ(1,25)NR
   25 FØRMAT (10I4)
```

EXAMPLE 2

The program written in the above application is first tested with a small sample of data consisting of the number of reservations for 4 cities, 3 flights per day for two days. The data is punched on the cards in the order shown below.

	1-4	5-8	9-12	13-16
CARD 1	$c_1f_1d_1$	$c_2f_1d_1$	$c_3f_1d_1$	$c_4f_1d_1$
CARD 2	$c_1f_2d_1$	$c_2f_2d_1$	$c_3f_2d_1$	$c_4f_2d_1$
CARD 3	$c_1f_3d_1$	$c_2f_3d_1$	$c_3f_3d_1$	$c_4f_3d_1$
CARD 4	$c_1f_1d_2$	$c_2f_1d_2$	$c_3f_1d_2$	$c_4f_1d_2$
CARD 5	$c_1f_2d_2$	$c_2f_2d_2$	$c_3f_2d_2$	$c_4f_2d_2$
CARD 6	$c_1f_3d_2$	$c_2f_3d_2$	$c_3f_3d_2$	$c_4f_3d_2$

Using the same DIMENSION statement above, write a READ and FORMAT to read in the test data as follows:

```
123456789...
C  EXAMPLE 2
      DIMENSIØN NR (10,3,7)
      READ (1,35)(((NR(I,J,K),I=1,4),J=1,3),K=1,2)
   35 FØRMAT (4I4)
```

EXAMPLE 3

In the previous example, when less than the entire array was read in, even though the data was punched in a similar manner, it was necessary to change the FORMAT to specify the number of values per card. A general way to read in the number of data values (that is, the dimensions of the data) and then read the data in such a way that it is not necessary to change the FORMAT each time the dimensions of the data case change is shown below. The dimensions read in may not exceed those specified in the DIMENSION statement.

```
12345 6 789...
        DIMENSIØN NR(10,3,7)
        READ(1,5) NC, NF, ND
     5  FØRMAT(3I2)
        DØ 20 K=1, ND
          DØ 20 J=1, NF
            READ(1,15)(NR(I,J,K),I=1,NC)
    20  CØNTINUE
    15  FØRMAT(10I4)
```

The FORMAT specifies the maximum number of values that would be on a card. At each READ, only NC values are read so the remaining format codes are ignored, NC can be any number from 1 to 10. Each execution of the READ reads one card. The inner DO loop (DO 20 J=1, NF) reads the following data cards:

```
CARD 1   NR(1,1,1),NR(2,1,1)... NR(NC,1,1)
  .        .
  .        .
  .        .
CARD NF  NR(1,NF,1) NR(2,NF,1) ... NR(NC,NF,1)
```

The outer DO loop would repeat the above pattern ND times, incrementing the third index each time. A total of NF times ND cards would be read.

EXAMPLE 4

The array NR contains the number of reservations for 10 cities, 3 flights per day, 7 days a week as explained in Example 3. The report below beginning with the blank line at line 2, is written by the statements below.

```
             1         2         3         4         5         6
    123456789012345678901234567890123456789012345678901234567890...
 1  FLIGHT     S         M         T         W         T         F         S
 2
 3                                        CITY  1
 4
 5      1     nnn       nnn       nnn       nnn       nnn       nnn       nnn
 6
 7      2     nnn        .         .         .         .         .         .
 8
 9      3     nnn        .         .         .         .         .         .
10
11
12                                        CITY  2
13
14                                           .
15
16                                           .
17
```

```
123456789...
      DIMENSIØN NR(10,3,7)
      DØ 20 I=1,10
        WRITE(3,15) I,((NR(I,J,K), K=1,7),J=1,3)
   15   FØRMAT(/T32,'CITY',1X,I2//(T5,I1,7I8/))
   20 CØNTINUE
```

CHAPTER EXERCISES

1. Three-dimensional arrays are initialized by means of three DO loops or by means of a DATA statement just like two-dimensional arrays are.

   a) Write three DO statements to initalize ARAY, which is a 3X4X5 array, to 0.

```
123456789...



```

b) Write one DATA statement for the above.

```
123456789...
```

2. Write a DIMENSION, READ, and FORMAT statement to read in a 3 row by 4 column integer matrix. Each card contains one column of elements punched consecutively in I3 format.

```
123456789...
```

3. Write necessary statements to input the matrix in problem 2 if each card contains one row of elements punched consecutively in I3 format.

```
123456789...
```

4. How would the following WRITE and FORMAT statements print out the array C?

```
123456789...
      INTEGER C(3,3)
      WRITE(3,10)((C(I,J),I=1,3),J=1,3)
   10 FØRMAT('0',4(I3,2X))
```

$$C = \begin{vmatrix} 3 & 2 & 7 \\ 5 & 8 & 1 \\ 4 & 6 & 0 \end{vmatrix}$$

```
           1         2         3         4
1234567890123456789012345678901234567890123456789...
1
2
3
4
5
```

5. Using the data cards

```
CARD 4  435637924
CARD 3  765722813
CARD 2  549217382
CARD 1  965843231
```

what values will be read by the following:

```
123456789...
      DIMENSIØN K(2,3)
      DØ 15 I=1,2
      READ(1,10)(K(I,J),J=1,3)
   10 FØRMAT(3(I2,1X))
   15 CØNTINUE
```

K(1,1) = ________ K(1,2) = ________ K(1,3) = ________

K(2,1) = ________ K(2,2) = ________ K(2,3) = ________

CHAPTER PROGRAMMING PROBLEMS

TOPIC APPLICATION
a) Dimension statement b) Reading and writing two-dimensional array c) Arithmetic statements with subscripted variables

Problem 9.1

PROBLEM STATEMENT

Write a FORTRAN program to read any NxN square matrix D. Program for a maximum of a 10 x 10 matrix. Calculate the sum of the elements $(a_{ij};i=j)$ on the main diagonal of the matrix, the sum of the elements in the third row (a_{3j}) and the sum of the elements in the second column (a_{i2}).

INPUT

On the first card provide a value for the dimension (N) of the given square matrix. Each following data card will contain one row of the matrix. On these cards, each element is punched consecutively in F4.1 format.

To test the program, use the following matrix, (or one supplied by your instructor):

$$
D = \begin{bmatrix} 2.1 & 0 & -5.2 & 6.0 \\ 8.0 & -2.5 & -1.9 & 9.0 \\ 4.2 & 3.6 & 2.9 & 1.2 \\ 7.0 & 2.6 & 2.8 & 4.3 \end{bmatrix}
$$

OUTPUT

Provide output statements to printout the dimension of the square matrix, the given matrix, and the required sums. Arrange the output in the following form.

```
         1         2         3         4
1234567890123456789012345678901234567890123

  N=nnn

       nn.n nn.n nn.n nn.n

       nn.n nn.n nn.n nn.n

       nn.n nn.n nn.n nn.n

       nn.n nn.n nn.n nn.n

  SUMD =nnnn.n

  SUMR3=nnnn.n

  SUMC2=nnnn.n

```

Problem 9.2

PROBLEM STATEMENT

The students in FORTRAN programming take up to 15 tests each semester. The instructor wishes to have a program to read in all the grades and compute the average grade for each student and compute the average test score on each test.

EXERCISE

Write a program that will read in the data cards in the form shown below. The first card gives the number of students in the class and the number of tests given. The remaining cards give the scores. There is one card per student containing his test scores. Read the cards into a 2-dimensional array called SCOR, which is dimensioned for a maximum of 25 students and a maximum of 15 tests each. Print the input information with appropriate titles.

Compute the average test score for each student and store it in the single-dimensioned array, STAVE.

Compute the average test score on each test and store it in the single-dimensioned array, TSTAVE.

Write out each of these arrays with appropriate titles as follows:

```
STUDENT                   TEST AVERAGE

   1                          XX.X
   2                          XX.X
  ...



   TEST                  AVERAGE SCORE

   1                          XX.X
   2                          XX.X
                              XX.X
```

Note: Although one 2-dimensional array could be used to store the students' averages and the average test score, the use of two one-dimensional arrays is frequently easier to understand.

INPUT DATA

```
         1         2
12345678901234567890123
    5    4
95.0 87.5 85.0 92.0
69.0 87.5  0.0 70.0
75.0 90.0 87.0 69.0
50.0 55.5 62.0 65.0
90.0 87.0 83.5 78.0
```

Problem 9.3

PROBLEM STATEMENT

In order to collect heights at uniform distances for a large section of the country, a 1" grid was made on detailed relief maps and the heights recorded at each grid point. This data lends itself to a 2-dimensional array. Because of the size of the area, the job was divided among several data collectors who recorded the heights on data sheets for key punching.

EXERCISE

Write a program that will read in the data if it is input in blocks with a card giving the row and column indexes of the first and last heights of the block as shown below. The blocks are not in any order, and the program must assign the heights to the proper locations in a 2-dimensional array. The heights are punched, 10 per card, in column order. As the number of heights will be different for different blocks, the program must determine the number of heights per block from the first card containing the indexes for the block.

A diagram of four blocks is given in Figure 9.3-2. Before the diagram, is an input sample with the blocks ordered as follows: D, B, C, and A. This data generated the output of Figure 9.3-2.

Run your program with this input sample, and print the heights out as shown in Figure 9.3-2. Do not input or print the block designations, A-D, or boundary lines, which are given only to aid your visualization of the data.

INPUT DATA

```
Block  Card                1         2         3         4
            1234567890123456789012345678901234567890123...
  D     1   4  3  6  6
        2   75. 69. 57. 62. 80. 85. 90. 92. 87. 85.
        3   92. 91.

  B     4   4  1  6  2
        5   85. 87. 92. 91. 90. 60.

  C     6   1  4  3  6
        7   48. 66. 67. 69. 80. 85. 87. 92. 99.

  A     8   1  1  3  3
        9   85. 90. 80. 72. 71. 75. 65. 59. 62.
```

Figure 9.3-1. Input Sample

		A			C		
	85.	72.	65.	48.	69.	87.	
	90.	71.	59.	66.	80.	92.	
	80.	75.	62.	67.	85.	99.	
	85.	91.	75.	62.	90.	85.	
B	87.	90.	69.	80.	92.	92.	D
	92.	60.	57.	85.	87.	91.	

Figure 9.3-2. Output Sample

Problem 9.4

PROBLEM STATEMENT

The Light Opera Company requests your services in aiding it to keep track of tickets sold. At the end of its ticket drive, the seats sold are input to your program, and a map is printed out by rows with a '0' indicating an unsold seat, a '1' indicating a sold seat. Each ticket is represented by two indexes; the first giving the row, and the second giving the seat, hence, column.

EXERCISE

Write the program described above. It should do the following:

1. Dimension array, NSOLD, for a maximum of 10 x 10. Initialize NSOLD to 0 at the start of the program and read in the number of tickets sold, NS, on the first card.

2. Read the tickets sold into array, INDX, dimensioned 2 x 100. INDX(1,I) stores the row and INDX (2,I) stores the column of the Ith ticket sold.

   For example, the first ticket 6,5 meaning row 6, seat (column) 5, would be assigned:

   INDX(1,1)=6
   INDX(2,1)=5

3. Use these numbers for array, NSOLD, and set a value of NSOLD to '1' for each pair of numbers.

   For example, 6,5 would set

   NSOLD(6,5)=1

4. Print out a map of '0''s by row showing which seats are sold and unsold. Have one space between each 0 and 1.

INPUT

```
                    1         2         3         4
Card       1234567890123456789012345678901234567890

  1        32
  2         5 4 5 5 5 610 110 210 3 1 5 1 6 3 7 3 8
  3         6 7 6 8 6 9 7 1 7 2 8 5 8 6 2 1 2 2 2 3
  4         4 3 4 4 4 5 4 6 4 7 1 9 110 4 8 4 9 410
  5         1 1 1 2
```

PARTIAL OUTPUT

```
  1         1 1 0 0 1 1 0 0 1 1
  2         1 1 1 0 0 0 0 0 0 0
  3         0 0 0 0 0 0 1 1 0 0
  4         0 0 1 1 1 1 1 1 1 1
            . . .
```

Problem 9.5

PROBLEM STATEMENT

The product of two 2X2 matrices is given by the following equations:

$$C_{11} = a_{11}b_{11}+a_{12}b_{21}$$

$$C_{12} = a_{11}b_{12}+a_{12}b_{22}$$

$$C_{21} = a_{21}b_{11}+a_{22}b_{21}$$

$$C_{22} = a_{21}b_{12}+a_{22}b_{22}$$

EXERCISE

Write a program that will read in the elements of two 2X2 matrices A and B and compute the product matrix C by the above method.

Print out the input data and the product in the following form:

```
A = 12.5    6.3
     8.9   -4.2

B =  8.7    2.3
    -4.1   -1.0

C = nn.n   nn.n
    nn.n   nn.n
```

Test your program by reading in two cards, card 1 contains the elements of A; card 2 contains the elements of B ordered as follows:

	1-5	6-10	11-15	16-20
CARD 1	12.5 (a_{11})	8.9 (a_{21})	6.3 (a_{12})	-4.2 (a_{22})
CARD 2	8.7 (b_{11})	-4.1 (b_{21})	2.3 (b_{12})	-1.0 (b_{22})

Problem 9.6

PROBLEM STATEMENT

The daily hours worked for each of four teenage lawn mowers are given below. Each one's pay is computed at $1.50 per hour with no overtime paid.

EXERCISE

Write a program that will read the hours into a 2-dimensional array, HRS, and compute the pay in a 2-dimensional array, PAY. Print out the pay with headings as shown below. Test your program by reading in the hours below with the five hours for each employee punched on separate cards.

OUTPUT

	HOURS WORKED						
						TOTAL	
EMPLOYEE	MON	TUES	WED	THURS	FRI	HRS	PAY
1	8.0	8.0	7.0	8.0	8.0	nn	nn.nn
2	8.0	9.0	5.0	8.0	8.0	nn	nn.nn
3	7.5	10.0	0.0	8.0	7.0	nn	nn.nn
4	8.0	9.5	8.0	8.0	8.0	nn	nn.nn

FORTRAN 10

10.1 . . . identify the control statements that modify the sequential execution of a program.

10.2 . . . identify the branching and looping operation.

10.3 . . . construct and use the unconditional GO TO statement.

10.4 . . . construct and use the computed GO TO statement.

10.5 . . . construct and use the arithmetic IF statement.

10.6 . . . construct and use the logical IF statement.

10.7 . . . compare the arithmetic IF statement and the logical IF statement.

10.8 . . . specify logical constants and logical variables and use them in statements.

10.9 . . . specify the three logical operators and use each in statements.

10.1

OBJECTIVE: . . . identify the control statements that modify the sequential execution of a program.

Programming discussed to this point has been relatively straightforward with little modification of the sequential execution of statements. Three groups of control statements, branching, looping, and terminating, modify the sequential flow. They allow for a greatly expanded utilization of the computer's capability.

The basic FORTRAN statements available for altering the sequential execution of statements are:

Branching

IF statement
computed GO TO statement
unconditional GO TO statement

Looping

DO statement
CONTINUE statement

Terminating

STOP or CALL EXIT statement

Figure 10.1-1 shows the effect of each group of control statements on the flow of execution.

Altering the Normal Sequence

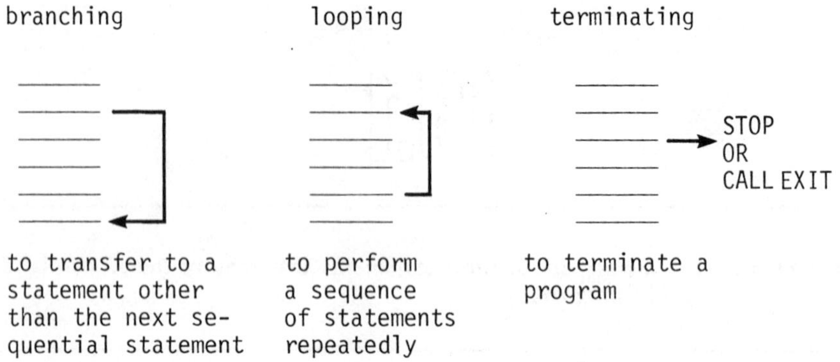

Figure 10.1-1. Program Control

The DO statement for looping and the STOP statement for terminating a program were discussed in Chapter 4. Branching statements will be presented in this chapter, enabling you to write your own looping sentences.

In programs written to this point, one terminating statement was used at the end of the program. When branching statements are used, termination may be desirable at more than one point in the program and not necessarily as the last executable statement. The END will always be the last statement in the program deck since it is a signal for compilation to end.

EXERCISE

1. Name the three groups of control statements that interrupt the normal order of program execution.

   1) ______________________________

   2) ______________________________

   3) ______________________________

2. TRUE OR FALSE. One or more terminating statements may be used anywhere within the executable statements in the program deck.

   T ______ F ______

10.2

OBJECTIVE: ... identify the branching and looping operation.

Branching allows the programmer to specify two or more different paths of computation automatically during the execution of the program. The branch can either

Figure 10.2-1. Normal Flow and Branching

be forward or backward, as shown in Figure 10.2-1. A branch may be unconditional, or it may be based upon a condition which is tested. Looping is a special form of branching.

Looping is the process of repeating a sequence of instructions a number of times with a different assigned value for at least one variable within the loop. Since looping is a repetitive process, some means must be provided to stop the repetition. The DO loop introduced in Section 4.9, is one form of looping. In it the number of repetitions is controlled by an integer index or counter. This index is initialized at a value and incremented by integral increments at each pass through the loop. The loop terminates when the index exceeds the terminal value specified on the DO statement. Such a loop is a counting loop, and many iterative processes fit this form. However, certain iterative processes are more naturally terminated by means of a condition because no specific number of times is associated with the process. In such cases, rather than strain to fit the iteration to the form of the DO statement, it is better to write your own loop. The branch statements provide the means to do this, and the pattern of statements is similar to those performed automatically by the DO statement, namely,

1. initialize a control variable

2. execute a block of statements

3. increment the control variable by any number, integer or real

4. test the control variable and either repeat steps 2-4 or terminate the loop.

By writing your own looping statements, you remove the restrictions of the DO statement. The incremental amount need not be an integer. The order of performing the steps may vary, for example, step 2 and 3 may be reversed and step 4 may be done before or after 2 and 3.

The following shows an example each of a counting loop and non-counting loop.

Angel Loaf Cake

DIRECTIONS

1. Sift flour with 1/4 c. sugar.
2. Do step 1 two times.
3. Beat egg whites with tartar, salt, vanilla, and almond extract until it forms soft peaks.
4. Add remaining 1/2 c. sugar, 2 T at a time to egg whites, beating as in step 3. 1/2 c. = 4T.
5. Sift 1/3 of flour mixture over whites, fold in.
6. Repeat step 5, folding flour in two additions.
7. Bake at 350 for 1 hour.

Three iterations are done in this recipe, as indicated by the dashed lines, and all are done a counted number of times.

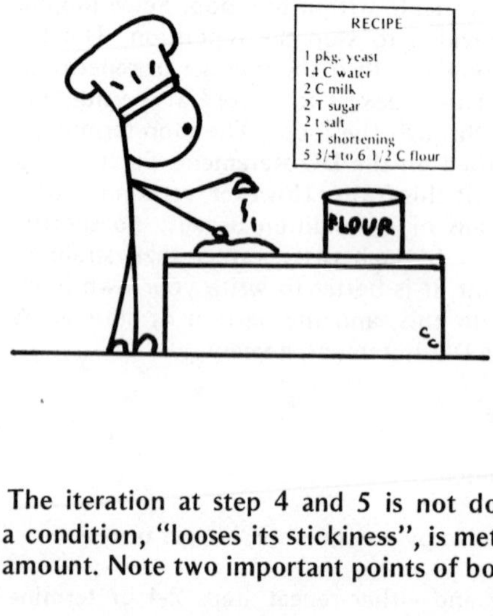

Perfect White Bread

DIRECTIONS

1. Soften yeast in water.
2. Combine milk, sugar, salt and shortening.
3. Stir in 2 c. flour and the yeast.
4. Mix all together.
5. Add a 'handful' of flour at a time repeating step 4 until dough looses its stickiness.
6. Shape dough into loaf and bake at 350 for 50 minutes.

The iteration at step 4 and 5 is not done a specific number of times but rather until a condition, "looses its stickiness", is met. The increment, a 'handful ' is not an integral amount. Note two important points of both loops:

1. Some variable must change to make the looping meaningful (i.e., flour).
2. Some means must be provided to halt the loop (test or count).

10.3

OBJECTIVE: . . . construct and use the unconditional GO TO statement.

The simplest of the branching statements is the unconditional GO TO which causes a branch to be taken with "no strings" attached. The unconditional GO TO statement is often used with other branching statements when it becomes necessary to branch back to the normal sequence of statements. The general form of this statement is:

GENERAL FORM

```
12345 6 789...
nnnnn   GØ TØ m
```

COMPONENTS

nnnnn	is the statement number (optional)
GØ TØ	is the keyword
m	is the statement number

EXAMPLE

```
12345 6 789...
        GØ TØ 66
```

'm' may be any valid statement number used in the program. A variable name may not be used.

Note: A statement number is required after each unconditional GO TO statement if that statement is ever to be executed. Failure to give the statement following the GO TO a statement number results in a compiler error with most computers.

Unconditional Branch

One use of the GO TO is to set up a loop in unit processing. Unit processing refers to the process shown in Figure 10.3-1.

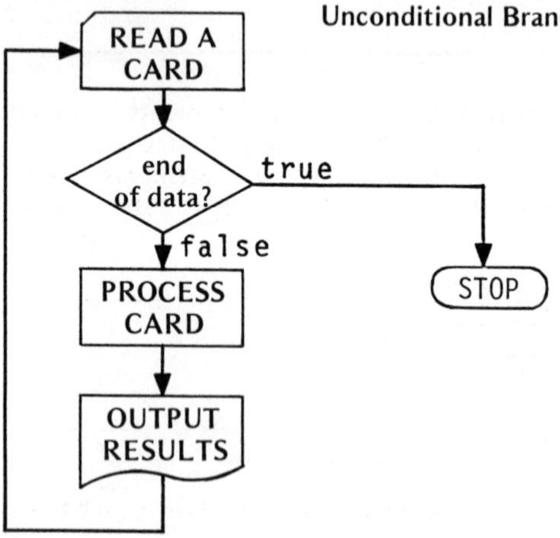

Figure 10.3-1. Unit Processing

Unit processing makes possible the processing of quantities of sets of data with a minimum of memory used. Only one set of data is read and stored at a time. It is processed and the results printed. The GO TO transfers control back to the READ statement, and each successive set of data uses the same memory locations.

An example of this is shown for the program segment given in Figure 10.3-1. It uses the END= option in the READ statement to branch at the end-of-data. If your computer does not support this option, Section 10.5 will show you how to write your own end-of-data test.

```
123456789...
    5 READ(1,90,END=10) A,B,C
      AVE=(A+B+C)/3
      WRITE(3,92) AVE
      GØ TØ 5
   10 ...
```

In chapter 4, the DO loop was introduced, which allowed you to do exactly the same process. Why then, not just use the DO loop? With the DO loop, it was necessary to first count the number of input data cards and then read in that number, which becomes the terminal number of the DO.

However, as the number of data cards increases, the chance for error increases in either miscounting the data cards or in forgetting to change the number read in as new data cards are added. Therefore, instead of a counting loop, a loop based on a test for the end-of-data is used, as will be shown in Section 10.5.

10.4

OBJECTIVE: ... construct and use the computed GO TO statement.

Another branching statement is the computed GO TO statement, which allows branching to more than the three different statements.

The general form is:

GENERAL FORM

```
123456789...
nnnnn GØ TØ (m1,m2,m3,...mn),iv
```

COMPONENTS

```
nnnnn          is the statement number (optional)

GØ TØ          is the keyword

m1,m2,m3,...are statement numbers

iv             is an integer variable
```

EXAMPLES

```
123456789...
      GØ TØ(5,10,50,65),IFLAG
      GØ TØ(10,20,30,40),INDEX
```

The computer will branch to statement m_1 when iv=1, to statement m_2 when iv=2, to m_3 when iv=3. If the value of iv is less than 1, or greater than n, the next statement following the GO TO will be executed on some computers. FORTRAN 66 did not permit this condition. What does your computer do if iv< n or iv> n?

My computer ______________________________________.

EXERCISE

A program is to be written for a system having 5 modes of operation. The program is to branch to a set of statements for each mode depending on the value of a mode index M that is set to a value between 1 through 5. The first set starts with statement number 100; the second with 200,ect. Write the necessary computed GO TO statement.

```
12345|6|789

```

10.5

OBJECTIVE: ... construct and use the arithmetic IF statement.

The arithmetic IF statement allows for three alternate paths to be taken in the program based upon a decision. The general form of the arithmetic IF is given as follows:

GENERAL FORM

```
12345|6|789...
nnnnn| |IF(e) m1,m2,m3
```

COMPONENTS

nnnnn	is the statement number
IF	is the keyword
e	is the argument of the IF and may be any valid arithmetic expression
m_1	is the label of statement branched to if e<0
m_2	is the label of statement branched to if e=0
m_3	is the label of statement branched to if e>0

EXAMPLES

```
12345|6|789...
     | |IF(A-1.0)5,10,20
     | |IF(A**2-B**2)5,5,10
```

The e is any valid arithmetic expression. An arithmetic expression is a sequence of numerical constants and/or variables connected with the arithmetic operators, such as X or (X+2.*Y-4.) The arithmetic expression has a numerical value; and this value is either less than zero, exactly equal to zero, or greater than zero. This condition determines the statement that is executed after the IF. A branch is made to statement m_1 if $e < 0$, to statement m_2 if e=0, and to statement m_3 if $e > 0$. This is shown in the flow diagram in Figure 10.5-1.

Decision

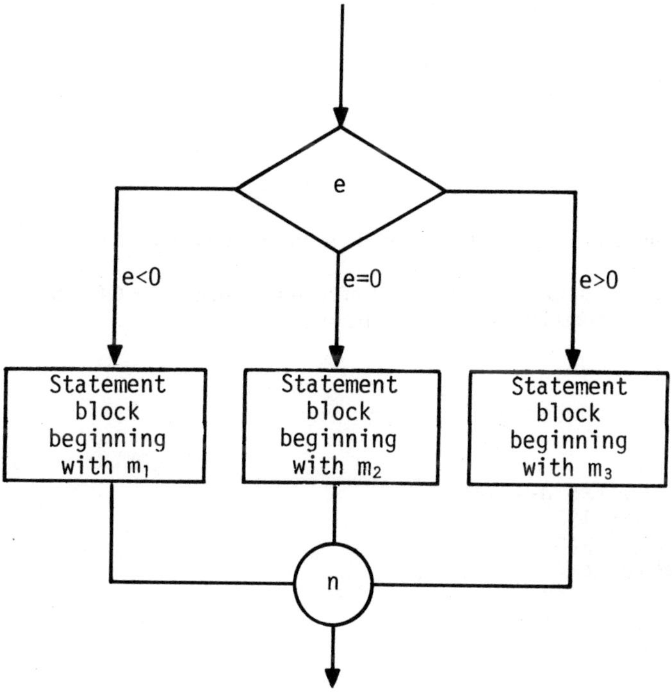

Figure 10.5-1. Flow Diagram for Arithmetic IF Statement.

An example of the arithmetic IF is given below.

EXAMPLE 1

A program is to be written to find the roots of a quadratic equation ax^2+bx+c using the formula

$$R_1, R_2 = \frac{-b \pm \sqrt{b^2 - 4ac}}{2a}$$

The necessary statements to calculate the radicand (b^2-4ac) and branch to program segments identified by statement 10 if $(b^2-4ac)<0$, to statement 20 if $(b^2-4ac)>0$ and to statement 15 if $(b^2-4ac)=0$, are

```
12345|6|789...
     | |IF(B**2-4.*A*C)10,15,20
   10| |...
   15| |...
   20| |...
```

The statement following an arithmetic IF must always have a label.

In order to "jump" over unwanted program segments, the GO TO is used, as shown in the next, more complete, solution of the quadratic equation.

EXAMPLE 2

```
12345|6|789...
     | |...
     | |DISC=B*B-4.*A*C
     | |IF(DISC)10,15,20
   10| |WRITE(3,90)
   90| |FØRMAT('NØ REAL RØØTS')
     | |GØ TØ 25
   15| |X1=-B/(2.*A)
     | |X2=X1
     | |GØ TØ 22
   20| |X1=(-B+SQRT(DISC))/(2.*A)
     | |X2=(-B-SQRT(DISC))/(2.*A)
   22| |WRITE(3,92)X1,X2
   92| |FØRMAT('bTHE REAL RØØTS ARE', 2F10.1)
   25| |CØNTINUE
```

EXAMPLE 3

Write statements to sum the positive integers from one to 100.

Without using a DO loop

```
12345 6 789...
        I=1
        ISUM=0
    8   ISUM=ISUM+I
        I=I+1
        IF(I-100)8,8,6
    6   CØNTINUE
```

Using a DO loop

```
12345 6 789...
        ISUM=0
        DØ 6 I=1,100
           ISUM=ISUM+I
    6   CØNTINUE
```

In Example 3, the DO loop provides a shorter, simpler method. Writing your own loop is particularly advantageous when there is no "count" naturally associated with the loop, and when the initial, terminal and incremental values are not integers, even though it is possible to determine the count and use a DO loop. Example 4 illustrates such a situation.

EXAMPLE 4

Write the statements to evaluate y=sinx+cosx for x from -10 to 10 radians in increments 0.1.

```
12345 6 789...
        X=-10.1
    5   X=X+.1
        IF(X-10.)6,6,10
    6   Y=SIN(X) + CØS(X)
        WRITE(3,90)X,Y
        GØ TØ 5
   10   CØNTINUE
   90   FØRMAT('b',2E13.5)
        ...
```

Pitfall

In Example 5 the value of the expression must be exactly zero for a branch to 20.

EXAMPLE 5

This program would cause the computer to go into

```
12345 6 789···
        A=0
    5   A=A+.1
        Y=A**3
        WRITE(3,10)A,Y
   10   FØRMAT('0',2F7.1)
        IF(A-1.0)5,20,5
   20   CØNTINUE
```

PT's*

Inspect all loops to prevent endless loops.
- Does the loop have an exit condition that can be met?
- Beware of "equals" as a condition with reals. Test on "non equal" conditions or use integers for testing.

*Preventive Tactics

an endless loop, since the value of (A-1.0) would never be exactly zero. Situations such as this can be avoided by never testing for "equals", but rather testing for "less than or equals" or "greater than or equals" when using real numbers.

The **IF** statement in the above example should read,

```
12345 6 789···
        IF(A-1.0)5,20,20
```

since A will always exceed 1.0 at some point.

Another method of avoiding the endless loop is by using integer or "exact" arithmetic, as shown in Example 6.

EXAMPLE 6

```
12345 6 789···
        I=0
    5   I=I+1
        A=SIN(FLØAT(I)/3.)
        Y=A**3
        WRITE(3,10)A,Y
   10   FØRMAT('0',2E12.5)
        IF(I-10)5,20,5
   20   CØNTINUE
```

Do not enter unless
you can exit!

The next example shows how to create your own unit processing loop (see the example in Section 10.3) without using the END = option. A procedure for handling the end-of-data condition is to use a <u>sentinel</u> <u>card</u> as the last data card. This card contains some value, such as 9999, in an unused field or a data value outside the range of possible values for one of the data items read in. Directly after reading in the data value, the field containing the indicator is tested for the end-of-data. The arithmetic IF provides one means for this.

EXAMPLE 7

Read in all the student cards and print the information they contain. The first field in each card contains the student ID, an integer between 100000 and 999999. Since any negative number is an invalid ID, we arbitrarily select -99999 and punch it in the field for student ID. (Any negative number or simply a blank card could be used.) This sentinel card is placed after the last valid data card.

The program reads each card, tests the student ID field for a negative number, and branches to STOP when it reaches it. This is shown below:

```
123456789...
     5 READ(1,90)ID,CLASS,GRPT
    90 FØRMAT(I6,4X,A2,4X,F10.1)
       IF(ID)99,99,10
    10 ...process card
       GØ TØ 5
    99 STØP
```

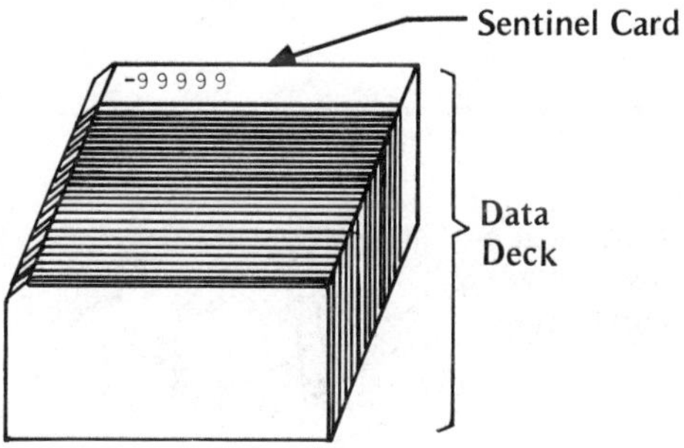

Sentinel card

EXERCISE

1. Write an arithmetic IF to branch to statement 10 if A is less than 25, to statement 20 if A is equal to 25, and to statement 30 if A is greater than 25.

12345	6	789···

2. Write an arithmetic IF to branch to statement 10,20, or30 depending on whether `IMØ<0, IMØ=0 or IMØ>0,` respectively.

12345	6	789···

10.6

OBJECTIVE: . . . construct and use the logical IF statement.

The logical IF statement is another conditional branch statement. It provides for two alternate paths of program execution based upon a logical condition, that is, a condition which is either true or false.

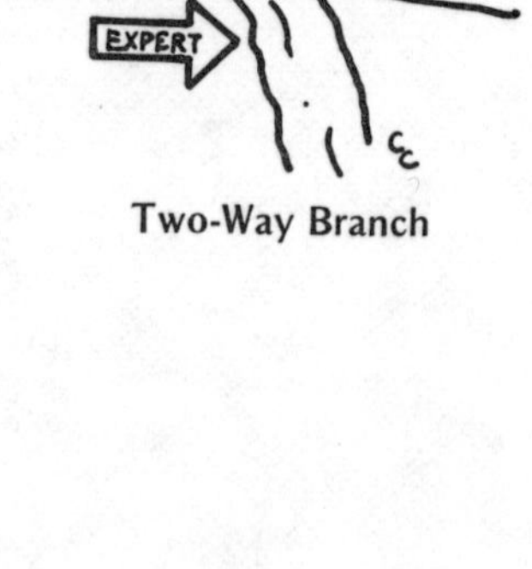

Two-Way Branch

GENERAL FORM	
1 2 3 4 5 | 6 | 7 8 9 · · ·	
nnnnn IF(e_1 reop e_2)s	
COMPONENTS	
nnnnn	is the statement number
IF	is the keyword
e_1 reop e_2	is a logical expression
e_1	is any valid arithmetic expression
reop	is a relational operator
e_2	is any valid arithmetic expression
s	is any executable statement except another logical IF or a DØ

Note: e_1 and e_2 must both be the same type, either REAL or INTEGER, if mixed-mode expressions are not allowed on your computer.

EXAMPLE

```
123456789...
      IF(A.LT.B)GØ TØ 15
      IF(X**2.GT.Y**2)Z=X-Y
```

A logical expression is an expression that has a value of 'true' or 'false'. A relational expression is one type of logical expression, and it has the form:

$$e_1 \quad \text{reop } e_2$$

Logical Expression

The e's are arithmetic expressions; reop is a relational operator. There are six relational operators which are always preceded and followed by a period. They are given in Table 10.6-1.

Table 10.6-1
Relational Operators

RELATIONAL OPERATOR	DEFINITION
.EQ.	Equal to (=)
.GE.	Greater than or equal to (≥)
.GT.	Greater than (>)
.LE.	Less than or equal to (≤)
.LT.	Less than (<)
.NE.	Not equal to (≠)

A relation is 'true' if e_1 and e_2 satisfy the relation specified by the reop; otherwise, it is 'false'. Relational expressions can be expressed as arithmetic expressions. For example, p.EQ.q is equivalent to the question, does p - q = 0?

The two expressions must each satisfy the rules for an arithmetic expression. Only arithmetic expressions whose type is integer or real are permitted.

Some examples of valid and invalid logical expressions follow.

<u>VALID</u>

```
(I .LT. I)
(E**2.7 .EQ. (5.*R + 4.) )
(.5 .GE. .6*R)
(E    .LT. 27.3E + 05)
```

<u>INVALID</u>

```
(E**2  .EQ 91.E09)  missing period
(  .GT. 9)          missing expression
```

The flow diagram in Figure 10.6-1 shows the flow of the logical IF statement.

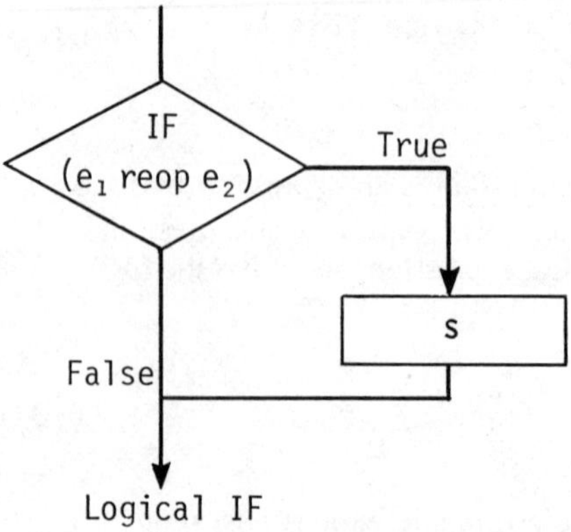

Figure 10.6-1. Flow Diagram of Logical IF Statement

If (e_1 reop e_2) is true, the statement s is executed. If (e_1 reop e_2) is false, the statement immediately following is executed.

The following example shows a program segment where the discriminant of a quadratic equation is tested and alternate branches taken. Compare this solution with Example 2 in Section 10.5, which uses the arithmetic IF statement.

> **PT's***
>
> The computer cannot divide by zero! When division by zero is a possibility, the denominator should be tested and the computation branched around to avoid division by zero. An example when this is necessary is in evaluating the following expression for $-1. < X < 1.$
>
> $$Y = \frac{1}{X}$$
>
> *Positively Taboo

EXAMPLE

```
12345|6|789···
     | | ···
     | |DISC=B*B-4.*A*C
     | |IF(DISC.GE.0.) GØ TØ 10
     | |  WRITE(3,90)
   90| |  FØRMAT('bNØ REAL RØØTS')
     | |  GØ TØ 25
   10| |IF(DISC.GT.0.)GØ TØ 20
     | |  X1=-B/(2.*A)
     | |  X2=X1
     | |  GØ TØ 22
   20| |X1=(-B+SQRT(DISC))/(2.*A)
     | |X2=(-B-SQRT(DISC))/(2.*A)
   22| |WRITE(3,92)X1,X2
   92| |FØRMAT('bTHE REAL RØØTS ARE',2F10.1)
   25| |CØNTINUE
```

EXERCISE

1. Write logical IF statements to go to statement 10, 20 or 30 depending on whether IM<0, IM = 0, or IM>0, respectively.

```
12345|6|789···
     | |
     | |
     | |
```

2. Write a logical IF statement to branch to statement 23 if the value of A is greater than or equal to the value of B.

```
12345|6|789···
     | |
```

3. Write a logical IF statement to change the sign of X if it is less than zero.

```
12345|6|789...
     | |
```

10.7

OBJECTIVE: . . . compare the arithmetic IF statement and the logical IF statement.

The logical IF adds no new capability and the arithmetic IF is sufficient to handle all the decision making and branching that is done. However, the logical IF is a recommended usage, because of its English-like readability, and because it permits you to test exactly what you want to test without the need to shift the test so as to obtain a negative-zero-positive result.

For example, write an IF statement that causes a branch to statement 5 if the temperature, TEMP, is greater than 55, otherwise go to statement 10.

```
12345|6|789...
     | |IF(TEMP.GT.55.)GO TO 5
   10| |...
```

```
12345|6|789...
     | |IF(TEMP-55.)10,10,5
```

Additional points to notice in comparing the two IF statements are:

1. When the arithmetic IF specifies a two-way branch only, it translates directly into a logical IF. When the arithmetic IF specifies a three-way branch, two logical IF statements are required.

2. The logical IF is based on a logical condition--true or false. The arithmetic IF is based on a numerical condition, negative, zero, or positive.

3. The logical IF allows for execution of one statement if the argument is true. If more than one statement is required, or if it is required to jump over the false branch, then the GO TO is used as the one statement. The arithmetic IF specifies statement numbers to which a branch is always required.

EXAMPLE 1

If the angle, A, is negative, add 180 to it.

```
123456789...
      IF(A.LT.0.0)A=A+180.
```

Logical IF

```
123456789...
      IF(X)10,5,10
    5 A=A+180.
   10 ...
```

Arithmetic IF

In this logical IF, no branch is taken. The statement following this IF statement is executed whether or not A is negative. It need not have a statement label. In the arithmetic IF, a branch is always taken; the statement following it must have a statement label.

EXAMPLE 2

If the value of X is equal to 0., set the angle, A, to 90. Otherwise, compute A as follows: $A = \arctan\left(\frac{1}{X}\right)$

```
123456789...
      IF(X.NE.0.0)GØ TØ 5
      A=90.
      GØ TØ 10
    5 A=ATAN(1./X)
   10 ...
```

Logical IF

```
123456789...
      IF(X)10,5,10
    5 A=90.
      GØ TØ 15
   10 A=ATAN(1./X)
   15 ...
```

Arithmetic IF

EXERCISE

1. Write the following IF statement using a relational expression.

IF (IX-IY) 5,6,6

2. Write logical IF statements to branch to 10 if the value of I is 6 or 7.

____

____

3. Write the above without logicals.

____

____

4. The following program segment computes the sum of the integers from one to 100.

   a) Write an arithmetic IF statement to test for terminating the loop.

   b) Write a logical IF statement to test for terminating the loop.

```
123456789...
      I=1
      ISUM=0
    6 ISUM=ISUM+I
      ____________________ or ____________________
    7 I=I+1  (arithmetic IF)      (logical IF)
      GØ TØ 6
    8 ...
```

10.8

OBJECTIVE: . . . specify logical constants and logical variables and use them in statements.

Up to this time, the word, constant, has been used for a numerical constant, which has a type, integer or real. There is a second type of constant called a <u>logical constant.</u>

LOGICAL CONSTANT
A logical constant has two forms: .TRUE. .FALSE.

These logical constants represent values of true and false, respectively.

A logical constant can be assigned to a variable of type, LOGICAL.

LOGICAL VARIABLE
A logical variable is a variable of type, LOGICAL, that is, it assumes a logical value of .TRUE. or .FALSE. only.

A variable is assigned the type, LOGICAL, in a specification statement. The general form and use of this statement is similar to the REAL and INTEGER specification statements (see Section 3.7).

GENERAL FORM

```
12345 6 789...
        LØGICAL a,b,c
```

COMPONENTS

```
LØGICAL   is the keyword

a,b,c     is a list of variable names designated as LØGICAL
```

EXAMPLE

```
12345 6 789...
        LØGICAL T,F
```

The assignment statement, a=b, can be used to set logical variables to logical expressions. The variable name on the left, a, must be declared LOGICAL and b must be a logical expression.

EXAMPLE G = .TRUE. The value of G is replaced by the logical constant .TRUE. G has been declared LOGICAL.

The logical IF statement can be used to test logical expressions. G has been declared LOGICAL, i.e.,

```
12345 6 789...
        IF (G) GØ TØ 5
```

In the following example, some data cards have a "-" in a column, called ICOL1, to signal special handling. Logicals are used to test for the "-". ISWTCH equals .TRUE. for non-minus cards. ISWTCH equals .FALSE. for minus cards.

EXAMPLE

```
123456789...
      LØGICAL ISWTCH
      DATA MINUS /'-'/
      .
      .
      .
      ISWTCH=.TRUE.
   15 IF(ICØL1.EQ.MINUS)GØ TØ 20
C NONMINUS CARD
      GØ TØ 25
   20 ISWTCH=.FALSE.
   25 IF(ISWTCH)GØ TØ 30
C PROCESS MINUS CARDS
      .
      .
      GØ TØ 40
C PROCESS NØN-MINUS CARDS
   30 .
      .
   40 .
```

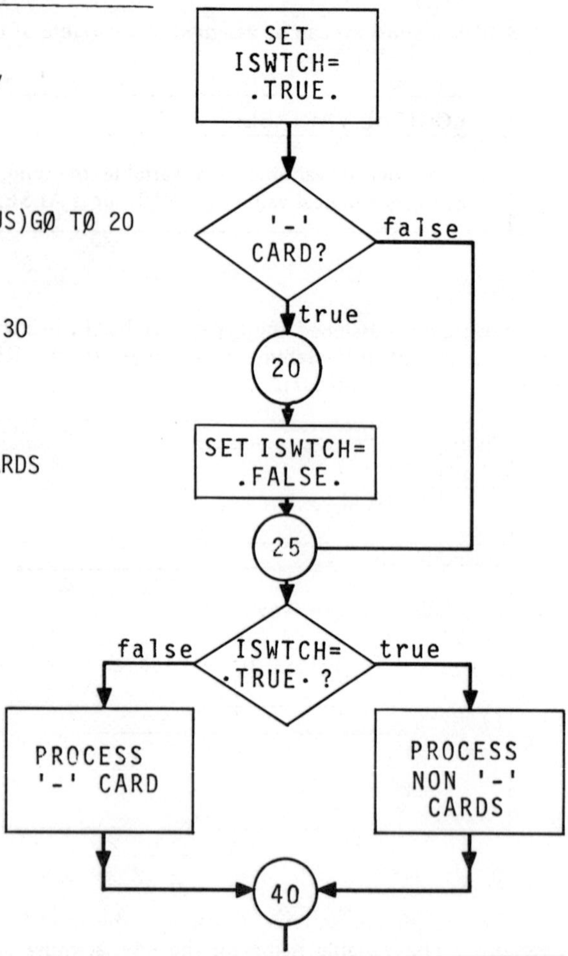

Notes:

In this example, we might have eliminated the logicals and simply used the test of statement 15 at statement 25. However, if statement 15 involved a complicated expression that would be tested several times throughout the program, the most efficient way is to evaluate it once and set a switch to be tested at all other times.

Another way would have been to let the switch, ISWTCH, be an integer, and simply set it to 0 and 1, and change statement 25 to a test for '0', i.e.,

IF (ISWTCH .EQ.0) GO TO 30

However, if other logical expressions might be tested in combination with the switch, the logical gives a convenient way to do it. An example of this is shown in the following test:

IF(ISWTCH .AND. X.LT.Y) GO TO 100

In this statement, if ISWTCH is true (card is non-minus card) and X is less than Y, branch to 100. If ISWTCH is false (a minus card) or if X is not less than Y the branch is not taken. (.AND. is discussed below.)

10.9

OBJECTIVE: ... specify the three logical operators and use each in statements.

There are three logical operators, each of which is preceded and followed by a period. (A and B are logical expressions.) They are given in Table 10.9-1.

Table 10.9-1
Logical Operators

Logical Operator	Use	Meaning
.NØT.	.NØT.A	If A is true, .NØT. A has value false;if A is false, .NØT. A is true.
.AND.	A.AND.B	If A and B are both true, (A.AND.B) is true. If either A or B or both are false,(A.AND.B) is false.
.ØR.	A.ØR.B	If either A or B or both are true,(A.ØR.B)is true; if both A and B are false, (A.ØR.B) is false.

Two logical operators may appear in sequence only if the second one is .NOT.. (See example below.)

Only those expressions which, when evaluated, have a value of true or false may be combined with logical operators to form logical expressions. Examples of valid logical expression using both logical and relational operators follow: (Note: L is logical).

VALID LOGICAL EXPRESSIONS

```
(R*R.GT.E)    .AND.    (A.GT.R)
(R.LT.E)      .AND.    (I.EQ.1)
(I.LT.J)      .ØR.     .NOT. (R.LE.E)
     L        .ØR.     R.GT.E
```

The order in which the operations are performed is as follows:

ORDER	OPERATION
1	Evaluation of functions, i.e., SIN(X)
2	Exponentiation (**)
3	Multiplication and division (*and /)
4	Addition and subtraction (+ and –)
5	Relational operators (.EQ., .GE., .GT., .LE., .LT., .NE.)
6	Logical operator .NØT.
7	Logical operator .AND.
8	Logical operator .ØR.

Logical expressions may not have to have all parts evaluated. For example, in (I.LT. 0 .AND. J.GT.2), if I.LT.0 is false, the statement is false. J.GT.2 need not be evaluated. If we had (I.LT.0 .OR. J.GT.2) and I.LT.0 is true, the statement is true and J.GT.2 need not be evaluated.

The following example shows the order of evaluating an expression.

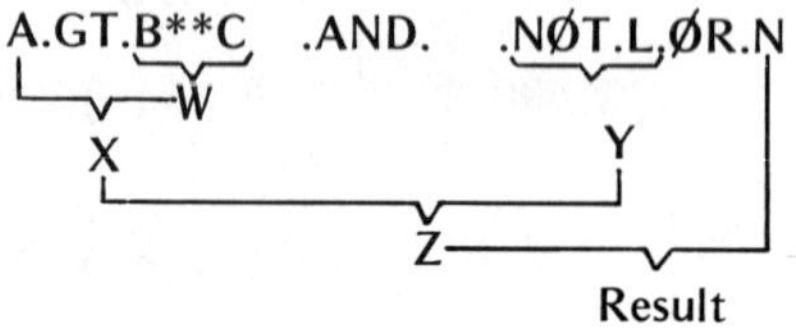

1. B**C (Call result W)	Exponentiation
2. A.GT.W (Call result X)	Relational operator
3. .NØT.L (Call result Y)	Logical operator .NØT.
4. X .AND. Y (Call result Z)	Logical operator .AND.
5. Z.ØR.N (Final result)	Logical operator .ØR.

Parentheses may be used in logical expressions for clarification and to specify the order of operations. If parentheses are inserted in the above example as follows:

A.GT.B**C .AND. .NØT. (L.ØR.N)

steps 1 and 2 remain the same but 3 - 5 change, as follows:

3.L.ØR.N (Call result T)
4..NØT. T (Call result S)
5.X .AND. S (Final result)

CHAPTER PROGRAMMING PROBLEMS

TOPIC APPLICATION

a) Branching and Looping
b) IF Statement
c) Unconditional GO TO Statement
d) ATAN FORTRAN Supplied Subprogram

Problem 10.1

PROBLEM STATEMENT

Write a program to calculate and printout a table of arctangents.

$$\theta = \tan^{-1} (A/(1-A)) \text{ degrees}$$

where A ranges from 0.1 to 1.5 in steps of 0.1. A flow diagram is given below.

INPUT

Not required - values of A are to be generated within the program.

CALCULATION of θ (THETA)

Use the FORTRAN supplied subprogram ATAN to calculate the various values of θ. In using this subprogram the following must be considered:

a) the subprogram output will be in radians and must be converted to degrees.
b) the subprogram will not work for A = 1.0. For this case, a statement must be written setting θ to 90 degrees.
c) for A greater that 1.0, 180 degrees must be added to the value obtained from the subprogram (after conversion to degrees) to place the value of θ obtained from the subprogram ATAN in the second quadrant.

OUTPUT

Write out the table of arctangents as follows:

```
           1         2         3
• • •7890123456789012345678901234567890123• • •
       TABLE ØF ARCTANGENT(A/(1-A))

                 A     THETA

              n.nn     nnn.nn
                -        -
                -        -
                -        -
                -        -
              etc.     etc.
```

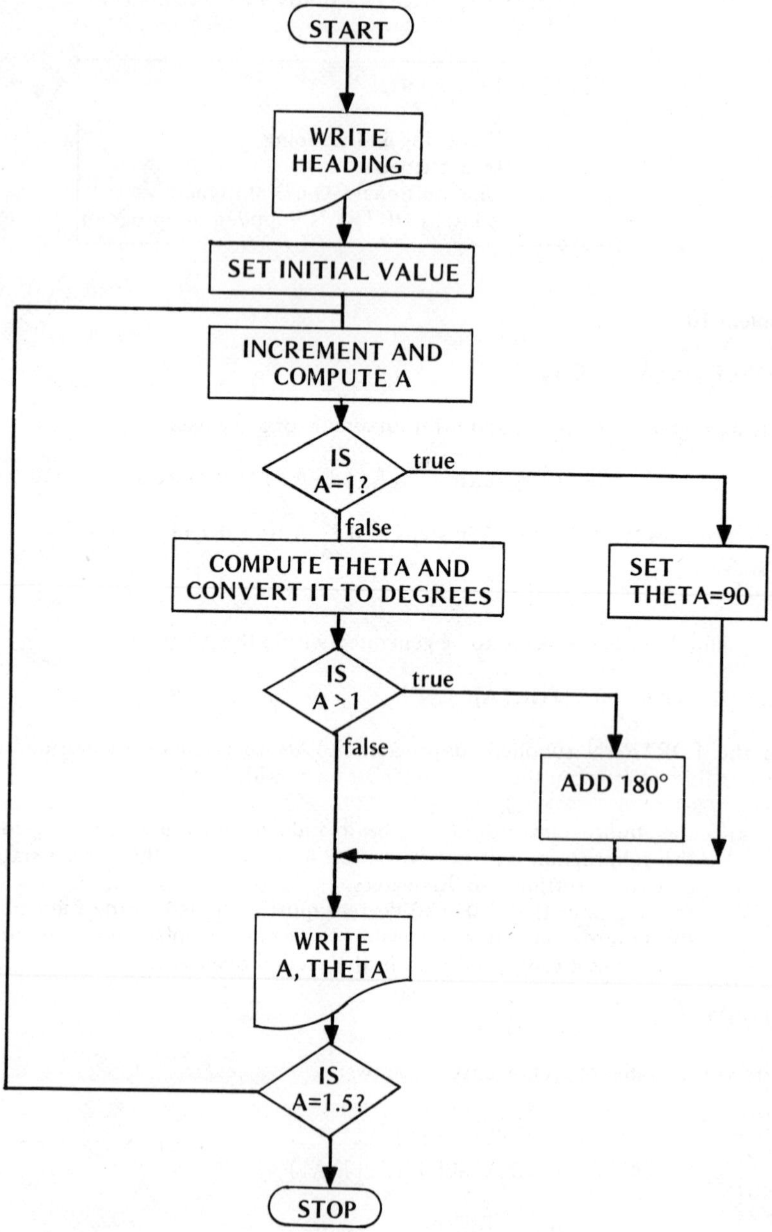
START
WRITE HEADING
SET INITIAL VALUE
INCREMENT AND COMPUTE A
IS A=1?
true
false
COMPUTE THETA AND CONVERT IT TO DEGREES
SET THETA=90
IS A>1
true
false
ADD 180°
WRITE A, THETA
IS A=1.5?
STOP

Problem 10.2

PROBLEM STATEMENT

A frequency table is a tabular arrangement of data grouped together into classes or categories. For example, instead of working with all the heights of female students at Yale University, the heights might be grouped into five classes and the number of students in each class counted. A frequency table of the heights of 100 students is shown below:

HEIGHT(INCHES)	NO. OF STUDENTS
72+	6
68-71	18
64-67	42
60-63	27
less than 60	7

The range of the data is the difference between the largest and smallest number in a group. For example, if the largest height was 75 inches and the smallest height was 58 inches, then 75-58 = 17 inches is the range.

EXERCISE

Write a complete program that will generate a frequency distribution and compute the range of the final grades in mathematics of 80 students at Western State College. Group the grades into class intervals and print out the results as follows:

```
123456789012345678901234567890123456789...

        GRADE                  NØ. ØF STUDENTS

        90-100                      nn
        80-89                       nn
        70-79                       nn
        60-69                       nn
        less than 60                nn

     Range is nn
```

INPUT

Test your program with at least 25 grades chosen between 50 and 100. Choose a convenient card format for your data.

Problem 10.3

PROBLEM STATEMENT

The inner diameters of washers produced by Bolts Tool Company are measured to the nearest thousandth of an inch. For quality control, randomly selected washers are chosen and measured to see if they fit the required error tolerance. The measurements are recorded on sheets which are keypunched. This data is used for statistical analysis. Before this analysis, the data is pre-processed for errors such as faulty measurements or keypunch errors.

EXERCISE

Write a program which will read up to 500 measurements into a single-dimensioned array, WASH. Any measurement greater than 1.0 or less than .1 is disregarded as being in error. The remaining "good" measurements are transferred to the array, WASHED. A count of the number of "good" measurements is kept.

The measurements are punched 14 per card in fields of F5.3. The program should count the number of measurements. The end-of-data is signaled by a negative number in the first field of a last end-of-data card. The last good data card may be only partially filled. Remaining fields are read in as 0.0 and counted. These are eliminated when each value is tested for less than .1 and the count adjusted accordingly.

INPUT DATA

14 per card in fields of F5.3

.337 .333 .321 .336 32.5 .003 .327 .033 .332 .329 .338 .328 .328 .329 .333
.323 .337 .341 .337
-1.

OUTPUT

Print out both the input data, and the "good" data, and the number of new data points. Choose any format that will print them out in a compact and readable form.

Problem 10.4

PROBLEM STATEMENT

The employee records for REEDY'S HARDWARE are kept on cards. For each employee there is one card which contains the name, the hourly wage, the number of hours worked that week, and a code for insurance. This code means : 1, deduct $2.68 for individual insurance; 2, deduct 5.23 for family plan; 3, not covered. Any hours greater than 40 are paid at twice the regular rate. Every employee should have 6.8% deducted from the gross pay for social security tax.

EXERCISE

Write a program to compute the pay for REEDY'S HARDWARE. Be sure to make a Data Table and Flow Diagram of the problem first. Include some means of testing for end-of-data that allows for varying the number of input cards. Output should be in columns as given below with heading printed over the columns.

Columns	1-20	21-25	30-39	40-49	50-59	60-69
	NAME	HOURS WORKED	GROSS PAY	S.S. TAX	INSUR.	NET PAY

```
C
A     NAME                 HOURLY      HOURS      CODE
R                           RATE      WORKED
                 1         2         3         4         5
D 1234567890123456789012345678901234567890123456789012345678 9
1 ANDERSØN, MARY            2.45        40          1
2 ANDREWS, JØE              2.65        40          2
3 ASCØT, JUNE               3.20        45          3
4 ATWØØD, MICHAEL           2.75        36          2
5 AZARS, LØUIS              3.10        42          1
```

Problem 10.5

PROBLEM STATEMENT

The weather bureau needs a program that will prepare a weather report which outputs temperature in Farenheit and in Celsius, and gives the present sky condition. Input will be the temperature (in Farenheit) and a number code for the sky condition.

Codes are as follows:

1 - clear and sunny
2 - partly clear
3 - cloudy

The time of day in in 24 hour time and should be converted to 12 hour time

800 = 8:00AM   1300 = 1:00PM

EXERCISE

Write a program that reads in the time of day, the temperature in Farenheit and the sky condition code. Compute the temperature in Celsius using the formula

$$T_C = 5/9\ (T_F - 32)$$

Test the sky condition code and print out the words CLEAR, PARTLY CLEAR, or CLOUDY along with the temperature as shown below.

INPUT

Test your program with the following data:

```
C
A             FARENHEIT
R TIME     TEMPERATURE     SKY CODE
D 1234567890123456789012345678901234567890123456789...
1 / 830        78            2
2 |1120        83            1
3 |1200        94            1
4 |1500        86            2
5 |1800        97            2
6 |2200        75            3
```

OUTPUT

The temperature at xx xx (AM / PM) is xxx.x degrees Farenheit, xx.x degrees Celsius. The skies are ------

(CLEAR
PARTIAL CLEAR
CLOUDY)

Problem 10.6

PROBLEM STATEMENT

This is a modification to Problem 9.4. If you did not do it, read it and write a program fitting the criteria of both problem descriptions.

EXERCISE

1. Input to this program consists of the output of Problem 9.4. Punch it up on 10 cards and read it into the 10X10 array, NSOLD. NSOLD no longer needs to be initialized.

2. Next, read into array, INDX, the additional tickets sold given below.

3. Test each location for which there is a ticket sold to be sure it is unsold. If it is "0" for unsold, change it to "1" for sold. It is already "1", print an error message reading:

   DUPLICATE TICKET SOLD FOR ROW nn SEAT nn

4. Print out a map of "0" and "1"'s as done in Problem 9.4 after all additional tickets sold have been processed.

5. Do not count the tickets sold. Instead, test for end-of-data or use END= option. As the last card may not be full, test also for a 0 row which would also signal end-of-data- and DO NOT use 0,0 as index.

INPUT

First input the output of Problem 9.4 into NSOLD. Next, input the following additional tickets sold into INDX.

CARD	1–4	5–8	9–12	13–16	17–20	21–24	25–28	29–32	33–36	37–40
1	6 5	6 6	1 3	1 4	4 1	4 2	5 6	5 7	5 8	5 9
2	7 3	7 4	8 4	8 5	10 4	10 5	10 6	9 1	9 2	7 5
3	9 3	9 4	9 9	10 10	3 4	3 5	3 6			

Problem 10.7

PROBLEM STATEMENT

In computing the average grade, Ms. Generous uses the best 10 of the 14 quizzes given.

EXERCISE

Write a program to read in 14 quiz grades, and compute the average of the best 10 grades.

Input should consist of 14 grades from 0 to 100, and output should consist of the 14 grades and the average of the best 10 grades.

FORTRAN 11

11.1 . . . use character data for testing and manipulation.

11.2 . . . override the explicit type specification for a group of specified variables.

11.3 . . . state the need for and advantages of using structured FORTRAN coding techniques . . . list the four major elements . . . identify FORTRAN '77 extended (structured) statements.

11.4 . . . use the block IF (IF-THEN) statement in writing FORTRAN program blocks.

11.5 . . . use the ELSE statement along with the block IF and END IF statements (IF-THEN-ELSE)

11.6 . . . use the ELSE-IF along with the block-IF and END IF statements.

11.7 . . . write the block-IF and IF-THEN-ELSE statements using the logical IF, GO TO, and CONTINUE statements along with appropriate comment statements.

11.1

OBJECTIVE: . . . use character data for testing and manipulation.

In chapter 5, character data was introduced as alphanumeric information used to supply headings and titles to make output more meaningful. Two ways were presented to designate character data. One way was as a string of characters enclosed in apostrophes (or H format code) in a FORMAT statement. This method gives no control over the characters in the string, except for specifying the starting position on writing it out. A second way was to read alphanumeric data into variable names, using the A format code. This method provides some measure of control over character data. If the data is read using A1 format code, each character is stored in one memory location and this location can be tested and assigned to other locations by means of the assignment statement. In this section, we will explore examples using character data for testing and manipulation.

As was stated in Chapters 5 and 6, there is variation in the exact manner of specifying character data, further complicated at the time of this writing, by the inclusion in FORTRAN 77 of a separate type specification, CHARACTER, which is not available on many computers. Different methods of dealing with character data will be presented; then, one method will be adopted for the examples used. Four characters per cell will be assumed although this, too, varies with the computer.

EXAMPLE 1

Frequently, there is a need to test some character code and do alternative processing based on the different codes. For example, suppose that the name of each of the college students of State College is punched in columns 1-20 of a card, along with a class code in column 25 which is defined as follows: F, freshman; S, sophomore; J, junior; R, senior. It is desired to read the cards and to print out a list of the freshmen only, but count the number in each of the other classes.

In order to test the class code, which we call, ICODE, some predefined characters must be stored. Otherwise, a test would result in undetermined branching as the code would be tested against an undefined variable, as follows:

```
12345 6 789...
        READ(1,90)NAME,ICØDE
        IF(ICØDE.EQ.F)GØTØ 6
   90   FØRMAT(5A4,4X,A1)
```

garbage	Fbbb
contents of F in memory	Contents of ICODE

The 'F' in the test is a variable name or a memory location, not the internal code for a (F), which is the contents of ICODE for a freshmen whose class code is read in by A1 format code. (The remainder of the location is filled with blanks.) Instead, F is undefined. Although F contains some number, this number is unknown and useless to the user, so we shall just call it 'garbage'. What needs to be done is to assign the configuration of (F) to the memory location F so that a valid test can be made. There are two ways this can be done.

METHOD 1

One way to store the character (F) into location F is to read a defining card containing F and any other characters that need to be tested, as follows:

```
123456789...
      INTEGER F,S,J,R
      READ(1,90)F,S,J,R
   90 FØRMAT(4A1)
```

```
FSJR
123456789...
```

Fbbb

contents of
F after READ

This assigns the coded 'F' to the location designated by F, which has been typed, INTEGER. If all character data is typed INTEGER, problems are minimized. Although some computers permit REAL names to be used, some do not; and care must always be taken when both INTEGER and REAL names are used so that a type conversion is not erroneously caused by the assignment of a REAL character name to an INTEGER character name by means of an assignment statement.

METHOD 2

Method 1. is the most universal method of defining characters for testing. A second method, simpler because it eliminates the need for reading data is, unfortunately, less standard. It is to define the character data in a DATA statement. This brings up the Hollerith versus apostrophe dilemma, and you will have to determine which form your computer accepts. Both ways are presented below and then the apostrophe method is used in remaining examples in this chapter. It is the FORTRAN 77 recommended method, if a CHARACTER type statement is included. However, many extended versions of FORTRAN exist today which do not have a type CHARACTER. Confusing? Yes! You will have to check to see the specifics of defining character data by means of the DATA statement for your computer (or simply use METHOD 1!).

If the DATA statement is used instead of reading in a defining card, the characters are defined in one of the following ways:

```
123456789...
      INTEGER F,S,J,R
      DATA F,S,J,R/'F','S','J','R'/

         or using the Hollerith code,

      DATA F,S,J,R/1HF,1HS,1HJ,1HR/
```

Which of the above DATA statements could you use on your computer?
Check one or both.
Apostrophe ________ Hollerith ________

Do you have a CHARACTER type? _____
If yes, the INTEGER statement is replaced with the following:

```
123456789...
      CHARACTER F,S,J,R,ICØDE
```

Now that the characters F, S, J, and R have been stored by one of the above methods, let us return to the example and see how the entire program would look. In order to signal the end of the data, a 'Z' is placed in the class code column of a sentinel card. Hence, a 'Z' is predefined in location Z. Although only the code, F, is needed in order to test for freshmen, all the possible codes have been defined as a count is made of the number in each of the other classes. Assume that the name of the student is in columns one through twenty, ICODE is in column 25.

```
123456789...
      DIMENSIØN NAME (5)
      INTEGER F,S,J,R,Z
      DATA NS,NJ,NR/3*0/
      DATA F,S,J,R/'F','S','J','R'/,Z/'Z'/
    5 READ(1,90)NAME,ICØDE
   90 FØRMAT (5A4,4X,A1)
      IF(ICØDE.EQ.Z)GØTØ 99
      IF(ICØDE.EQ.F)GØTØ 8
      IF(ICØDE.EQ.S)NS=NS+1
      IF(ICØDE.EQ.J)NJ=NJ+1
      IF(ICØDE.EQ.R)NR=NR+1
      GØ TØ 5
    8 WRITE(3,92)NAME
   92 FØRMAT(1X,5A4)
      GØ TØ 5
   99 WRITE(3,94)NS,NJ,NR
   94 FØRMAT(//1X,'NUMBER ØF SØPHØMØRES',I6/
     1          1X,'NUMBER ØF JUNIØRS   ',I6/
     2          1X,'NUMBER ØF SENIØRS   ',I6)
      STØP
      END
```

EXAMPLE 2

Suppose that in a search for ones 'roots', a search is made of all the names on the city census cards, looking for the name,REILLY. Assume the names are punched one per card, last name first, in column 1 through 20. Depending on the number of character per location permitted on the computer used, 'REILLY' may or may not fit in one location. We will use four characters per location, so REILLY will be assigned to two locations and require dimensioning, which can be done in the INTEGER type statement. The end of the data is signified by a sentinel card containing the name, END.

```
12345 6 789...
      DIMENSIØN NAME(5),NUMB(2)
      INTEGER REILLY(2),END
      DATA REILLY/'REIL','LYbb'/,END/'ENDb'/
    7 READ(1,90)NAME,NUMB
   90 FØRMAT(5A4,2X,2A4)
      IF(NAME(1).EQ.END)GØTØ 99
      IF(NAME(1).NE.REILLY (1))GØTØ 7
      IF(NAME(2).NE.REILLY (2))GØTØ 7
      WRITE(3,92)NAME,NUMB
   92 FØRMAT(1X,5A4,2X,2A4)
      GØ TØ 7
   99 STØP
      END
```

Figure 11.1-1 shows how REILLY looks in memory, and how NAME looks for two different cards read in.

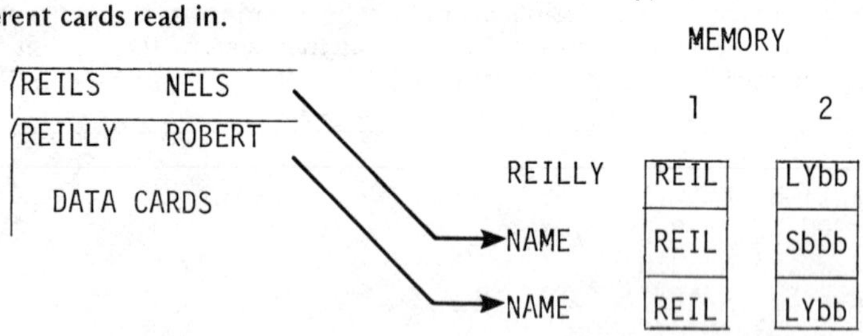

Figure 11.1-1. Memory Using Character Data.

Both memory locations of REILLY must be compared to the two locations for NAME before a match is found. All the relational operators (Chapter 10) can be used to test character data as long as both data items tested are character data with the same type names. In this example, all character data names have been typed, INTEGER. The phone number is treated as alphanumeric data since it is not a number for computation; and also someone may list it as PE05000 instead of 7305000.

EXAMPLE 3

Now consider a more complicated data card. Suppose the name may be placed anywhere in the first 20 columns, last name, then first name, separated by a comma. It would then be necessary to test and eliminate any beginning blanks and then test the next five characters or until a comma is found. This requires that each character be assigned to a single location, so each character can be tested. A dollar sign ($) in column 1 signals the end-of-data.

```
12345 6 789...
      INTEGER BLK,CØMMA,REILLY,END
      DIMENSIØN REILLY(6),NAME(20), NUMB(2)
      DATA BLK/' '/,CØMMA/','/,REILLY/'R','E','I','L','L','Y'/
      DATA END/'$'/
    5 READ(1,90)NAME,NUMB
   90 FØRMAT (20A1,4X,2A4 )
C *** TEST FØR END ØF DATA
      IF(NAME(1).EQ.END)GØ TØ 99
C *** SEARCH FØR FIRST NØN BLANK CHARACTER
      DØ 8 I=1,20
        IF(NAME(I).NE.BLK)GØ TØ 9
    8 CØNTINUE
C *** SET PØINTER TØ FIRST NØN BLANK CHARACTER
    9 ISTART = I
      IEND=ISTART+5
      ICØM=IEND+1
      K=1
      DØ 10 I=ISTART,IEND
C *** SEARCH FØR END ØF LAST NAME SIGNIFIED BY CØMMA
        IF(NAME(I).EQ.CØMMA) GØ TØ 5
C *** DØ CHARACTER BY CHARACTER TEST AGAINST REILLY
        IF(REILLY(K).NE.NAME(I)) GØ TØ 5
        K=K+1
   10 CØNTINUE
      IF(NAME(ICØM).NE.CØMMA)GØTØ5
C *** A MATCH HAS BEEN FØUND
      WRITE(3,92)NAME,NUMB
   92 FØRMAT(1X,20A1,5X,2A4)
      GØ TØ 5
   99 STØP
      END
```

EXERCISE

Answer the following questions about your computer, and re-write the above program for your computer, and run it on your computer with input data including the name REILLY and your own name.

My computer can store______characters per memory location.

I [must / need not] specify character data with a CHARACTER type statement.

I [can / cannot] use apostrophes to specify character in a DATA statement.

I [do / do not] have a DATA statement capability. (BASIC FORTRAN does not)

Character data can be used to generate plots as is shown in the next example.

EXAMPLE 4

Generate a plot of the waveform $y = 45 + 30 \sin x$

for x = .25 to 50 in .25 increments.

Since y is bounded for this function by 15 and 75, it is convenient to make the horizontal scale the Y axis. The scale for the y-axis is generated and assigned to ISCALE. It is printed across the top. The INTEGER array WAVFOR, is initialized to blanks and it is used to print each line across the page which is blank except for one asterisk, STAR. As each value of y is generated, it is truncated to an integer which is used as the index of WAVFOR for storing the asterisk, overriding the blank for the Y value of WAVFOR.

```
123456789.........
C THIS PRØGRAM PLØTS A WAVEFØRM
C
      DIMENSIØN ISCALE (16)
      INTEGER WAVFØR(80), BL, STAR, DOT
      DATA WAVFØR/ 80*' '/, BL/' '/, STAR/'*'/
      DATA DØT/'.'/
      DØ 5 I=1,16
        J=I-1
        K=5*(J-1) + 5
        ISCALE(I)=K
    5 CØNTINUE
      WRITE(3,90)ISCALE
      DØ 10 I=1,200
        X=.25*FLØAT(I)
        Y= 45.+3Ø.*SIN(X)
        M=Y
        WAVFØR(M)=STAR
        WRITE(3,94)X,WAVFØR,DØT
        WAVFØR(M)=BL
   10 CØNTINUE
      STØP
   90 FØRMAT('1',5X,'X',45X,'F(X)' // 14X,16I5/)
   94 FØRMAT(' ',F6.3,13X,80A1,T64,A1)
      END
```

PLOTTED OUTPUT

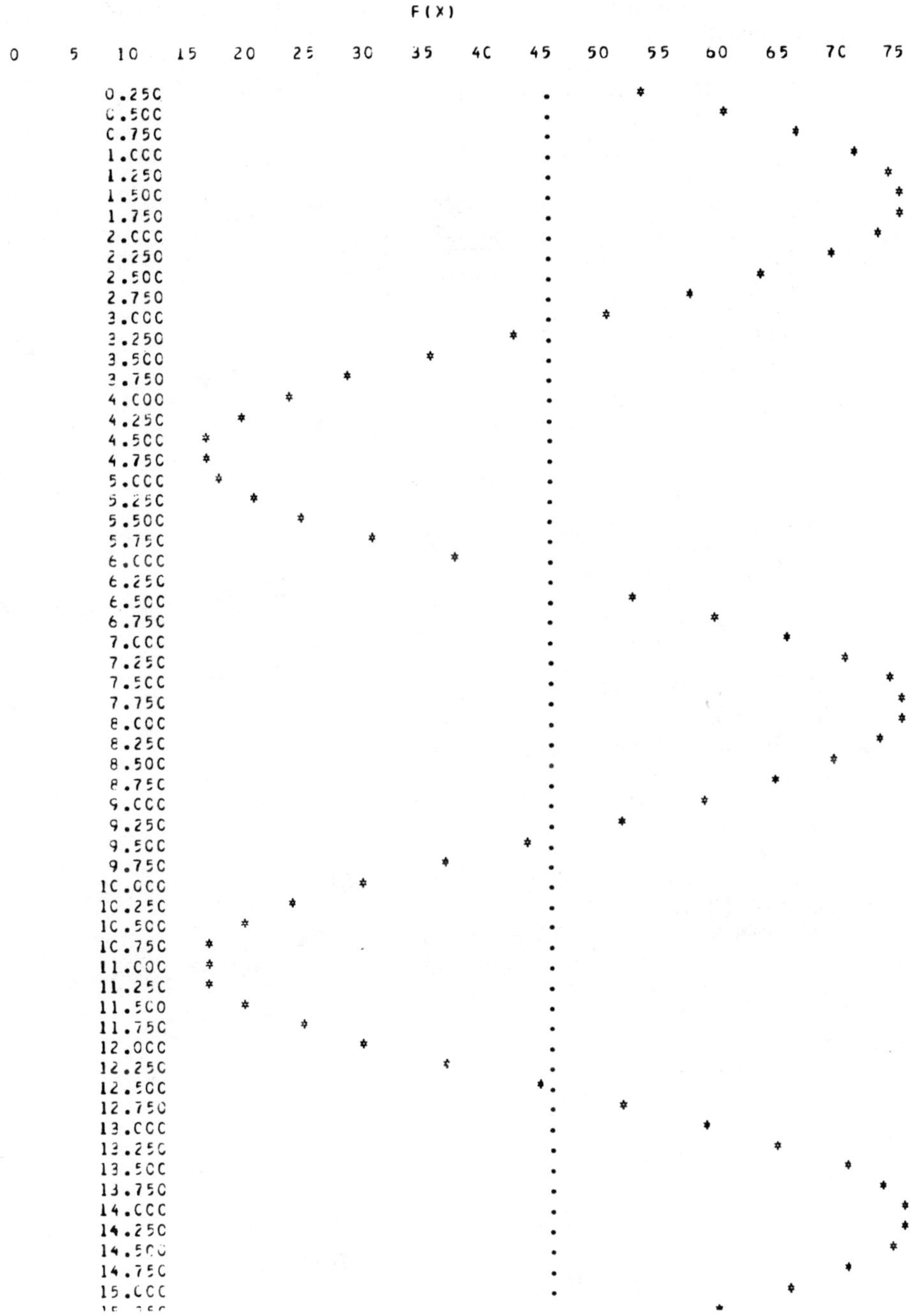

EXERCISE

1. The language BASIC is a popular language on most micro-computers today. In many respects, it is "easy" FORTRAN with similar keywords but with format-free input/output. The following partial program shows how FORTRAN could be used to write a BASIC compiler.

```
C  THIS PARTIAL PROGRAM ANALYZES BASIC STATEMENT TYPES
      DIMENSION ICARD(80),ISTMT(5,4),LEN(4)
      DATA LEN / 3,5,5,4  /, IBLK/' '/
      DATA IBLK/' '/
      DATA ISTMT     / 'L','E','T',' ',' ',
     1                 'I','N','P','U','T',
     2                 'P','R','I','N','T' ,
     3                 'G','O','T','O',' ' /
    2 READ(1,5,END=90)ICARD
    5 FORMAT(80A1)
      WRITE (3,8) ICARD
    8 FORMAT (' ',80A1)
C  SET POINTER TO START OF BASIC STATEMENT
   10 IS=6
C  SETUP LOOP TO PROCESS STATEMENT TYPES                    ________
   11 DO 20 I=1,4
C  SET LENGTH OF STATEMENT
   12   L=LEN(I)
C  SETUP LOOP TO PROCESS EACH CHARACTER IN STATEMENT
   13      DO 30 J=1,L
              IF(ICARD(IS).EQ.IBLK) IS=IS+1
   14         IF(ICARD(IS).NE.ISTMT(J.I)) GO TO 20
   15         IS=IS+1
   30      CONTINUE
C  A MATCHING STATEMENT HAS BEEN FOUND
      WRITE (3,50) I
   50 FORMAT(' STATEMENT TYPE IS NO.', I2)
   16      GO TO (100,200,300,400),I                        ________
   20 CONTINUE
C  NO MATCHING STATEMENT FOUND
   22 WRITE(3,40) ICARD
   40 FORMAT(' INVALID STATEMENT TYPE' , 80A1)
      GO TO 2
C  PROCESS LET STATEMENT
```

SAMPLE INPUT CARD

```
LET B=A
```

Questions:

a. What value is assigned to each of the following?

ISTMT(1,1)___	ISTMT(2,1)___	ISTMT(3,1)___
ISTMT(1,2)___	ISTMT(2,3)___	ISTMT(3,2)___
ISTMT(1,3)___	ISTMT(2,3)___	ISTMT(3,3)___
ISTMT(1,4)___	ISTMT(2,4)___	ISTMT(3,4)___

b) List the order of executions of the statements after the first card has been read, beginning with statement 10 and continuing until either statement 16 or 22 is reached.

2. Write FORTRAN statements that will read in a card and set INDX equal to the column in which the first non-blank character is found.

```
12345|6|789···
```

3. Write FORTRAN statements that will read in a sequence of cards and count the number that have a '–' punched in column 80. The end of the data deck is signified by a '$' in column 80.

```
12345|6|789···
```

4. Write FORTRAN statements that will test the alphanumeric word, UNIT, and if 'DEG' is found, divide XLAT by 57.296. (Assume UNIT has already been read in.)

```
12345|6|789···
```

5. Write FORTRAN statements that will test the MEAT field, column 1-4, for 'PORK' or 'BEEF' and print out HOG or COW, respectively, depending upon what is found. (Assume the MEAT field has already been read in as an alphanumeric field.) If neither is found, print 'LAMB'.

12345 6 789···

11.2

OBJECTIVE: . . . override the explicit type specification for a group of specified variables.

The IMPLICIT type statement has been a feature of extentions of Standard FORTRAN on many computers and it is now included in FORTRAN 77. However, some systems will not have this feature, and this section may be skipped without the loss of any computing capability.

Complete the following:

My computer system [does / does not] support the IMPLICIT type statement.

The IMPLICIT type statement is a specification statement that permits changing the explicit type of a group of variable names, beginning with a specified letter. The general form of the IMPLICIT type statement is as follows:

GENERAL FORM

```
12345|6|789...
       IMPLICIT type1(a1,b1,...),type2(a2,b2,...),...
```

COMPONENTS

IMPLICIT	is the keyword
$type_i$	is one of the following: INTEGER,REAL,OR LOGICAL
Each a_1,b_1...	is a single alphabetic character or range of characters separated by a minus sign, such as A-D.

EXAMPLE

```
12345|6|789...
       IMPLICIT REAL (M),INTEGER(A-C)
```

In the above example, all variable names beginning with M will be of type, REAL, and all variable names beginning with A, B, and C will be type, INTEGER.

Rules For Use Of The IMPLICIT Statement

1. The IMPLICIT statement is a specification statement, and it must be before any other specification statement or any executable statement.

2. Only one IMPLICIT statement may appear in a program unit.

3. The IMPLICIT statement applies only to the program unit in which it appears.

4. The IMPLICIT statement does not change the type names of the system-supplied subprograms.

5. The same letter may not appear more than once in an IMPLICIT statement of a program unit.

EXAMPLE

A programmer wishes to keep track of the use of all his program variable names by using the following naming conventions. The input data items, all of which are real numbers, begin with I, all output data items, begin in Ø, data items storing constants begin with C, and all temporary data items begin with T.

In order to do this, the explicit type of all variables, beginning with I, must be changed to REAL. The following statement does that:

```
123456789
      IMPLICIT INTEGER (I)
      READ(1,20) IRAD,IHT,ILGTH,IWDTH
   20 FØRMAT(4F5.1)
```

The IMPLICIT statement makes IRAD, IHT, ILGTH, IWDTH all real variables at every occurence in this program unit.

EXERCISES

1. Write one statement that will cause all names beginning with Z be integers within the program unit.

   123456789 . . .

   ____

2. Write one statement that will make only ZOO, ZULA, and ZEBRA integers within the program unit.

   123456789 . . .

   ____

3. Write one statement that will make integers of all program variable names.

   123456789 . . .

   ____

4. Write one statement that will make all names beginning with M or N be real variable names.

   123456789 . . .

   ____

11.3

OBJECTIVE: . . . state the need for and advantages of using structured FORTRAN coding techniques . . . list the four major elements . . . identify FORTRAN 77 extended (structured) statements.

In recent years there has been a move to write programs in a structured form. New structured statements have been added to some compilers to aid in this process. This development has been somewhat haphazard since no standards were available. The FORTRAN 77 standard has now provided for a set of structured statements.

Sections 11.3 through 11.6 provide an introduction to structured programming along with the nature and use of FORTRAN 77 extended (structured) statements. Section 11.7 shows the use of standard FORTRAN statements (IF, GO TO, CONTINUE) to simulate FORTRAN 77 structured statements.

Sections 11.3 to 11.7 may be skipped without loss of continuity in the study of standard FORTRAN.

As the complexity of your FORTRAN program increases, so does the need for a systematic and organized method of design and programming. Conventional methods of programming tend to produce programs that are difficult to understand, debug, maintain, and modify. This is especially true when there is unrestricted use of the GO TO statement.

Structured programming provides an effective means to organize the total programming process. It consists of four major elements:

a) top down design
b) data list
c) codable diagrams
d) coding with new structured language

The first three elements have been discussed previously, and various aspects of the structured program concept have been used throughout this book. This chapter provides the nature and use of the structured statements included in the FORTRAN 77 Standard: The BLOCK IF, ELSE IF, ELSE, and END IF statements.

Programs using these structured statements are less likely to contain logical errors. They allow direct top-down programming. Use of these techniques eliminates the unnecessary use of the GO TO statement and eliminates random branching.

11.4

OBJECTIVE: . . . use the block-IF (IF THEN) statement in writing FORTRAN program blocks.

The block-IF statement has the form:

```
GENERAL FORM
123456789...
nnnnn IF(e) THEN

COMPONENTS
nnnnn          is the statement number (optional)
e              is a logical expression
IF and THEN are keywords

EXAMPLES
123456789...
      IF(A-B.GT.Ø.)THEN
      IF(X.GE.Y)THEN
```

The logical expression (e) is constructed in the same manner given for the logical IF in Chapter 10.

It is used with the END IF statement.

```
GENERAL FORM
123456789...
      END IF

COMPONENTS
END IF is a keyword
```

These two statements are used in pairs as follows:

```
12345|6|789...
       IF(e)THEN
         S
         S    IF-block
         S
         S
       END IF
```

Figure 11.4-1 shows the flow diagram for the IF-block statement. The IF-block consists of all executable statements between the IF(e) THEN and END IF statements.

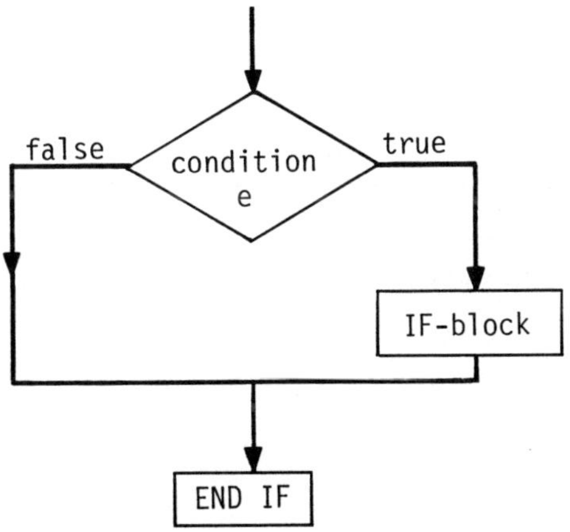

Figure 11.4-1. IF-block Flow Diagram

The IF-block is executed in normal execution sequence, if e is true. If e is false, control is transferred to the END IF statement. In both cases, the normal sequential operation continues after the END IF is reached. Transfer of control into an IF-block from outside the IF-block is prohibited.

EXAMPLE 1

Write a program segment that will determine the square root of the expression

$$(b^2-4ac)$$

if positive, and continue with no action if negative.

```
12345|6|789...
       RAD=B**2-4.*A*C
       IF(RAD.GT.Ø.)THEN
         D=SQRT(RAD)
       END IF
```

EXAMPLE 2

Write IF-blocks to perform the following: if an insurance code ISUR is equal to 0, a deduction for insurance, DEDINS, is computed as 3% of the amount of pay, PAY. If ISUR is equal to 1, DEDINS is 5% of PAY.

```
123456789...

      IF(ISUR.EQ.0)THEN
        DEDINS=.03*PAY
      END IF
      IF(ISUR.EQ.1)THEN
        DEDINS=.05*PAY
      END IF
```

EXERCISE

Draw an IF-block flow diagram, and write the corresponding program segment for each of the following:

a) Compare A to B and set C equal to the larger of the two.

```
123456789...




```

b) The serial number, ISERNO, is tested for less than or equal to 0 which indicates an error. If it is in error, a message is written out "ERROR" and the card, CARD, printed. Otherwise, the number of cards, NCARD, in incremented.

```
123456789...




```

11.5

OBJECTIVE: . . . use the ELSE statement along with the block IF and END IF statements (IF-THEN-ELSE).

The ELSE statements has the form

```
GENERAL FORM
123456789...
nnnnn ELSE

COMPONENT
ELSE is the keyword
```

The ELSE statement is used with the block IF and END IF as follows:

```
123456789...
      IF(e)THEN
        s
        s    IF-block for (e) true
        s
      ELSE
        s
        s    IF-block for (e) false
        s
      END IF
```

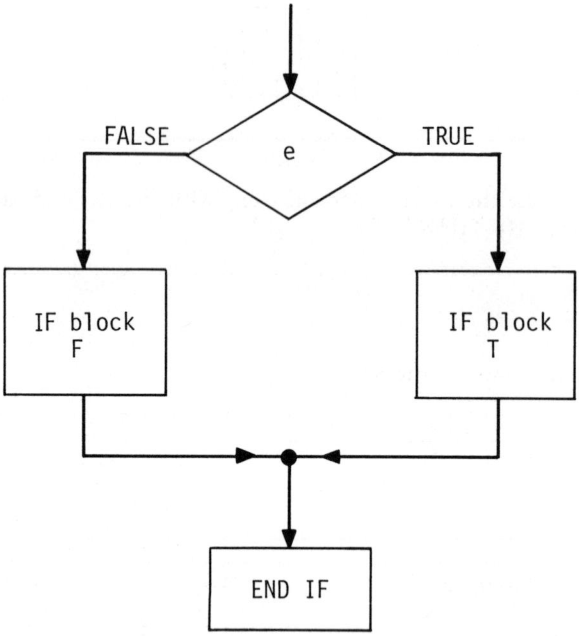

The condition (e) is tested for a true or false condition. If (e) is true, IF block T is executed. If (e) is false, IF block F is executed. In structured FORTRAN, this selection is called the IF-THEN-ELSE structure. Standard FORTRAN does not have the IF-THEN-ELSE statements, but this structure can be implemented by the IF statement, the CONTINUE, and the GO TO statement in conjunction with the logical operations as shown in Section 10.6 of your textbook.

Transfer of control into either the IF-block or ELSE-block is prohibited.

EXAMPLE

Write a program to read three numbers (X,Y, and Z). Determine the largest of the three, and write the largest.

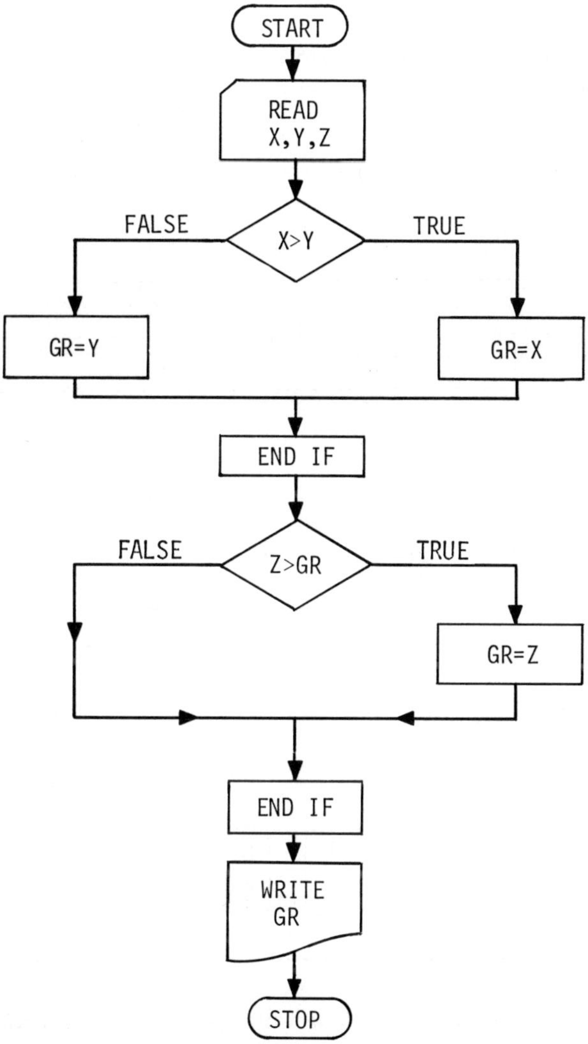

PROGRAM CODE

```
123456789···
      READ(1,90)X,Y,Z
      IF(X.GT.Y)THEN
        GR=X
      ELSE
        GR=Y
      END IF
      IF(Ƶ.GT.GR)THEN
        GR=Ƶ
      END IF
      WRITE(3,92)GR
      ...
   90 FØRMAT(3F8.1)
   92 FØRMAT(F10.1)
```

EXERCISE

Write a program to determine the largest of four numbers (N1, N2, N3, N4).

1 2 3 4 5 6 7 8 9 . . .

11.6

OBJECTIVE: . . . use the ELSE-IF along with the block-IF and END IF statements.

FORTRAN 77 also provides an ELSE IF statement to be used in conjunction with the block-IF and END IF statements. The form of this statement is

GENERAL FORM

```
12345|6|789...
     | |ELSE IF(e)THEN
```

COMPONENTS

```
ELSE IF  is a keyword

      e  is a logical expression

   THEN  is a keyword
```

EXAMPLE

```
12345|6|789...
     | |ELSE IF(A.NE.B)THEN
     | |   s┐
     | |   s├  ELSE IF-block
     | |   s┘
     | |next ELSE IF,ELSE OR END IF statement
```

The ELSE IF-block consists of all the executable statements following the ELSE IF statement up to, but not including the next corresponding ELSE IF, ELSE, or END IF statement.

The expression (e) is first evaluated. If (e) is true, normal execution continues with the first statement of the ELSE IF-block. If the value of (e) is false, control is transferred to the next ELSE IF, ELSE or END IF statement.

Various combinations of block IF, ELSE, and ELSE IF statements can be used with the END IF.

```
12345|6|789...
     | |IF(e1)THEN
     | |   s
     | |      block 1
     | |   s
     | |ELSE IF(e2)THEN
     | |   s
     | |      block 2
     | |   s
     | |ELSE IF(e3)THEN
     | |   s
     | |      block 3
     | |   s
     | |ELSE
     | |   s
     | |      block 4
     | |   s
     | |END IF
```

Figure 11.6-1 Example Using the ELSE-IF Structure.

```
      N1=0
      N2=0
      N3=0
      N4=0
      SUM1=0
      SUM2=0
      SUM3=0
      SUM4=0
      IF(ICØDE.EQ.1)THEN
        N1=N1+1
        SUM1=SUM1+X
      ELSE IF(ICØDE.EQ.2)THEN
        N2=N2+1
        SUM2=SUM2+X
      ELSE IF(ICØDE.EQ.3)THEN
        N3=N3+1
        SUM3=SUM3+X
      ELSE IF(ICØDE.EQ.4)THEN
        N4=N4+1
        SUM4=SUM4+X
      END IF
```

11.7

OBJECTIVE: . . . write the block-IF and IF-THEN-ELSE statements using the logical IF, GO TO, and CONTINUE statements along with appropriate comment statements.

Some programming standards by firms require writing structured code using standard FORTRAN statements. This section is provided to demonstrate this process. This will also provide a means of simulating structured code at these installations using standard code only.

In coding the decision block in FORTRAN, a restrictive use of the GO TO statement, with the IF and the CONTINUE is used to make a structure similar to the IF-THEN-ELSE of structured FORTRAN.

Examples of decisions coded in both standard FORTRAN and structured FORTRAN are given below to show the parallel structures of each.

EXAMPLE 1 -Double Alternative Decision

To avoid a division by zero in evaluating the expression,

$$\theta = \arctan \frac{A}{A-1}$$

A should be tested for 1.0. If A=1.0, θ should be set to 90°. If A is not equal to 1.0, θ is computed by the formula. The library function for arctan, ATAN, is used. It returns the angle in radian measure, which is then converted to degrees.

Figure 11.7-1 shows the flow diagram for this example.

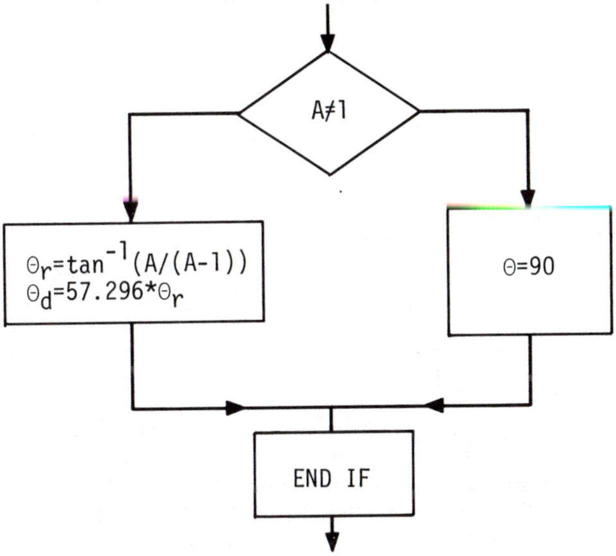

Figure 11.7-1 Example Flow Diagram

The code corresponding to this structure is

```
123456789...
      IF(A.NE.1.0) GØ TØ 10
        THETAD=90
        GØ TØ 15
   10   THETAR=ATAN(A/(A-1.))
        THETAD=57.296*THETAR
C     ENDIF
   15 CØNTINUE
```

Figure 11.7-2A Example in STANDARD FORTRAN of the IF Statement

```
12345 6 789...
      IF(A.EQ.1.0)THEN
        THETAD=90
      ELSE
        THETAR=ATAN(A/(A-1.))
        THETAD=57.296*THETAR
      END IF
```

Figure 11.7-2B Example in STRUCTURED FORTRAN of the IF-THEN-ELSE Statement

EXPLANATION

1. Using the logical IF, in Figure 11.7-2A, if the result of the condition is true, the statement following the condition is executed. The GO TO is used to branch to the statement block for TRUE. If the condition is not true, the statement block immediately following is executed.

2. The statements within the IF block up to the CONTINUE are indented to make the IF block clear. Although FORTRAN 66 does not have the ENDIF terminator, a comment card is used to insert it prior to the CONTINUE statement which ends our simulated 'structured' IF. As you code your IF, indent on your coding paper prior to keypunching.

3. In the Structured FORTRAN example, the IF THEN ELSE is used. If the condition is true, the THEN block follows immediately. After the THEN block, control transfers to the first statement after ENDIF. If the condition is false, the ELSE block is executed. This is terminated at the ENDIF and control passes to the next statement following ENDIF.

4. The statements within the TRUE block and FALSE block are indented for clarity. This is either done manually at coding time, or as a compiler option, some structured compilers indent for you.

5. Notice the inverse condition is used in the FORTRAN 66 from the Structured FORTRAN because of the difference in the flow of control using the logical IF from the IF-THEN-ELSE. The following shows the inverse conditions for all the logical operations.

OPERATOR	INVERSE OPERATOR
.EQ.	.NE.
.NE.	.EQ.
.GT.	.LE.
.GE.	.LT.
.LT.	.GE.
.LE.	.GT.

EXAMPLE 2 -- Single Alternative IF

The single alternative decision has no statement to be performed if the condition is false. For example, the amount of purchase is tested, and the tax is computed only if the amount exceeds $.15.

```
123456789···
      IF(AMØUNT.LT..15) GØ TØ 5
        TAX=.05*AMØUNT
        AMØUNT=AMØUNT+TAX
C     ENDIF
    5 CØNTINUE
```

Figure 11.7-3A Example in FORTRAN 66 of Single Alternative Statement

```
123456789···
      IF(AMØUNT.GE..15)THEN
        TAX=.05*AMØUNT
        AMØUNT=AMØUNT+TAX
      ENDIF
```

Figure 11.7-3B Example in STRUCTURED FORTRAN of Alternative IF-THEN Statement

EXPLANATION

1. In Example A, if the condition is true, (amount is less than .15), then no statement block is executed and flow of control transfers to the end of the IF signified by the CONTINUE. If the condition is false, the statement block immediately following is executed which terminates at the CONTINUE.

2. In Example B, if the condition is true (amount is greater than or equal to .15), then the statements following are executed. If the condition is false, control passes to the statement following the ENDIF terminator.

3. Note that the inverse conditions are expressed in the two examples.

EXAMPLE 3 -- Single Statement Alternatives

A single alternative statement can be stated in one statement of the alternatives. When this occurs, the coding can be reduced as follows:

```
123456789
      IF(A.GT.1.0)THETAD=THETAD+180.
```

This reduces considerably the amount of coding while preserving the intent of structured programming, namely, clarity.

CHAPTER PROGRAMMING PROBLEMS

TOPIC APPLICATION

a) Errors in data
b) Review of DO and IF statements
c) Review of character data

Problem 11.1

PROBLEM STATEMENT

A list of males and females in a computer programming class and their weights have been recorded and listed below. No more than 100 sets of data will be encountered. Write a program to determine:

a) the average weight of the males (total weight of males/number of males)
b) the total number of males
c) the number of males weighing over 200 pounds
d) repeat a-c for women

INPUT

On the first card read in the total number of data sets (type, weight). Then read in type and weight data using five sets for each card. Use the following data to make up four cards of data sets:

CARD	TYPE	WEIGHT	CARD	TYPE	WEIGHT
	1	188		2	95
	1	0*		2	105
2	2	108	4	1	350*
	1	208		1	175
	1	164		1	50*
	1	199		2	250
	1	200		1	125
3	*3	333	5	1	198
	1	226		2	125
	2	205		1	205

type 1 = male student
type 2 = female student
*errors in data to be removed by the computer program

Print out your input data to check for errors made in keypunching it.

Errors in data:

Quite frequently data cards contain errors. The program should be constructed to "throw out" these obvious inaccuracies in the data set. For this problem discard the data set if:

a) type is not 1 or 2 b) weight $\geq$ 350 c) Weight $\leq$ 50

OUTPUT

Start printing at the top of a new printout page. Printout the results with double spacing in the following form:

```
           1         2         3         4
  1234567890123456789012345678901234567890123456789012345678...
1 | AVERAGE WEIGHT OF MALES =
2 | TOTAL NO OF MALES =
3 | MALES OVER 200 LB =
4 | AVERAGE WEIGHT OF FEMALES =
5 | TOTAL NO OF FEMALES =
6 | FEMALES OVER 200 LB =
7 |
8 |
9 |
```

A flow diagram should be constructed before attempting to write the program on the FORTRAN coding sheet.

Problem 11.2

PROBLEM STATEMENT

Write a FORTRAN Program to calculate the mean, variance, and standard deviation of a given sample. N the sample size will not exceed 500. The three statistical measures can be calculated as follows:

$$\text{AVE} = \frac{\Sigma x_j}{N} \qquad \text{VAR} = \frac{\Sigma x_j^2 - \frac{(\Sigma x_j)^2}{N}}{N-1} \qquad \text{STD} = \sqrt{\text{VAR}}$$

INPUT

Data cards will be supplied with the following format:

first card
- COL 1 - 5 value of N in I format
- COL 6 - 10 code (integer)
- COL 11 - 78 title of program (alphanumeric)

remaining cards
- divided into ten fields of seven columns per field using the form nnnnn.n for each field.

OUTPUT

Start printing on the top of a new page.
The printout of results should be arranged in the following form:

```
          1         2         3   8
 1234567890123456789012345678901...1
1|               CØDE     nnnnn
2|               TITLE    aaaaaaaa........a
3|               N        nnnnn
4|               AVE      nnnnn.n
5|               VAR      nnnnn.n
6|               STD      nnnnn.n
7|
```

Note: Print out your input data to check for errors!

Problem 11.3

PROBLEM STATEMENT

Many products, such as dairy products, must be dated with the last date that they can be used. The company knows the "life" of each one of its products, and it stamps the last date that each product can be used on the product.

EXERCISE

Write a program that will compute and print the ending date given a starting date and the number of days to be counted from this starting date.

For example, 10 days after the current date of Feb. 2, 1977 is Sunday, Feb. 12, 1977. Ten days after Wed., Dec. 28, 1977 is Sat., Jan, 7, 1978.

Input should consist of the month, day, year and number of days to be counted to the ending date. Input the date in the form of integers 020277 for Feb. 2, 1977.

Output should be in the following form:

STARTING DATE IS TUES., DEC. 13, 1977
NUMBER OF DAYS TO BE COUNTED IS 40
ENDING DATE IS SUN., JAN. 22, 1978

FORTRAN 12

12.1 . . . identify the two types of subprograms and state the characteristics and use of each type.

12.2 . . . use system-supplied FUNCTION subprograms.

12.3 . . . define the FUNCTION subprogram statement.

12.4 . . . reference a FUNCTION subprogram in a FORTRAN statement.

12.5 . . . use the RETURN statement in subprograms.

12.6 . . . write FUNCTION subprograms.

12.7 . . . define and write statement FUNCTIONS.

12.8 . . . use execution-time dimensions.

12.1

OBJECTIVE: . . . identify the two types of subprograms and state the characteristics and use of each type.

Up to this point, each program that has been considered has been a single, executable program unit. Frequently, however, in the writing of a program the same procedure which requires a sequence of statements appears several times. To avoid repeating the procedure several times, it can be defined as a subprogram, which is referenced whenever it is needed. The program unit, which is not the subprogram, is called the main program. Every program must have one and only one main program, but it may have any number of subprograms that can be accommodated by the system. Since a subprogram may call another subprogram, the program calling a subprogram is called the calling program. A subprogram may not call itself.

Subprograms are categorized as follows:

1. FUNCTIONS
   - . System-supplied FUNCTIONS
   - . Statement FUNCTIONS
   - .User-written FUNCTIONS
2. SUBROUTINES

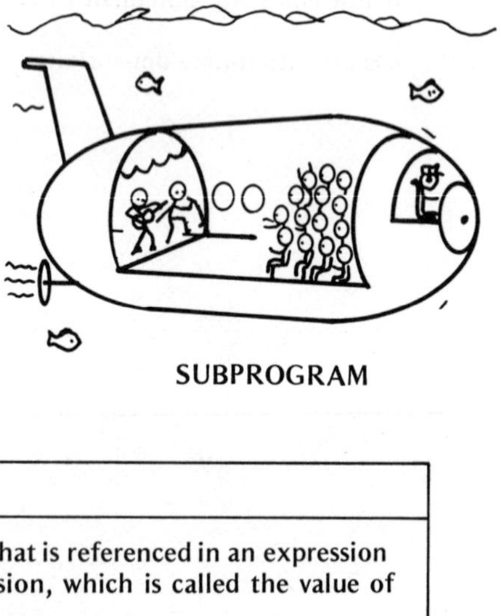

SUBPROGRAM

FUNCTION
A FUNCTION is a procedure that is referenced in an expression and supplies a value to the expression, which is called the value of the FUNCTION.

There are three types of FUNCTIONS. The first type, the system-supplied or intrinsic FUNCTION, is supplied by the computer system. You have already used several of these FUNCTIONS which were introduced in Section 4.5, namely, SIN, COS, TAN, EXP, and SQRT.

SYSTEM-SUPPLIED FUNCTION
The system-supplied FUNCTION is supplied by the computer system and has a special meaning. The specific names of the most commonly used FUNCTIONS and their meanings are given in Section 12.2.

STATEMENT FUNCTION
A statement FUNCTION is a procedure that is specified in a single statement. This single statement is placed within the program unit referencing it, before any executable statement. It is not an executable statement itself.

USER-SUPPLIED FUNCTION
The user-supplied FUNCTION is a procedure, consisting of one or more statements, which is external to the program unit referencing it.

SUBROUTINE
A SUBROUTINE is a procedure that is external to the program unit referencing it. It is referenced by a special statement called the CALL statement.

The two classes of subprograms differ mainly in the manner in which they are referenced and in the number of values that they return. A SUBROUTINE subprogram uses a special statement, the CALL statement, whereas a FUNCTION subprogram is called by mentioning its name in an expression. A SUBROUTINE subprogram may return any number of values or perform a task without returning any values. The FUNCTION subprogram always returns a single value through the FUNCTION name.

If a value is returned by a subprogram, the value is dependent upon one or more values, called <u>arguments</u>, which are supplied in parentheses after the name of the subprogram. A FUNCTION subprogram must have at least one argument; a SUBROUTINE subprogram may have any number or none at all.

Table 12.1-1 shows a comparison of the two classes of subprograms.

Table 12.1-1

Comparison of the FUNCTION and SUBROUTINE Subprograms

SUB- PROGRAM	NAMING RULES	DOES NAME TELL TYPE?	IS NAME ASSIGNED A VALUE?	NUMBER OF ARGU- MENTS	NUMBER OF VALUES RETURNED	HOW CALLED
FUNCTION	1-6 alpha- numeric; 1st alpha- betic	Yes	Yes	1 or more	At least 1 through the name of the FUNCTION	Name (arg,..) appears in an expression in a FORTRAN statement
SUB- ROUTINE	same as above	No	No	0 or more	0 or more	CALL name (arguments)

In the flow diagram for a calling program, the symbol used to show that the processing is done by a subprogram is given in Figure 12.1-1. A separate flow diagram would be made showing the details of the subprogram. The symbol used to return to the calling program is also given in Figure 12.1-1.

Figure 12.1-1. Flow Diagram Symbols for Subprograms.

The hierarchy chart, discussed in Chapter 7, is a particular aid in breaking a program into functional units, each of which can be written as a subprogram. The following example shows how this is done.

EXAMPLE

Test scores on a college entrance examination from several high schools are sent in for processing. It is desired to compute the arithmetic mean and the standard deviation of the scores from each school.

We begin by making a data table, Table 12.1-2, and a hierarchy chart, Figure 12.1-2.

Table 12.1-2
Data Table

DATA ITEM	DEFINITION	UNIT	DATA TYPE[1]	USE[2]	FORTRAN NAME
N	number of test scores for school		I	I	NT
t_i	test scores		R	I	TEST
$\bar{A}$	arithmetic mean		R	0	AMEAN
σ	standard deviation		R	0	STD

[1] DATA TYPE: I = Integer, R = Real, A = Alphanumeric,
[2] USE: I = Input, Ø = Output, T = Temporary, C = Constant

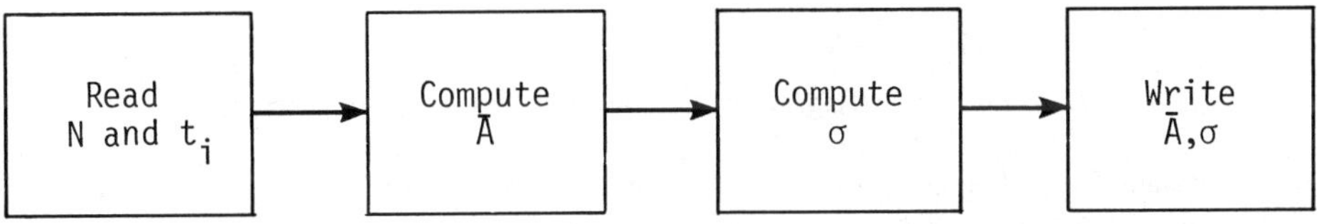

Figure 12.1-2. Hierarchy Chart.

As this problem is not very long, we would not object to its being written as one program unit. However, there are two distinct procedures to be done; each of them could be written as a subprogram. In fact, if general subprograms are written for the mean and the standard deviation, they can be saved and used in other application. Most installations maintain a library of commonly used, user-written subprograms to which these could be added.

Figure 12.1-3 shows the detailed flow diagram for the main program.

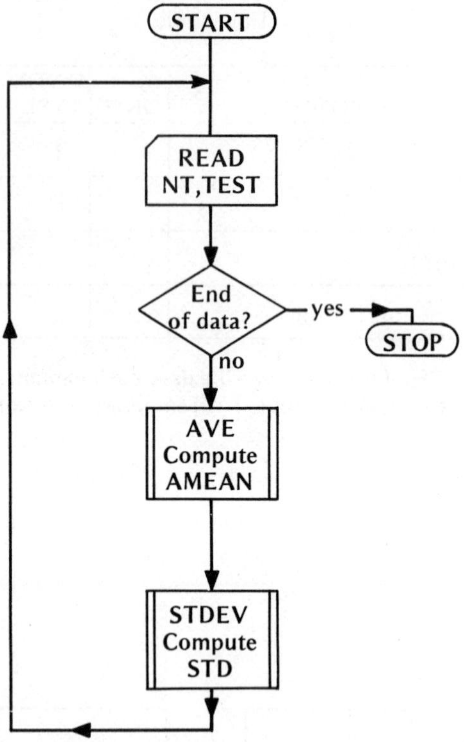

Figure 12.1-3. Detailed Flow Diagram of a Program using Subprograms.

Detailed flow diagrams for each subprogram would also be made. These are left as an exercise for the reader. The formulas needed for this problem were given in Programming Problem 11.2.

When a subprogram is called, a sequence of steps must be executed to pass control to the subprogram and to enable returning to the calling program. This calling sequence consists of the following steps which are performed automatically by the computer for each subprogram reference.

1. Make available to the subprogram the address of the argument list. The argument list is made by the compiler, consisting of the memory addresses of each of the arguments.

2. Make available to the subprogram the address in the calling program to which to return after the subprogram has executed.

3. Branch to the address of the subprogram.

The above sequence requires some additional execution time that is not required if the statements were written within the main program. However, the time is so small that it should not be a factor in determining whether or not to write a subprogram.

The details of writing and using each type of FUNCTION subprogram are presented in the sections of this chapter. The SUBROUTINE subprogram is discussed in Chapter 13.

12.2

OBJECTIVE: ... use system-supplied FUNCTION subprograms.

The use of five of the system-supplied FUNCTIONS (SIN, COS, TAN, SQRT and EXP) was discussed in Section 4.5. There are a number of other FUNCTIONS which are available as system-supplied FUNCTIONS. Table 12.2-1 gives the names and definitions of the most common system-supplied FUNCTIONS. Check your local installation for a complete list of your system-supplied FUNCTIONS, and for the specific name to be used in cases where two names are given here. Each of these FUNCTIONS is used in a similar way as the FUNCTIONS previously discussed. The general form for referencing the FUNCTION subprogram is as follows:

GENERAL FORM
name $(a_1, a_2, a_3, \ldots, a_n)$
COMPONENTS
name   is the FUNCTION name $a_1, \ldots, a_n$ are the actual arguments
EXAMPLES
ATAN (ALPHA) ALØG (X) IABS (JJ)

Some computers treat certain system-supplied FUNCTION subprograms that require very few machine instructions (such as ABS) as in line FUNCTIONS. The machine instructions of an in line FUNCTION are inserted directly among the machine instructions of the expression which references the FUNCTION. More complicated FUNCTIONS are treated as external FUNCTIONS. The machine instructions of these FUNCTIONS are stored in a system library and made available to a user's program automatically. System-supplied FUNCTION subprograms are used in exactly the same manner regardless of how they are handled by the computer.

Table 12.2-1
System-Supplied FUNCTIONS

	Definition	FUNCTION Name	Number of Argument	Type of Argument	Type of Result
Type Conversion	Conversion to integer	INT IFIX	1 1	Real Real	Integer Integer
	Conversion to real	REAL FLOAT	1 1	Integer Integer	Real Real
Truncation	integer (a)	AINT	1	Real	Real
Absolute value	$\|a\|$	IABS ABS	1 1	Integer Real	Integer Real
Remainder	$a_1 - \text{int}(a_1/a_2)*a_2$	MOD AMOD	2 2	Integer Real	Integer Real
Transfer of Sign	$\|a_1\|$ if $a_2 \geq 0$ $-\|a_1\|$ if $a_2 < 0$	ISIGN SIGN	2 2	Integer Real	Integer Real
Positive Difference	$a_1 - a_2$ if $a_1 > a_2$ 0 if $a_1 \leq a_2$	IDIM DIM	2 2	Integer Real	Integer Real
Choosing Largest Value	$\max(a_1, a_2, \ldots)$	MAX0 AMAX1 AMAX0 MAX1	≥2 ≥2 ≥2 ≥2	Integer Real Integer Real	Integer Real Real Integer
Choosing Smallest Value	$\min(a_1, a_2, \ldots)$	MIN0 AMIN1 AMIN0 MIN1	≥2 ≥2 ≥2 ≥2	Integer Real Integer Real	Integer Real Real Integer
Square Root	$\sqrt{a}$	SQRT	1	Real	Real
Exponential	e**a	EXP	1	Real	Real
Natural logarithm	$\log_e(a)$	ALØG	1	Real	Real

Table 12.2-1
(Continued)

FUNCTION Performed	Definition	FUNCTION Name	Number of Argument	Type of Argument	Type of Result
Common Logarithm	$\log_{10}(a)$	ALØG10	1	Real	Real
Sine	sin (a)	SIN	1	Real	Real
Cosine	cos (a)	CØS	1	Real	Real
Tangent	tan (a)	TAN	1	Real	Real
Arcsine	arcsin(a)	ASIN ARSIN	1	Real	Real
Arccosine	arccos(a)	ACØS ARCØS	1	Real	Real
Arctangent	arctan(a) arctan (a_1/a_2)	ATAN ATAN2	1 2	Real Real	Real Real
Hyperbolic Sine	sinh(a)	SINH	1	Real	Real
Hyperbolic Cosine	cosh(a)	CØSH	1	Real	Real
Hyperbolic Tangent	tanh(a)	TANH	1	Real	Real

In evaluating expressions containing FUNCTIONS and other operations, FUNCTIONS are performed before exponentiation, multiplication and division, addition and subtraction. The actual arguments supply the values that will be used to determine the result of the FUNCTION.

The following examples show the use of system-supplied FUNCTIONS in coding FORTRAN statements for each of the following formulas.

EXAMPLES

	FORMULA STATEMENT
	123456789···
$d = \lvert a-b \rvert \cdot c$	D=ABS(A-B)*C
$x = A-\log^{e} \sin(B-C)$	X=A-ALØG(SIN(B-C))
$d = \dfrac{\tan^{-1}\sqrt{a^2+b^2}}{\lvert c \rvert}$	D=ATAN(SQRT(A**2+B**2))/ABS(C)
$y = e^{(\cos^2 2\theta+E)^{\frac{1}{2}}}$	Y=EXP(SQRT((CØS(2.*THETA))**2+E))

EXAMPLE

The following FORTRAN statement assigns the remainder of 121 divided by 7 to IREM.

```
12345 6 789...
        IREM=MØD(121,7)
```

FUNCTION MOD gives the remainder in a division. MOD is defined as $arg_1 - X*arg_2$ where X is the greatest integer less than or equal to arg_1 divided by arg_2. The greatest integer less than 121÷7 is 17. Hence,

121-17*7=2

EXAMPLE

The following FORTRAN statement assigns the largest value of A, B, C, D, E, F, and G to XLARG.

```
12345 6 789...
        XLARG=AMAX1(A,B,C,D,E,F,G)
```

12.3

OBJECTIVE: ... define the FUNCTION subprogram statement.

The first statement in a subprogram defines what class of subprogram it is. The statement to define a FUNCTION subprogram is as follows:

GENERAL FORM
123456789···
type FUNCTIØN name (a,b,c,...)
or
FUNCTIØN name(a,b,c,...)

COMPONENTS	
type	is INTEGER, REAL, DØUBLE PRECISIØN, or LØGICAL
FUNCTIØN	is a keyword
NAME	is the name assigned to the FUNCTIØN
a,b,c,...	are dummy arguments

EXAMPLES
123456789···
FUNCTIØN RØØT(A,B,C)
REAL FUNCTIØN IBS(X,Y)
INTEGER FUNCTIØN ZIP(I,G,H)

The name of the FUNCTION subprogram must consist of one to six alphabetic and numeric characters, the first being alphabetic. Special characters are not allowed.

The type declaration for the FUNCTION subprogram is optional. If it is omitted, the name of the FUNCTION assigns a type to the value of the FUNCTION depending upon the type of the variable name of the FUNCTION according to the I-N rule. If the type is used, it overrides the type assigned by the naming convention. For example, FUNCTION RAND(N) returns a real value; INTEGER FUNCTION RAND(N) returns an integer value.

The arguments in the FUNCTION statement are dummy arguments in that they will be replaced by the actual arguments at the time the FUNCTION is referenced. A FUNCTION must have at least one argument. A dummy argument may be a non-subscripted variable, array name, or a dummy name of a subprogram. A dummy argument may not be an array element.

Although a FUNCTION always returns a single value through the FUNCTION name, one or more of the arguments may also be used to return values to the calling program. This is done by changing the value of the dummy argument within the FUNCTION subprogram which, in turn, changes the corresponding actual argument when the FUNCTION is called.

If the dummy argument is changed within the FUNCTION, the corresponding actual argument must be a variable or an array element, but not a constant.

12.4

OBJECTIVE: . . . reference a FUNCTION subprogram in a FORTRAN statement.

A FUNCTION subprogram is referenced in the following form:

GENERAL FORM	
name(a,b,c,...)	
COMPONENTS	
name	is the name of the FUNCTION called
a,b,c,...	are the actual FUNCTION arguments
EXAMPLES	

```
123456789...
      AVE=SUM(A1,A2,A3)/3.
      RI=RØØT(X,Y,Z)
      Z=FUNX(ALP,SIN)
```

The reference to a FUNCTION may be in any expression of an arithmetic statement or in a relational expression.

The actual arguments may be any of the following:

1. variable name
2. literal or arithmetic constant
3. array name

4. array element

5. arithmetic or logical expression

6. name of another subprogram

The actual argument list must agree in number, order,and type to the dummy arguments in the FUNCTION.

A FUNCTION subprogram may not reference itself.

12.5

OBJECTIVE: . . . use the RETURN statement in subprograms.

All external subprograms must have at least one RETURN statement.

GENERAL FORM
1 2 3 4 5 6 7 8 9 · · · nnnnn RETURN
COMPONENTS
nnnnn is an optional statement number RETURN is a keyword

The RETURN statement returns control back to the calling program. In FUNCTION subprograms, control returns to the statement containing the name of the FUNCTION, and the computed FUNCTION value is returned through the FUNCTION name, as shown in Figure 12.5-1.

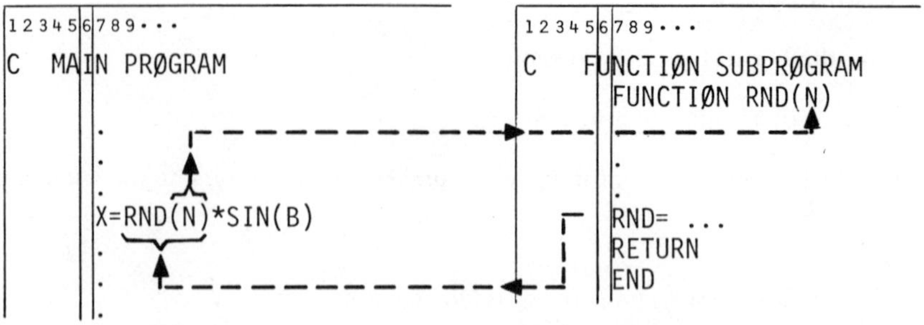
1 2 3 4 5 6 7 8 9 • • •
C MAIN PRØGRAM
X=RND(N)*SIN(B)
1 2 3 4 5 6 7 8 9 • • •
C FUNCTIØN SUBPRØGRAM
FUNCTIØN RND(N)
RND= ...
RETURN
END

Figure 12.5-1. Transfer of Data Using FORTRAN Subprogram

A FUNCTION subprogram may have more than one logical returning point, as shown in the following example:

```
123456789···

      FUNCTIØN QDRT1(A,B,C,IRØØT)
C     THIS FUNCTIØN CØMPUTES ØNE RØØT ØF A QUADRATIC EQUATIØN
      IRØØT=-1
      DISC=B**2-4.*A*C
      IF(DISC.LT.0.)GØ TØ 5
      IRØØT=+1
      QDRT1=(-B+SQRT(DISC))/(2.*A)
    5 RETURN
      END
```

If a subprogram has a number of logical points from which to return, a more efficient object program will result from branching to one common RETURN statement.

12.6

OBJECTIVE: . . . write FUNCTION subprograms.

The general form of a FUNCTION subprogram is as follows:

GENERAL FORM

```
12345|6|789
          type FUNCTIØN name (a1,a2,...an)
          ...
          name = e
          RETURN
          END
```

COMPONENTS	
type	is an optional explicit type declaration
FUNCTIØN	is the keyword
name	is the name of the FUNCTION
$a_1 \ldots a_n$	are dummy arguments
e	is any valid expression
RETURN	is the statement that returns control to the calling program
END	is the end of the program unit

EXAMPLE

```
12345|6|789
      FUNCTIØN BIGGER(A,B)
C  THIS FUNCTIØN RETURNS THE LARGER ØF A ØR B
      BIGGER=A
      IF(A.LT.B)BIGGER=B
      RETURN
      END
```

A FUNCTION subprogram may contain any FORTRAN statement except the SUBROUTINE definition statement, another FUNCTION definition statement, and a BLOCK DATA statement (discussed in Chapter 14). The following application illustrates the form of FUNCTION subprogram.

DUMMY ARGUMENT

EXAMPLE 1

This example shows a FUNCTION subprogram, called RAD, which will compute the radius of a circle inscribed in a triangle of sides a, b, and c using the following formulas:

$$r = \sqrt{\frac{(s-a)(s-b)(s-c)}{s}} \qquad s = \frac{(a + b + c)}{2}$$

A main program, which reads in the values for a, b, and c and prints out the diameter using FUNCTION RAD to compute the radius, is given below the FUNCTION.

```
123456789..

C  EXAMPLE 1
C  FUNCTIØN RAD CØMPUTES THE RADIUS ØF A CIRCLE
      FUNCTIØN RAD(A,B,C)
      S=(A+B+C)/2.0
      RAD=SQRT((S-A)*(S-B)*(S-C)/S)
      RETURN
      END

C  THIS PRØGRAM CØMPUTES THE DIAMETER ØF A CIRCLE INSCRIBED
C     IN A TRIANGLE
C
    5 READ(1,10,END=90)S1,S2,S3
   10 FØRMAT(3F8.1)
   15 D=RAD(S1,S2,S3)*2.0
      WRITE(3,20)S1,S2,S3,D
   20 FØRMAT('bSIDESb=b',3F10.1,3X,'DIAMETER=',F10.1//)
      GØ TØ 5
   90 H=1.4*(S1+S2+S3)
      S=3.14*D*H
      ...
      END
```

Note the following:

1. The name of the FUNCTION appears on the left-hand side of "=" symbol.

2. The actual arguments, S1, S2, and S3 replace the dummy arguments A, B, and C in FUNCTION RAD. They agree in order, number, and type.

3. The variable name S used in the FUNCTION and in the main program have no relation to each other and present no conflict.

4. The result of the FUNCTION is returned through the name RAD and replaces the name and arguments in statement 15. This result is then multiplied by 2 and assigned to D. In evaluating expressions with FUNCTIONS and other operations, FUNCTIONS are evaluated first.

The following example shows the use of the type declaration on the FUNCTION statement to override the implicit REAL type which the FUNCTION name connotes.

EXAMPLE 2

The FUNCTION subprogram called TIME converts time from the civilian 12-hour basis to military time which is on a 24-hour basis. It uses INTEGER type declaration so TIME will return an integer value. FUNCTION will have three arguments as follows:

IH - hour on 12 hour basis

IM - minutes on 12 hour basis

ICODE - AM/PM code. 0=AM; 1=PM

The FUNCTION subprogram computes as follows:

9:15 AM - input would be 9,15,0 and TIME should return 0915. For 4:35 PM, TIME would return 1635, 12:00 Noon would be input as AM and equal 1200, and 12:00 Midnight would be input as PM and equal 2400. A portion of the main program is given below:

```
123456789...

C  EXAMPLE 2
C  MAIN PROGRAM
      INTEGER TIME
      READ(1,5)MHR,MIN,MAPM
    5 FØRMAT(3I2)
      ITIME=TIME(MHR,MIN,MAPM)
      WRITE(3,10)ITIME
   10 FØRMAT(T50,'TIME IS',I5)

C  FUNCTIØN TIME CØMPUTES 24 HØUR TIME
      INTEGER FUNCTION TIME(IH,IM,IAM)
      TIME=1200*IAM+100*IH+IM
      IF(IH.NE.12)GØ TO 4
      IF(IAM.EQ.0.AND.IM.NE.0)TIME=IM
      IF(IAM.EQ.1.AND.IM.NE.0)TIME=1200+IM
    4 RETURN
      END
```

It is necessary to use a type declaration in the main program for TIME since the value returned from INTEGER FUNCTION TIME will be an integer.

The following example has an array as one of the FUNCTION arguments. Note, it is necessary to dimension the array in the FUNCTION subprogram to show it is an array. However, memory is reserved for the DIMENSION statement in the main program only.

EXAMPLE 3

A FUNCTION subprogram called AVE computes the average of N real numbers in an array. A portion of the main program referencing AVE is given below.

```
123456789...

C  EXAMPLE 3
C  CØMPUTE THE AVERAGE PØWER CØNSUMPTIØN
      DIMENSIØN PC(100)
    5 READ(1,10)N,(PC(I),I=1,N)
   10 FØRMAT(I3/(10F6.1))
   15 S=AVE(N,PC)
      WRITE(3,20)S
   20 FØRMAT('bAVERAGE PØWER USED ISb',F8.2)
      ...

C  CØMPUTES THE AVERAGE OF N REAL NUMBERS
C
      FUNCTIØN AVE(N,ARY)
      DIMENSION ARY(100)
      S=0.
      DØ 10 I=1,N
          S=S+ARY(I)
   10 CØNTINUE
      XN=N
      AVE=S/XN
      RETURN
      END
```

Although the actual arguments in a subprogram may be constants, if constants are used as arguments, care must be taken so that the subprogram does not change the value of the dummy variable corresponding to the constant for this can change the value of the constant! This is shown in the example below. Note that although L is set to 2 and then printed, the value of L is 3.

```
123456789...

C  MAIN PRØGRAM

      IX=6
      K=5
      J=ITEST(IX,2,K)
      L=2
      WRITE(3.10)IX,K,J,L
   10 FØRMAT('bIX=',I3,'bK=',I3,'bJ=',I3,'bL=',I3)
      STØP
      END
C  THIS FUNCTION SHØWS WHAT HAPPENS IF CØNSTANT IS USED
C  AS AN ARGUMENT AND IS CHANGED IN THE FUNCTIØN SUBPRØGRAM
      FUNCTION ITEST(N,M,K)
      M=3
      ITEST=N+M+K
      RETURN
      END
```

RESULT

```
         1         2         3         4
1234567890123456789012345678901234567890
IX=   6 K=   5 J= 14 L=   3
```

Constants are also stored by the computer. The address of the constant is passed as the argument. In the example, when M is set to 3, the 3 is stored at the address of the actual argument, hence, the address of the constant, 2. For the remaining program, the constant 2 has a value of 3. A 'tricky' bug to find!

> PT*
>
> Do not use constants as actual arguments in subprograms.
>
> *Prevent Trouble

12.7

OBJECTIVE: . . . define and write statement FUNCTIONS.

A statement FUNCTION is a special type of FUNCTION subprogram. The statement FUNCTION is written as a part of the same program unit that uses it whereas other FUNCTION subprograms are not in the same program unit that references them. The general form for defining a statement FUNCTION is as follows:

GENERAL FORM

```
name(a1,a2,a3...an) = expression
```

COMPONENTS

name	is the statement FUNCTION name
$a_1, a_2, \ldots, a_n$	are the dummy arguments
expression	is any arithmetic or logical expression

EXAMPLES

DEFINITION	REFERENCE
`FUNC(A)=3.*A**2+A-7`	`Y=FUNC(X)`
`AVE6(A,B,C,D,E,F)=(A+`	`SA=AVE6(S1,S2,S3,S4,`
`*B+C+D+E+F)/6.` (continuation, column 6)	`*S5,S6)` (continuation, column 6)

Rules for statement FUNCTIONS are as follows:

1. The statement FUNCTION must be defined by a single statement, although it may be continued on several lines as any other statement may be.

2. The statement FUNCTION itself is a non-executable statement and it must appear before all executable statements.

3. There must be at least one argument.

4. The statement FUNCTION may include references to library FUNCTIONS, FUNCTION subprograms and previously-defined statement FUNCTIONS.

5. The name of a statement FUNCTION may be any valid FORTRAN variable name except array element names. The type of the name determines the type of statement FUNCTION and, hence, the type of result returned from it. The type may be overridden in an explicit type statement.

6. The arguments enclosed in parentheses following the FUNCTION names are dummy names for which the arguments given in the reference to the FUNCTION are substituted when the FUNCTION is used. These names may be used in more than one statement FUNCTION, and they may be used as variables in the program outside the statement FUNCTION definition. The actual argument in the reference to the statement FUNCTION must agree in type to the dummy argument.

7. The expression to the right of the '=' character defines the operations to be performed each time the statement FUNCTION is referenced.

8. A statement FUNCTION is used by writing its name followed by the actual arguments that are to replace the dummy arguments.

EXAMPLE 1

In a program the diagonals of various rectangular solids are computed. The diagonal is given by the formula $d=\sqrt{a^2 + b^2 + c^2}$. To avoid coding this formula each time, a statement FUNCTION is written for it. The statement is used to compute the diagonal of a solid whose sides are given by X1,X2,X3.

```
123456789...
C  EXAMPLE 1
      DIAG(A,B,C)=SQRT(A*A+B*B+C*C)
        .
        .
        .
    5 D1=DIAG(X1,X2,X3)
```

At the time statement 5 is executed, the actual arguments X1, X2, and X3 replace the dummy arguments A, B, C in the expression; and hence,

D1 = SQRT(X1*X1+X2*X2+X3*X3)

EXAMPLE 2

Assume that a FUNCTION subprogram named IFACT already was written which returns the factorial for n, the one argument of IFACT. A statement FUNCTION to compute the number of permutations is written, and it is used to compute the permutations of NMEN working JMEN at a time.

```
123456789···
C EXAMPLE 2
      INTEGER PERM(N,L)=IFACT(N)/IFACT(N-L)
        .
        .
        .
      NP=PERM(NMEN,JMEN)
```

NMEN replaces N and JMEN replaces L in statement FUNCTION PERM. PERM returns an integer value because of the explicit statement overriding the I-N rule for integers.

12.8

OBJECTIVE: . . . use execution-time dimensions.

When an array is passed as an argument to a FUNCTION subprogram, both the actual array in the main program and the dummy array in the FUNCTION subprogram must be dimensioned. In Example 3 of Section 12.6, the array PC is passed to FUNCTION AVE replacing the dummy array argument ARY. Both PC and ARY are dimensioned at 100; however, memory is reserved only once from the DIMENSION statement in the main program. The purpose of the DIMENSION statement in the subprogram is to show the compiler that ARY is a one-dimensional array but the size of the array is a 'dummy' in that it does not cause memory to be reserved. Therefore, it could be any arbitrary positive INTEGER constant and the number 1 is frequently used for this purpose. On most systems, the first two statements in FUNCTION AVE in Example 3 of Section 12.6 could be replaced with the following:

```
123456789···
      FUNCTIØN AVE(N,ARY)
      DIMENSIØN ARY(1)
```

When the FUNCTION is executed, the actual argument N determines how many elements of the array PC, which replaces ARY, will be used. In the main program, the array PC must be dimensioned for the maximum number of elements.

On some computers, checks are made to see if the dimensions of arrays are exceeded, and the DIMENSION statement information in a subprogram is used for this check of the arrays in the subprogram. Therefore, on such systems the dummy array argument could not be set to the arbitrary size 1 but must be set equal to the DIMENSION size of the actual argument in the main program, or it may be set as a variable as the following alternate method shows.

This alternate method allows for execution-time dimensioning of the arrays in a subprogram, and it is acceptable on all systems whether or not checks are performed to see if a dimension is exceeded.

This execution-time dimensioning uses a variable for the DIMENSION size of the dummy arrays in the subprogram. The actual DIMENSION size of the actual argument must still be set in the main program to the maximum positive INTEGER constant needed.

```
123456789...

C   THIS FUNCTIØN RETURNS THE LARGEST NUMBER IN A 2-D ARRAY
C
      REAL FUNCTIØN MAX(RAY,NR,NC)
      DIMENSIØN RAY(NR,NC)
      MAX=RAY(1,1)
      DØ 10 IR=1,NR
         DØ 20 IC=1,NC
            IF(RAY(IR,IC).GT.MAX)MAX=RAY(IR,IC)
   20    CØNTINUE
   10 CØNTINUE
      RETURN
      END

C   MAIN PRØGRAM
      DIMENSIØN HT(50,50)
      REAL MAX
      READ(1,90)M,N
      READ(1,92)((HT(I,J),I=1,M),J=1,N)
      BIG=MAX(HT,M,N)
      WRITE(3,94)BIG
      STØP
   90 FØRMAT(2I3)
   92 FØRMAT(10F8.1)
   94 FØRMAT('bBIGGEST=',F10.1)
      END
```

The DIMENSION statement in the REAL FUNCTION MAX shows that the dummy array RAY is two-dimensional, but the size of RAY is variable. At execution time, the actual array HT replaces RAY and M and N replace NR and NC, respectively; and they determine the size of the array used.

CHAPTER EXERCISES

Answer TRUE or FALSE for 1-8.

1. At least once before the END statement in a FUNCTION subprogram there must be a RETURN statement. ______

2. If arrays are used as arguments in a FUNCTION subprogram, they must be dimensioned in both the FUNCTION and the calling program. ______

3. The same statement numbers may not be used in subprograms and the main program. ______

4. A FUNCTION subprogram may not call itself. ______

5. A FUNCTION subprogram may perform a task without returning a value. ______

6. An actual argument in a FUNCTION reference may be a constant. ______

7. A value must be assigned to the FUNCTION name at least once within the FUNCTION. ______

8. A FUNCTION must have at least one argument. ______

Answer questions 9-13 using system-supplied FUNCTIONS.

9. Write a FORTRAN statement that stores the smallest value of A, B, C, D, E, F into SMALL.

____

10. Write a FORTRAN statement that stores the largest value of I, J, K, L, M, N into LARGE.

____

11. Write a FORTRAN statement for each of the following mathematical formulas.

a. $$Y=\sin\left(\frac{\tan^{-1}\sqrt{a^2 + b^2}}{|C|}\right)$$

____

b. $$Z=\sqrt{\frac{a_1-b_2}{\sin 2\pi L}}$$

____

12. What is the value of IY after the following statement is executed?

IY = MØD(75,7)   Answer ________

13. The following program prints out some sample values of X. Which values would be printed? How many would be printed out in all?

```
12345 6789...
      DEL = .01
      DØ 5 I = 1,300
        X=2.*SIN(DEL)
        IF (MØD(I,5) .EQ.0) WRITE (3,10) DEL, X
        DEL=DEL+.01
    5 CØNTINUE
   10 FØRMAT (F10.2,F10.4)
```

Values printed ________________________

Total number printed ______

14. Write a FUNCTION subprogram statement that defines a REAL FUNCTION named MATXS which has three arguments, A, B, and N.

```
12345 6789
```

15. Write a complete FUNCTION subprogram called STEP which will return a value of 0 if X < -1. or X > +1. and return a value of 1 if -1. ≤ X ≤ + 1. It should have one argument, X. The value returned is an integer code 0 or 1; and hence the FUNCTION must be INTEGER.

```
12345 6789...
```

16. Write a complete FUNCTION subprogram named SUM with arguments A, J and M. SUM computes the sum of M elements in the one-dimensional array A starting with the Jth element. A has a maximum dimension of 100.

```
12345 6789...
```

17. Write a complete FUNCTION called DØT which computes the dot product of 2 vectors in a 3-dimensional space. The dot product (·) for $A = (a_1, a_2, a_3)$ and $B = (b_1, b_2, b_3)$ is given by

$$A \cdot B = a_1 b_1 + a_2 b_2 + a_3 b_3$$

Write a main program which will read in values for A and B and use DØT to compute A · B. Print out A and B and A · B.

```
123456789...
```

18. Write a statement FUNCTION which computes the following mathematical formula

$$fn(a,b) = \sqrt{\sin(a) + \cos(b)}$$

```
123456789...
```

19. If the statement FUNCTION given below is referenced for G, H, T, and X, which have the values given, what will be the value of Z after statement 5 is executed?

```
123456789...
      FUNC(A,X,B,C) = A*X*X+B*X+C
      G = 3.0
      H = 1.5
      T = 2.0
      X = 1.0
    5 Z = FUNC(G,T,H,X)
```

ANSWER Z = ______

TOPIC APPLICATION

a) Write FUNCTION Subprograms
b) Call FUNCTION Subprograms

Problem 12.1

PROBLEM STATEMENT

Write a FORTRAN subprogram to calculate the factorial of N or N!. The meaning of N! is described by the expression:

$$N! = (N)(N-1)\ (N-2)\ldots(1) \qquad \text{where N is an integer}$$

for example

$$4! = (4)\ (3)\ (2)\ (1) = 24$$

An alternate way of writing this expression is:

$$N! = (1)\ (2)\ (3)\ldots(N)$$

Note: A subprogram is compiled separately from the main program. Additional control cards will be needed for the additional compilation. Set up your program deck in accordance with the requirements of your installation.

Your subprogram should be written to provide for the case when N=0. Note that 0!=1.

A main program has been written that utilizes such a subprogram to calculate a table of factorials from 0 to 50 as follows:

```
12345 6 789...
C   PR ØBLEM NØ. 12.1 MAIN LINE PRØGRAM
       WRITE(d0,5)
     5 FØRMAT ('1',T22,'N',T31,'N FACTØRIAL'//)
       DØ 20 I=1,51
         J=I-1
         X=FCTRL(J)
         WRITE(d0,30)J,X
    20 CØNTINUE
    30 FØRMAT ('b',T21,I2,T30,E13.6)
       STØP
       END
```

Note: Set d_0 to your output device number.

It will be necessary to label your subprogram FCTRL. An integer argument is used to transfer a value to the subprogram. Your program should return the value of n! as a real number.

No data cards are required for this program.

Check points:

0! = 0.100000E01
30! = 0.265252E33
50! = 0.304139E65

Note: 50! may exceed the capacity of some computers.

Problem 12.2

PROBLEM STATEMENT

A person has 2 parents, 4 grandparents, 8 great grandparents, and so on. The sequence of numbers representing the number of ancestors a person has with each new generation is a geometric progression with a ratio of 2. The total number of ancestors a person has after n generations can be found by using the formula for the sum of the terms of a geometric progression, which is as follows:

$$s = \frac{a - ar^n}{1-r}$$

where
n = number of generations
s = sum of n generations
a = first term = 2
r = common ratio = 2

EXERCISE

Write a FUNCTION subprogram, SUMGEO, that computes the sum of the terms of a geometric series. It should have arguments of a, r(both real numbers) and n (integer) Write a main program that computes the number of ancestors a person has each generation for 10 generations calling SUMGEO with 10 different values of n. Set up a DO loop to generate the 10 values of n and write out the sum for each of the 10 generations as follows:

```
         1         2         3         4
1234567890123456789012345678901234567890123456789 . . .
  GENERATIØN        TØTAL NØ. ANCESTØRS
                         TØ DATE

       1                   2
       2                   6
       3                  14
      ...                 ...
      10                2046
```

Problem 12.3

PROBLEM STATEMENT

The reciprocal of a number, X, is 1/X

EXERCISE

Write a FUNCTION subprogram called RECP that calculates the reciprocal of a variable passed as the argument. Before calculation of the reciprocal, test to be sure it is not zero. If it is zero, set RECP to the maximum number of your computer.

Write a main program that reads in a number, calls RECP to compute the reciprocal, and prints out the number and reciprocal (use E-format code to print out both) for any number of data values supplied. Provide for termination at the end-of-data. Test your program with the following values:

Input Data

```
10.0
 0.0
 1.E25
```

Problem 12.4

PROBLEM STATEMENT

The harmonic mean, H is defined as follows:

$$H = \frac{n}{\Sigma \frac{1}{X}} \quad \text{where} \quad \Sigma \frac{1}{X} = \frac{1}{X_1} + \frac{1}{X_2} + \ldots + \frac{1}{X_n}$$

EXERCISE

Write a main program that will read and write a sequence of numbers and compute the harmonic mean, H. Call RECP (Problem 12.3) to compute the reciprocals and print out the result from MAIN. Recycle so any number of sets of data could be read in.

Test your program with the following numbers:

Input Data

Case 1	1.,	5.,	9.,	20.,	32.
Case 2	2.,	5.5,	11.,	17.5,	24.

Problem 12.5

PROBLEM STATEMENT

Stirling's approximation for N! is given by $N! \sim \sqrt{2\Pi n}\,\left(n^n e^{-n}\right)$

EXERCISE

Write a FUNCTION subprogram, called SFACT, to compute a factorial using the Stirling approximation.

Compute N! as a real number since the magnitude of N! increases rapidly and exceeds the maximum magnitude of an integer on most computers.

Modify the main program given in Problem 12.1 to compute the factorial using FCTRL and using SFACT and print out the differences for factorials starting at 5! and going to 45! in increments of 5.

There is no input data

Note: 40! = 0.814 E 48

45! = 0.119 E 57

Check to see that 45! does not exceed the capacity of your computer. Actually, 45^{45} must be computed and may exceed the maximum value of a real. If so, compute to a factorial that your computer can handle.

FORTRAN 13

13.1 . . . define SUBROUTINE subprograms by means of the SUBROUTINE statement.

13.2 . . . use the CALL statement to reference the SUBROUTINE subprogram.

13.3 . . . apply the rules for SUBROUTINE subprograms in writing SUBROUTINES.

13.4 . . . state the criteria involved in determining the type of sort to use . . . and apply basic sorting techniques to writing a sorting routine.

13.1

OBJECTIVE: . . . define **SUBROUTINE** subprograms by means of the **SUBROUTINE** statement.

The general form of the **SUBROUTINE** defining statement is:

GENERAL FORM

```
12345 6 789...

        SUBRØUTINE name
            or
        SUBRØUTINE name (a1,a2,...an)
```

COMPONENTS

SUBRØUTINE	is the keyword
name	is the name of the SUBROUTINE subprogram
$a_1, a_2, \ldots a_n$	are the dummy arguments

EXAMPLES

```
12345 6 789...

        SUBRØUTINE PAGE
        SUBRØUTINE SØRT(X,N)
```

The **SUBROUTINE** definition statement must be the first statement in the subprogram. The name of the subprogram must be one to six alphabetic and numeric characters with the first character alphabetic. Special characters are not allowed in the name. Unlike the **FUNCTION** subprogram, no value is returned through the name. Therefore, the type of the name has no significance and either a real or integer name may be used. The subprogram name may not be used as the name of a variable.

The argument list is optional. A **SUBROUTINE** may perform a task, such as providing heading information on each output page. In such cases, there would be no arguments. A **SUBROUTINE** may use one or more of its arguments to return values to the calling program. These arguments are considered dummy arguments in the subprogram as they are replaced at execution time by the actual arguments supplied in the calling statement.

A dummy argument may be a non-subscripted variable, an array name, or a dummy name of a subprogram. Any dummy array name must be dimensioned in the subprogram.

13.2

OBJECTIVE: . . . use the CALL statement to reference the SUBROUTINE subprogram.

One difference between the two types of subprograms is the manner in which they are referenced. The SUBROUTINE subprogram is referenced through the CALL statement.

GENERAL FORM

```
12345|6|789...

nnnnn| |CALL name
     | |     or
     | |CALL name (a1,a2,...an)
```

COMPONENTS

nnnnn	is an optional statement number
CALL	is a keyword
name	is the name of the SUBROUTINE subprogram
$a_1,a_2,\ldots a_n$	are the actual arguments

EXAMPLES

```
12345|6|789...

     | |CALL PAGE
     | |CALL MTXA(X,Y,100)
     | |CALL SØRT(A,N)
```

The CALL statement transfers control to the SUBROUTINE subprogram. The values of the actual arguments in the CALL statement replace the values of the dummy arguments in the subprogram. Each actual argument must agree in type, length and order to the corresponding dummy argument. Different variable names may be used for the corresponding arguments in the subprogram and in the calling program.

13.3

OBJECTIVE: . . . apply the rules for SUBROUTINE subprograms in writing SUBROUTINES.

The general form of the SUBROUTINE subprogram is as follows:

GENERAL FORM

```
123456789...

      SUBRØUTINE name(a1,...an)
      . . .
      RETURN
      END
```

COMPONENTS

SUBROUTINE	is a keyword defining a SUBROUTINE
name	is the name of the SUBROUTINE
$a_1,\ldots,a_n$	are dummy arguments(optional)
RETURN	is a statement to return control to calling program
END	is a statement to terminate the program unit

EXAMPLE

```
123456789...

      SUBRØUTINE HEAD
      WRITE(3,8)
    8 FØRMAT('1',T40,'CØMPATIBILITY ANALYSIS')
      RETURN
      END
```

The first statement must be the SUBROUTINE statement which gives the name of the subprogram and which lists the dummy arguments, if any. The arguments, if present, represent the actual arguments given in the CALL statement of the calling program. The arguments are used to transfer values between the subprogram and the calling program. The values may be set in either the subprogram or in the calling program or both.

The remaining statements may be any FORTRAN statements except a FUNCTION statement, another SUBROUTINE statement or a BLOCK DATA statement. BLOCK DATA is discussed in Chapter 14.

Unlike the FUNCTION subprogram which must have its name set to a value within the subprogram, the SUBROUTINE name may not appear in any statement in the subprogram except the SUBROUTINE statement.

The statement numbers and variable and array names other than the arguments that are used in the subprogram may be the same as those in the calling program or in other subprograms without conflict.

Control is returned from the SUBROUTINE to the calling program by means of the RETURN statement described in Section 12.5. Figure 13.3-1 shows the transfer of control between a calling program and the SUBROUTINE subprogram.

```
123456789...
C MAIN PROGRAM
      ...
      X=...
      DEL=...
      CALL SCAMLT(X,DEL,N)
   17 Z=.5*QRS/FLØAT(N)
      ...
```

```
123456789...
      SUBROUTINE SCAMLT(A,EPSI,K)
        .
        .
        .
      K= ...
      RETURN
      END
```

Figure 13.3-1. Transfer of Control Using SUBROUTINE Subprograms.

EXAMPLE

The following example computes the average of N real numbers in an array.

```
123456789...
C  THIS RØUTINE CØMPUTES THE AVERAGE ØF N NØS.
      SUBRØUTINE AVER(N,ARY,AVE)
      DIMENSION ARY(100)
      S=0.
      DØ 10 I=1,N
         S=S + ARY(I)
   10 CØNTINUE
      XN=N
      AVE=S/XN
      RETURN
      END
```

This example was written as a FUNCTION in Section 12.6. In making it a SUBROUTINE, the result AVE is made an argument since the name does not return a value in a SUBROUTINE.

The calling program is identical to that given for the FUNCTION in Example 3 of Section 12.6, except for the reference, statement 15. To use the above SUBROUTINE, the following statements would be used in place of statement 15.

```
123456789...
   15 CALL AVER(N,PC,AVE)
      S=AVE
```

The discussion of execution-time dimensions for FUNCTION subprogram in Section 12.8 also applies when using SUBROUTINE subprograms. Therefore, the first two lines of the above example could be either of the following:

Using the arbitrary dimension 1

```
123456789...
      SUBRØUTINE AVER(N,ARY,AVE)
      DIMENSIØN ARY(1)
```

Using a variable dimension

```
123456789...
      SUBRØUTINE AVER(N,ARY,AVE)
      DIMENSIØN ARY(N)
```

In some cases, as was shown above by computing an average in both a FUNCTION and a SUBROUTINE subprogram, either a FUNCTION or a SUBROUTINE may be used. However, in cases where there are no arguments or when an entire array is to be computed in the subprogram, a SUBROUTINE subprogram is used. The next two examples illustrate each of these cases.

EXAMPLE 1

Write a SUBROUTINE subprogram that will cause the printer to advance to a new page and print a heading when it is called by the following statement:

```
123456789...
C  MAIN PRØGRAM
      CALL HEAD
      ...

C  THIS SUBRØUTINE WRITES A HEADING ON A NEW PAGE
      SUBRØUTINE HEAD
      WRITE(3,10)
   10 FØRMAT('1',T40,'REGRESSIØN ANALYSIS'//)
      RETURN
      END
```

EXAMPLE 2

Write a SUBROUTINE subprogram called CMPRES which will test array, ARY, for positive values. ARY contains NE elements. Each positive value is transferred to the compressed array, CRAY. The number of positive values in CRAY is returned in NC. This subprogram would be used in statistical applications where missing or zero data values occur in collecting data from a number of observations, and they should not be included in the analysis.

A portion of the main program which calls CMPRES is given first.

```
123456789...

      DIMENSIØN DATA(100),GDATA(100)
      READ(1,5)NØ,(DATA(I),I=1,NØ)
    5 FØRMAT(I4/(10F6.1))
      CALL CMPRES(DATA,GDATA,NØ,NG)
      WRITE(3,8)(GDATA(I),I=1,NG)
    8 FØRMAT(1X,10F8.1)

      ...
```

```
C  THIS SUBRØUTINE CØPIES PØSITIVE ARRAY ELEMENTS
      SUBRØUTINE CMPRES(ARY,CRAY,NE,NC)
      DIMENSIØN ARY(100),CRAY(100)
      NC=0
      DØ 20 J=1,NE
          IF(ARY(J))20,20,10
   10     NC=NC+1
          CRAY(NC)=ARY(J)
   20 CØNTINUE
      RETURN
      END
```

EXAMPLE 3

The following complete program for computing bionomial coefficients uses a SUBROUTINE subprogram referencing a FUNCTION subprogram. A subprogram may reference any subprogram except itself. The subprogram referenced must, of course, be a part of the complete program deck submitted or stored on a program library accessible to your program.

The Binomial Theorem permits one to quickly expand the powers of a binomial. In the expansion of $(a+b)^n$, the coefficients of $a^{n-r}b^r$ are given by

$$\frac{n!}{(n-r)!r!}$$

where n and $r \geq 0$ and $n \geq r$, and $n! = 1 \cdot 2 \cdot 3 \cdots n$

```
123456789...

C
C   PROGRAM TØ CØMPUTE BINØMIAL  CØEFFICIENTS
C
      DIMENSIØN CØEF(25)
      WRITE(3,90)
      DØ 5 N=1,10
        CALL BIØCØE(N,CØEF)
        K=N+1
        WRITE(3,94)N,(CØEF(I),I=1,K)
    5 CØNTINUE
   99 CALL EXIT
   90 FØRMAT('1BINØMIAL  CØEFFICIENTS FØR PØLYNØMIAL ØF DEGREE N'/)
   92 FØRMAT(I2)
   94 FØRMAT('0',I2,2X,11F10.2)
      END

      SUBRØUTINE BIØCØE(N,CØEF)
C   THIS RØUTINE CØMPUTES BINØMIAL  CØEFFICIENTS FØR A PØLY. ØF
C        DEGREE N
      DIMENSIØN CØEF(25)
      K=N+1
      FN=FACT(N)
      DØ 5 I=1,K
        J=I-1
        M=N-J
        CØEF(I)=FN/(FACT(J)*FACT(M))
    5 CØNTINUE
      RETURN
      END


      FUNCTIØN FACT(N)
C   THIS RØUTINE COMPUTES FACTØRIAL N
C
      FACT=1
      DØ 5 I=1,N
        XI=I
        FACT=FACT*XI
    5 CØNTINUE
      RETURN
      END
```

13.4

OBJECTIVE: . . . state the criteria involved in determining the type of sort to use . . . and apply basic sorting techniques to writing a sorting routine.

One problem which is encountered in all types of applications in business and scientific work is that of constructing a list of sorted data items from a group of unsorted items. Frequently, this sorting process is written as a SUBROUTINE subprogram.

As sorting is a frequent process in many business applications, many installations have sort routines as a part of their library of subprograms available to the user. There are many sorting techniques which vary in speed and complexity and which vary depending on the volume of data involved in the sort and the devices and core available for use.

The FORTRAN programmer should be familiar with the basic methods involved so as to be able to choose, adapt, or write a sort suited to his problem. Appendix D contains information on basic sorting techniques. Study this before attempting to do Programming Problem 13.1.

CHAPTER EXERCISES

1. Write F for FUNCTION subprogram; S for SUBROUTINE subprogram; or B for both depending upon which the following description fits:

   a) Always returns a value ________

   b) The name implies the type of result unless explicitly declared otherwise ________

   c) May perform a task without returning any values ________

   d) Must have a RETURN statement ________

   e) Is compiled separately from the main program ________

2. Write a SUBROUTINE subprogram which causes the printer to skip to the top of a new page every time the statement CALL SKIP occurs in the main program.

1 2 3 4 5	6	7 8 9 . . .

3. Write a complete **SUBROUTINE** subprogram that will reverse the order of the elements in a one-dimensional array called AR1 which contains N1 values. Preserve the original values in AR1 and put the reversed order elements in an array called AR2. Hence, if AR1 elements are arranged low to high, the elements of AR2 would be from high to low. Although N1 may be less than the maximum dimension of 50, the values of the reversed array should be in elements AR2(1) through AR2(N1).

```
12345|6|789...
     | |
     | |
     | |
     | |
     | |
     | |
     | |
```

CHAPTER PROGRAMMING PROBLEMS

TOPIC APPLICATION

a) SUBROUTINE subprogram
b) DO and IF statements
c) Sorting Method

Problem 13.1

PROBLEM STATEMENT

Write a **SUBROUTINE** subprogram to sort a list of real numbers into ascending order. Use the following main program to call the **SUBROUTINE** defining the input and output devices of your installation in a **DATA** statement.

```
12345 6 789
        REAL LIST(100)
        READ(di,5,END=99)M,(LIST(K),K=1,M)
    5   FØRMAT(I3/(10F5.1))
        WRITE(do,50)(LIST(K),K=1,M)
        CALL SØRT(LIST,M)
        WRITE(do,50)(LIST(K),K=1,M)
   50   FØRMAT(//10(5X,F6.1))
   99   STØP
        END
```

Note: d_i = your input device number
d_o = your output device number

INPUT

Make up a set of M random positive real numbers (at least 25 and not more than 100) having values between zero and 999.9. Make up data cards as follows:
First card

Columns 1 to 3 contain the number of values (M) in I3 format.

Remaining cards

Divided into ten fields of five columns using the form nnn.n with values keypunched in the random order selected.

OUTPUT

The output will be a list of the given numbers followed by a list of these numbers listed in ascending order.

NOTE: Be sure to flow diagram your program prior to writing the necessary FORTRAN statements.

CONTROL CARDS:

Use control cards for the SUBROUTINE subprogram in the same sequence used for program number 12.1.

Problem 13.2

PROBLEM STATEMENT

The formulas for computing the mean, standard deviation and variance of a set of numbers was given in Problem 11.2.

EXERCISE

In Problem 11.2, the mean, standard deviation and variance were computed in one program. Re-write this problem making one subprogram, called STIX, which will compute the mean, standard deviation or variance depending on which is desired. One of the arguments to STIX is ICODE, defined as follows:

ICODE = 1 compute mean only
ICODE = 2 compute mean and standard deviation
ICODE = 3 compute all three

Test your program with the same data used for Problem 11.2. The main program should also read in ICODE.

Problem 13.3

PROBLEM STATEMENT

Matrix manipulations play an important role in the solution of many mathematical problems.

EXERCISE

Write a main program to read in a 2-dimensional array, ARY, whose dimensions M and N are read in on the first card. Maximum dimensions should be 25 x 25.

a) Write SUBROUTINE COPYR that will copy the row, NR, of a 2-dimensional array into a single dimensional array, VCTR.

   Call COPYR from your main program and write out VCTR from the main program. Arguments include the dimensions of the two-dimensional array, the array, and NR, which are all read in MAIN. Re-cycle so as to read in several NR values, and provide for termination at the end-of-data.

b) Write a SUBROUTINE, COPYC that will copy column, NC, of a 2-dimensional array into a single dimensional array, VCTC.

   Call COPYC from your main program and write VCTC from your main program. Main also reads in NC. Re-cycle so any number of NC values could be read in.

c) Write a SUBROUTINE, COPYD that will copy the diagonal of a two-dimensional array into a single-dimensional array.

   Call COPYD from your main program and write the diagonal from main.

Test Data for Problem:

$$ARY = \begin{vmatrix} 11.4 & 2.3 & 6.7 & 5.4 \\ 1.2 & 3.7 & 24.1 & 0.0 \\ 2.2 & -4.1 & 8.0 & 9.7 \end{vmatrix}$$

a) NR = 2
   NR = 3

b) NC = 1
   NC = 3

Problem 13.4

EXERCISE

Write a SUBROUTINE program called COPY that copies the non-zero elements of an array A into array B. The arguments of COPY are as follows:

A input array (maximum of 50), one-dimensional
B output array (maximum of 50), one-dimensional
NA number of elements in A
NB number of non-zero elements in B after copy

Write a main program which reads in NA and array A and calls COPY to generate B. Main should also print B and the number of non-zero elements in B.

Test your program by reading in 25 elements of which at least 5 are 0.

Problem 13.5

EXERCISE

Write a main program that will read in and write two matrices, A and B, whose maximum dimensions are 25 x 25. Read in M and N, the size of both A and B, on the first data card.

a) Write SUBROUTINE ADD that adds like elements of A and B and returns the sum in the 2-dimensional array, C.

b) Write SUBROUTINE SUBT that subtracts like elements of A and B and returns the difference in the 2-dimensional array, C.

c) Modify the main program to read in a code and test it to see if the sum or difference of the matrices A and B is desired and call ADD or SUBT depending upon the code.

Test your program with the 3 x 4 array given for Problem 13.3 and any other 3 x 4 array.

Problem 13.6

PROBLEM STATEMENT

A linear relationship exists between two variables if each separate relationship can be expressed by a linear equation and if there is an assumed relationship between the two. If a linear relationship between two variables is assumed, then the coefficient of correlation between the two variables can be determined by

$$r = \frac{N\Sigma(XY) - (\Sigma X)(\Sigma Y)}{\sqrt{(N\Sigma X^2 - (\Sigma X)^2)\,(N\Sigma Y^2 - (\Sigma Y)^2)}}$$

This coefficient is a ratio which varies between -1 and +1 where the larger positive coefficient means there is a strong relationship and a coefficient close to -1 means there is a negative relationship.

EXERCISE

Using the following data which you input on cards, write a SUBROUTINE subprogram, CCOR, to compute the coefficient of correlation between the heights of 12 fathers and the heights of their oldest sons. Write a main program to read and print the input data and call CCOR to compute the coefficient of correlation.

The main program should also print out this result.

INPUT DATA

Heights in Inches

Father	65	63	67	64	68	62	70	66	68	67	69	71
Son	68	66	68	65	69	66	68	65	71	67	68	70

FORTRAN 14

14.1 . . . state the purpose of specification statements . . . and identify the purpose of each different specification statement.

14.2 . . . state the purpose of the EXTERNAL statement and . . . use the external statement in a program.

14.3 . . . transfer arguments between program units by means of the COMMON statement.

14.4 . . . use labeled COMMON blocks.

14.5 . . . state the purpose of the EQUIVALENCE statement and . . . use the EQUIVALENCE statement in a program.

14.6 . . . write a BLOCK DATA subprogram to initialize variables in labeled COMMON.

14.1

OBJECTIVE: . . . state the purpose of specification statements and . . . identify the seven types of specification statements.

A specification statement is a statement that provides the compiler with information about the nature of the variables used in the source program. A specification statement is a non-executable statement and must precede all executable statements and statement functions. A list of the specification statements is given below. The first seven have been discussed. The remaining four are discussed in this chapter.

```
123456789...
      CHARACTER
      DIMENSION
      DOUBLE PRECISION
      IMPLICIT
      INTEGER
      LOGICAL
      REAL
      COMMON
      EQUIVALENCE
      EXTERNAL
      INTRINSIC
```

Five of the specification statements are explicit type specification statements. The INTEGER and REAL statements were discussed in Section 3.7. The DOUBLE PRECISION statement is used in a similar manner to specify that a real variable is to be a double precision real variable. That is, the value of the variable is assigned to two locations of memory for double precision constants.

The DIMENSION statement was discussed in Chapter 8. The last four specification statements are discussed in this chapter.

14.2

OBJECTIVE: . . . state the purpose of the EXTERNAL statement and . . . use the EXTERNAL statement in a program.

If the name of any subprogram is passed as an argument to another subprogram, the compiler must be told that it is a subprogram name instead of a variable name or array name. In general, this is done by means of an **EXTERNAL** statement regardless of the type of subprogram. However, **FORTRAN '77** specifies that a different statement, the **INTRINSIC** statement, is to be used for those subprograms that are system-supplied **FUNCTION** subprograms. Both statements are presented here, and you will have to determine which statement your system uses for system-supplied subprograms.

GENERAL FORM

```
123456789...

      EXTERNAL name_i...name_n
```

COMPONENTS

```
EXTERNAL           is a keyword

name_i,...name_n   are subprogram names that are passed as
                       arguments to another subprogram.
```

EXAMPLE

```
123456789...

      EXTERNAL SIN,CØS
```

The **EXTERNAL** statement is a specification statement and must appear before statement functions and all executable statements.

EXAMPLE

A subprogram is needed to print out the common logarithms or the natural logarithms of the numbers from **IS** to **IN** depending on the value of an input code, **ICODE**. A portion of the main program, which calls the subprogram, and the **SUBROUTINE** are as follows:

```
123456789...

C MAIN PRØGRAM
      DIMENSIØN RES(100)
      EXTERNAL ALØG10,ALØG
      READ(1,5)IS,IN,ICØDE
    5 FØRMAT(3I2)
      IF (ICØDE) 10,10,15
C CØMPUTE CØMMØN LØGS
   10 CALL SLØG (ALØG10,IS,IN,RES,J)
      GØ TØ 25
C CØMPUTE NATURAL LØGS
   15 CALL SLØG(ALØG,IS,IN,RES,J)
   25 WRITE(3,30) (RES(I), I=1,J)
      ...
      END
```

```
      SUBRØUTINE SLØG(FLØG,IS,IN,R,J)
      DIMENSIØN R(100)
      J=0
      DØ 5 I=IS,IN
        XI=I
        J=J+1
        R(J)=FLØG(XI)
    5 CØNTINUE
      RETURN
      END
```

Complete the following:

> My computer uses the [EXTERNAL / INTRINSIC] statement for system-supplied FUNCTION subprograms.

The general form of the **INTRINSIC** statement is as follows:

GENERAL FORM

```
123456789···
      INTRINSIC name_i,...name_n
```

COMPONENTS

INTRINSIC	is	a keyword
$name_i,...name_n$	are	system-supplied FUNCTION names that are passed as arguments to another subprogram

EXAMPLE

```
123456789···
      INTRINSIC SIN,CØS
```

In the example given above, the **INTRINSIC** statement below would replace the **EXTERNAL** statement.

```
123456789···
      INTRINSIC ALØG10,ALØG
```

14.3

OBJECTIVE: . . . transfer arguments between program units by means of the COMMON statement.

In the examples using subprograms given in Chapters 12 and 13, the values were passed between the subprogram and the calling program by means of arguments. A second means of communication between program units is the use of a common storage area. This special storage block in memory is called COMMON and the variables assigned to COMMON are accessible to all program units containing the COMMON statement, thereby eliminating long argument lists. The general form of this statement is as follows:

GENERAL FORM

```
123456789...
      CØMMØN a1(k1),a2(k2),...an(kn)
```

COMPONENTS

CØMMØN	is	the keyword
$a_1(k_1)$ ... $a_n(k_n)$	are	variable names or array names. Each (k) is optional. If present, it gives the dimensions of the array.

EXAMPLE

```
123456789...
      CØMMØN A,B,D(30),IM(3,4),NX
```

COMMON is a specification statement and must precede all executable statements and statement functions.

> **PT***
>
> For large programs that are maintained and revised for years, the use of arguments instead of COMMON has a decided advantage in that it is clearer which variables a subprogram effects. A hastily made change to a single COMMON variable may send repercussions through many subprograms that contain the COMMON statement, and it is less clear which variables are used by which subprograms.
>
> *Precipitous Tamperings

COMMON is the more efficient means of communication between program units both in time and space, and when these are a main concern, COMMON should be used for all the variables in the argument list that always correspond to the same variable in the calling program at every call of the subprogram. When a variable in the subprogram corresponds to a different variable in the calling program at different calls to the subprogram, it must be an argument. COMMON can be used for all variables in the first category and arguments for the second. Arguments passed in a COMMON block must agree in order, type and length in all program units that use them. The names of the members in COMMON in different program units need not be the same because the order listed on the COMMON statement determines which variables are the same.

The following COMMON statement creates a COMMON storage area containing 10 memory locations.

```
123456789...
      CØMMØN A,J,ALP,DELTA,XQ,N,M,CØDE,IZ,IX
```

The COMMON storage area may contain arrays. The arrays may be dimensioned in the COMMON statement. The following example creates a COMMON area containing 32 memory locations.

```
123456789...
      DIMENSIØN MAT(3,4),X(10),Y(10)
      CØMMØN MAT,X,Y
```

An equivalent form is as follows:

```
123456789...
      COMMON MAT(3,4),X(10),Y(10)
```

More than one COMMON statement may appear in which case all entries are strung together in the order of their appearance. The following two COMMON statements create a COMMON area exactly the same as the one COMMON statement above.

```
12345|6|789...
       COMMON MAT(3,4)
       COMMON X(10),Y(10)
```

EXAMPLE

The statements necessary to transfer all arguments between the main program and the subprogram via COMMON instead of by an argument list is shown in the following two program portions.

PT*

To avoid errors in COMMON definitions and save keypunching, keypunch one set of COMMON statements and duplicate the set for each routine using COMMON.

***Punching Time-saver**

Using Arguments

```
12345|6|789...
C     MAIN PROGRAM
      DIMENSION X(100)
      ...
      CALL STD (X,N)
      ...
      END
```

```
C     SUBROUTINE
      SUBROUTINE STD(A,N)
      DIMENSION A(100)
      ...
      RETURN
      END
```

Using Common

```
12345|6|789...
C   MAIN PROGRAM
      COMMON X(100),N
      ...
      CALL STD
      ...
      END
```

```
123456789...
      SUBRØUTINE STD
      CØMMØN A(100),N
      ...
      RETURN
      END
```

Note that the dimension information is supplied in the COMMON statement instead of in a DIMENSION statement.

EXAMPLE

A subprogram to add two matrices X and Y and assign the sum to S is given below. The variables NR and NC represent the number of rows and columns in X and Y. The maximum size matrices to be added is 10 by 10. A main program to read in NR, NC, and two arrays and print the sum of the two matrices as computed by the subprograms is given first. COMMON is used to pass the information from the main program to the subprogram.

```
123456789...
C   MAIN PRØGRAM
      CØMMØN A(10,10), B(10,10), SUM(10,10), NR, NC
      READ(1,5) NR, NC
      READ(1,8) ((A(I,J),I=1,NR),J=1,NC)
      READ(1,8) ((B(I,J),I=1,NR),J=1,NC)
    5 FØRMAT(2I3)
    8 FØRMAT(10F8.1)
      CALL MTXADD
      DØ  15 I=1,NR
        WRITE(3,10) (SUM(I,J),J=1,NC)
   10   FØRMAT(10F10.1)
   15 CØNTINUE
      ...
```

```
123456789...
      SUBRØUTINE MTXADD
      CØMMØN X(10,10), Y(10,10), S(10,10), NR, NC
      DØ 10 I = 1,NR
      DØ 10 J = 1,NC
        S(I,J)=X(I,J)+Y(I,J)
   10 CØNTINUE
      RETURN
      END
```

The actual arguments A and B are read in the main program and are passed through COMMON to MTXADD. A and B correspond to X and Y in COMMON; and hence, they replace X and Y in the above subprogram. Similarly, SUM replaces S. The values of NR and NC that are read in main are also transmitted to MTXADD through COMMON.

14.4

OBJECTIVE: . . . use labeled COMMON blocks.

The common memory area discussed in the preceding section is called blank COMMON as there is no special name assigned to it. The variables that appeared in the COMMON statements were assigned locations starting at the beginning of the common memory area in the order of their appearance in the COMMON statements. In a program which has several subprograms and uses many variables in COMMON, it may be desirable to use separate COMMON blocks so that only those variables used in a subprogram appear in the COMMON statement in that subprogram. To do this, several areas or blocks of common memory are given a name and those blocks with the same name occupy the same memory area. The name consists of one to six alphanumeric characters, the first of which is alphabetic. These separate blocks of common memory are called labeled COMMON blocks. A calling program may share one labeled COMMON block with one subprogram and another with another subprogram. As only the variables that are used by the subprogram appear in it, it facilitates debugging and documentation. (When programs are written for others to use, the program and a description of it called the documentation are frequently put in a library for others to use.)

GENERAL FORM

```
123456789...
      CØMMØN / name / a1(k1), . . . an(kn)
```

COMPONENTS

CØMMØN	is	the keyword
/ name /	is	the name of this labeled CØMMØN block
$a_1(k_1)\ldots a_n(k_n)$	are	variables assigned to this labeled CØMMØN block. The (k_i) is optional dimension information

EXAMPLES

```
123456789...
      CØMMØN / CØNV / A(100), X(100), M, N, SR, TQ
      CØMMØN / ØUT / Y(100), RVT, IJ, KPQ
```

The differences between blank and labeled COMMON are:

1. There may be only one blank COMMON area in a program and it has no programmer-assigned name. There may be many labeled COMMON areas, each with a name assigned by the programmer.

2. Variables and array elements in blank COMMON cannot be assigned initial values. Variables and array elements in labeled COMMON may be assigned initial values if a BLOCK DATA subprogram (Section 14.6) is used.

The order in which the variables are listed in the labeled COMMON statement determines the order in which the memory locations are assigned. Different names may be used in different program units as the association is by order not by name.

Labeled COMMON statements must precede any executable statement, DATA statement, or statement function.

An example using labeled COMMON blanks is given in the program segment below.

```
123456789...
C  MAIN PROGRAM
      CØMMØN /IP/X(100), Y(100), NI
      CØMMØN /ØP/Z(100), NØ
      ...
      SUBRØUTINE IN
      CØMMØN /IP/ A(100), B(100), IN
      ...
      SUBRØUTINE ØUT
      CØMMØN /ØP/ C(100), NØ
```

Figure 14.4-1 illustrates the association of variables in the program units.

MAIN	COMMON	SUBROUTINE IN	SUBROUTINE OUT
X(1)	IP	A(1)	
.		.	
.		.	
.		.	
X(100)		A(100)	
Y(1)		B(1)	
.		.	
.		.	
.		.	
Y(100)		B(100)	
NI		IN	
Z(1)	ØP		C(1)
.			.
.			.
.			.
Z(100)			C(100)
NØ			NØ

Labeled and blank COMMON blocks may be declared in the same statement. The blank COMMON is written first without slashes. If blank COMMON follows a labeled COMMON, it is written with two consecutive slashes but without a name.

For example, the following statement

```
12345|6|789...
     | |CØMMØN A,B,NAB/BLK1/R,S/BLK2/X(100),
     |+|Y(100)//K,ZRQ
```

is equivalent to the following three statements:

```
12345|6|789...
     | |CØMMØN A,B,NAB,K,ZRQ
     | |CØMMØN /BLK1/R,S
     | |CØMMØN /BLK2/X(100),Y(100)
```

The two consecutive slashes // indicate blank COMMON and the variables K and ZRQ are strung together with any prior entries in blank COMMON.

14.5

OBJECTIVE: . . . state the purpose of the EQUIVALENCE statement and . . . use the EQUIVALENCE statement in a program.

The EQUIVALENCE statement is a specification statement which permits two or more variables in the same program unit to share the same memory location. The form of this statement is as follows:

GENERAL FORM
1 2 3 4 5 6 7 8 9 · · ·
EQUIVALENCE $(a_1,a_2 \ldots a_n),(b_1,b_2,\ldots b_n),\ldots$

COMPONENTS		
EQUIVALENCE	is	the keyword
$(a_1,a_2,\ldots a_n)$, $(b_1,\ldots b_n)$	are	lists of variables names and/or array elements

EXAMPLE
1 2 3 4 5 6 7 8 9 · · ·
EQUIVALENCE (A,B),(A(1),ATS),(A(2),ALT)

Each list of variable names and/or array elements enclosed in parentheses share the same memory location. In the above example, A and B refer to the same location; A(1) and ATS refer to the same location; and A(2) and ALT refer to the same location.

The EQUIVALENCE statement provides a means of allocating the same memory locations to different variables. This means that the total of memory locations required by a program can be reduced by having two or more variables share the same location. Of course, the values of these shared variables must not be needed by the program at the same time. The reduction of the amount of total storage required for a program by using the EQUIVALENCE statement is particularly desirable when several large arrays are used in a program, but the values of one array are no longer needed when the values of the equivalenced array are assigned.

A second use of the EQUIVALENCE statement is to save the task of changing a variable name that inadvertently was changed within a program. Similarly, if two programmers supply coding for the same program unit but use different variable names for the same quantities, an EQUIVALENCE statement can equate the similar variable names.

PT*

It should be noted that the use of the EQUIVALENCE statement to repair misspelled words or to replace a data table for communication between programmers is a 'klutzy' way to program, and it is not recommended!

*Pretty Terrible

Rules for Using The EQUIVALENCE Statement

1. The EQUIVALENCE statement is a non-executable specification statement which must appear before all statement function definitions and executable statements.

2. Each list of elements to be equivalenced must contain at least two items. Dummy arguments may not be equivalenced. The following statement causes XIRST and XRIST to refer to the same location.

```
12345|6|789...
     | |EQUIVALENCE (XIRST,XRIST)
```

3. The subscript of an array may be any integer constant less than or equal to the dimension of the array. The subscript does not provide dimension information but rather it causes the array element designated to share the memory location of the other variables within the parentheses.

The following statement means that the sixth element of array A is also referred to as ALT.

```
12345|6|789...
     | |EQUIVALENCE (A(6),ALT)
```

4. Since array elements are stored sequentially, the equivalencing of two elements of two different arrays may equivalence other elements of the arrays. In the following example, the equivalencing of A(5) and B(1) causes the remaining elements of A to be equivalenced to elements of B, as shown under the MEMORY ALLOCATION

```
12345|6|789...
     | |DIMENSION A(8),  B(5)
     | |EQUIVALENCE (A(5),B(1))
```

MEMORY ALLOCATION

A(1)	A(2)	A(3)	A(4)	A(5)	A(6)	A(7)	A(8)	
				B(1)	B(2)	B(3)	B(4)	(B5)

5. Variables of different types may be equivalenced if they are used in different parts of a program unit. In the following program segment XDEG and I share the same location without conflict since XDEG is never used once it is converted to XRAD.

```
12345|6|789...
     | |EQUIVALENCE (XDEG,I)
     | |READ (1,5) XDEG
     | |XRAD = XDEG/57.296
     | |...
     | |I=J*K-L
     | |...
```

6. Two variables in one common block or in two different common blocks may not be equivalenced. A variable in a common block may be equivalenced to a variable not in a common block.

Care must be taken so that the equivalencing of an array element to a variable in COMMON does not equivalence other elements to locations before the start of COMMON. This is shown on the following page.

Equivalence (A(5),X) implies the equivalence of the four other elements of A to locations before the start of COMMON which is not permissible.

```
123456789...
      DIMENSIØN A(5)
      CØMMØN X,Y,Z
      EQUIVALENCE (A(5),X)
```

14.6

OBJECTIVE: . . . write a **BLOCK DATA** subprogram to initialize variables in labeled COMMON.

Variables in blank COMMON may not be initialized in a DATA statement. Variables in a COMMON block may be initialized but only by a separate subprogram, called a BLOCK DATA subprogram. The general form of a BLOCK DATA subprogram is:

GENERAL FORM

```
12345|6|789...

        BLØCK DATA
        CØMMØN /name1/a1,...an.../namen/b1,...bn
        DATA statement
        END
```

COMPONENTS

```
BLOCK DATA     is a keyword
COMMON /name/  is a labeled CØMMØN statement
END            is a keyword
```

EXAMPLE

```
12345|6|789...

        BLØCK DATA
        DIMENSION ARY (100)
        CØMMØN /CMPT/ARY,A1,A2,D/CNST/PI,R2D,FNM
        DATA ARY/100*0./,A2,A1/-1.,1.5/,
       + PI,R2D,FNM/3.14159,57.296,6076.2/
        END
```

Rules for Writing a BLOCK DATA Subprogram

1. The BLOCK DATA subprogram may not contain any executable statements. The only statements that it may contain are: BLOCK DATA, DATA, COMMON, DIMENSION, EQUIVALENCE, and type-statements pertaining to the data being defined.

2. The BLOCK DATA statement must be the first statement and END must be the last statement in the subprogram.

3. The COMMON statement defining the labeled COMMON for the variables being initialized must precede the statements which give the initial values to the variables.

4. All elements of a labeled COMMON block must be listed in the COMMON statement, even though they do not all have to be initialized. The variable D in COMMON CMPT in the example above is not initialized.

5. Data in different labeled COMMON blocks may be initialized in a BLOCK DATA subprogram. The order of the variables in the DATA statement does not need to be the same as their order in the COMMON statement. Note A1 and A2 in the COMMON and DATA statements above.

6. Only one BLOCK DATA subprogram may be used in a program.

CHAPTER EXERCISES

1. Indicate which of the following statements are valid by V, invalid by I.

```
12345|6|789...

        EQUIVALENCE (A,B,C(3)),(K,D)          ________
        EQUIVALENCE (X,3.,DELTA)              ________
        EQUIVALENCE (A(5,5),B(3,3))           ________
        EQUIVALENCE Z(1),ALT,Z(2),ACC         ________
        CØMMØN A,B,C(5,5),K,L                 ________
        CØMMØN XL,YL,3.0                      ________
        CØMMØN (QR(3,3),WIDTH)                ________
        CØMMØN /XYZ/X,Y,Z                     ________
        CØMMØN A,B,C/BLK1/D,E,F               ________
```

2. A program contains two arrays AR1 (50,50) and AR2 (25,25).

By the time that AR2 is used in the program the values of AR1 are no longer needed. Write a FORTRAN statement that will reduce the total storage requirement of this program by 625 locations.

____

3. The program portion below passes the arguments from the main program to SUBROUTINE MTXADD by arguments. Answer the questions using it.

PROGRAM

```
12345|6|789...

C MAIN  PRØGRAM
        DIMENSIØN A(10,10),B(10,10),C(10,10),IRØW,ICØL
        ...
      6 CALL MTXADD (A,B,C,IRØW,ICØL)
        ...
        END
```

```
C SUBRØUTINE FØR MATRIX ADDITIØN
        SUBRØUTINE MTXADD (X,Y,Z,IR,IC)
        DIMENSIØN X(10,10),Y(10,10),Z(10,10),IR,IC
        DØ 5 I=1,IR
          DØ 6 J=1,IC
             Z(I,J)=X(I,J)+Y(I,J)
      6   CØNTINUE
      5 CØNTINUE
        RETURN
        END
```

a. Write a statement that puts all the arguments into blank COMMON. Include the DIMENSION information in the COMMON statement so the DIMENSION statement can be eliminated.

1 2 3 4 5	6	7 8 9 • • •

b. Re-write statement 6 in the main program if the COMMON statement is used instead of the argument list.

1 2 3 4 5	6	7 8 9 • • •

c. Re-write the SUBROUTINE definition statement for MTXADD if the COMMON statement above is used.

1 2 3 4 5	6	7 8 9 • • •

d. Write the labeled COMMON statement that would be used if a labeled COMMON block called ARY were used for all the arguments instead of blank COMMON.

1 2 3 4 5	6	7 8 9 • • •

4. Write a BLOCK DATA subprogram which assigns the eight values given below to the array DAMP, which should be dimensioned at 8. The array DAMP is to be put in a labeled COMMON block called SHIFT. The values of DAMP are as follows:

DAMP = .1,.2,.3,.4,.5,1.0,2.0,3.0

1 2 3 4 5	6	7 8 9 • • •

5. When using COMMON to transfer arguments in a FUNCTION subprogram, why is it necessary to have at least one argument?

____

____

CHAPTER PROGRAMMING PROBLEMS

TOPIC APPLICATION
a) Comprehensive program b) Tabular Output Format

Problem 14.1

PROBLEM STATEMENT

Write a FORTRAN program to calculate the RMF (relative magnification factor) and phase angle for a forced MKD system where:

$$RMF = \frac{1}{\sqrt{(1-r_n{}^2)^2 + (2r_n\zeta)^2}}$$

$$\theta = \tan^{-1}\left(\frac{2r_n\zeta}{1-r_n{}^2}\right)$$

Have θ printed out in degrees.

ζ = damping factor
r_n = undamped frequency ratio

r_n should start at a value of .1 and increase as follows:

steps of .1 $0<r_n\leq .9$

steps of .02 $.9<r_n\leq 1.0$

steps of .2 $1.0<r_n\leq 3.0$

For each run ζ (a shift variable) should be held constant at the following values:

ζ = 0.1, 0.2,. 0.3, 0.4, 0.5, 1.0, 2.0, 3.0

Each answer should be rounded off to two decimal places. Many computers round off data in the last place specified by the FORMAT. If your computer does not round off, see note on the bottom of the next page. Complete the following:

My computer [does / does not] round off on printing output.

OUTPUT

Start printing at the top of a new page.
Arrange the output in the following form.

	ZETA = 0.1		ZETA = 0.2		ZETA = 0.3		...
r_n	RMF	THETA	RMF	THETA	RMF	THETA	...
.1	___	___	___	___	___	___	
.2	___	___	___	___	___	___	
.3	___	___	___	___	___	___	...
.4	___	___	___	___	___	___	
.5	___	___	___	___	___	___	
...	...	...	...	...	...	...	...

Use F4.2 format for RMF and F6.2 for θ

The printout must fit on a standard page. At most installations this can be at least 120 characters in one line and 57 lines on each printout page.

BONUS

After values have been obtained from the computer, make two plots (a) one of RMF vs. r_n and (b) phase angle vs. r_n for the various values of ζ used.

NOTE

If your computer does not round off the output, a statement function may be used to provide the roundoff as follows:

```
12345|6|789...
     | |ROUND (X,N) = X+(.5*.1**N)*X/ABS(X)
```

where N is the number of decimal places to which the number X is to be rounded.

Problem 14.2

PROBLEM STATEMENT

When people unfamiliar with computers are filling out data for a program, it is nice to provide a simple, more familiar input format that does not depend on card columns. Such free-format input is featured in the following program. This program will give you a slight glimpse at how a compiler program would be written.

A program is written to compute the average gas mileage on five major makes of automobiles. People were randomly selected at gasoline stations and asked to write on a card their auto make and the average miles per gallon they got in the following form, but starting in any column.

FORD = 15.

CHEVY = 17.

EXERCISE

Write a program that will read in the free-format input and compute the average miles per gallon for each of the following five makes of automobiles:

a)FORD
b)CHEVROLET
c)OLDSMOBILE
d) PONTIAC
e) BUICK

Your program must do the following:

a) Read the entire card in with 80A1 format code to be able to test each column.

b) Define all characters needed for testing, such as: F,C,Ø,P,B=,., in DATA statements.

Initialize all counters, and set printout message names, such as FORD, in DATA statements.

The main program should do the following:

a) Find the first non-blank character to start testing.

b) Test this first letter against prestored possible choices. Eliminate any non-match card with an error message.

c) Test each column until '=' is found.

d) Build the decimal number for gas mileage by testing each non-blank column before the decimal against a set of prestored alphanumeric digits. (Recall that even the gas mileage is read in A1 format code.)

e) End-of-data is signified by a STOP card so test each first non-blank character for S.

Test your program with the following input sample:

```
OLDS = 9.
 MERCURY = 13.
PONTIAC= 15.
  CHEVY = 15
     MERCURY = 14
 CHEVROLET= 18.
    FORD = 16
 FORD = 9.
MERCURY = 7.
CHEVY = 13.
CHEVY = 19.
 FORD= 15.
 FORD = 17.
 FORD = 12.
 CHEVY=11.
 PONTIAC = 6
 STOP
```

The output should consist of a statement for each automobile, as follows:

```
          1         2         3         4         5
 12345678901234567890123456789012345678901234567890123
1|AVERAGE OF 5 FORD       CARS  IS  13.8 MPG
2|
3|    ...
```

Problem 14.3

PROBLEM STATEMENT

Computers are used to aid in breaking complicated coded messages. The code we will use here is quite simple but will involve several computer concepts.

EXERCISE

Write a program to decode messages written using numbers instead of letters. The correspondence is as follows:

A	B	C	...	X	Y	Z	blank
26	25	24		3	2	1	99

Assign all the letters of the alphabet and blank to individual memory locations in array, ABC. Use a BLOCK DATA, INTEGER declaration, and COMMON to initialize and pass array, ABC.

Write a subroutine, DECOD, which does the decoding and returns the decoded letters to the main program in array, MSG. The main program reads the input and prints the decoded message.

INPUT

Card

```
1 |14122599142222071813209904222399260799131813229911114
2 |25262416990912121499201813120899111801012699112609151209
```

Problem 14.4

PROBLEM STATEMENT

A polynomial is of the form

$$a_0x^n + a_1x^{n-1} + a_2x^{n-2} + \ldots a_n$$

where a_i, $i=0 \ldots n$ are the coefficients

and n is an integer

The polynomial is said to be of degree, n.

For a given value of X and given coefficients, the polynomial has a value.

EXERCISE

Write a SUBROUTINE called POLYV which will compute the value of a polynomial. POLYV needs the following data which is passed through COMMON:

COEF -- a single dimensional array which stores the coefficients, a_0, $a_1 \ldots a_n$

N - degree of the polynomial

POLYV also has two arguments:

ARG -- the value of X for which the polynomial is to be evaluated

VAL-- the value of the polynomial for ARG

Write a main program that reads and prints the values of N followed by the coefficients of a polynomial. It should have a COMMON to pass N, and the coefficient array to POLYV. It should also read in any number of values for ARG, one at a time, and call POLYV to evaluate the polynomial. Provide for the end-of-data using a sentinel card or END= option.

INPUT

Test your program by computing the value of the following polynomial:

$2x^5-9.5x^4+3.1x^3+1.1x^2-1$ for $x = 4.5$ and

$x = 3.5$

OUTPUT

DEGREE OF POLYNOMIAL IS nn
COEFFICIENTS ARE nn.n nn.n nn.n . . .
FOR X = nn.n THE VALUE IS snnnnn.n

15

FORTRAN

15.1 . . . design a complex program requiring a number of subprograms and . . . code a subprogram as part of a larger comprehensive program.

15.1

OBJECTIVE: . . . design a complex program requiring a number of subprograms, and . . . code a subprogram as part of a larger comprehensive program.

One of the main reasons for the use of subprograms is to enable a long, complicated program to be broken up into smaller units. This is of particular importance in project programming, when more than one programmer is involved in writing a program. Without project programming, programs of the complexity of the moon launch could not be done. In project programming, over all design and planning and communication among all those involved becomes very important.

The HIPO is particularly helpful in designing a long program. It lists the functions that are to be performed as an aid in modularizing into shorter, more manageable units, or subprograms, which are called to perform a particular task by one main program. The following application shows how a long complex problem should be started at the top with a hierarchy chart, that lists the major functions to be performed and the flow of control between them. These major functions suggest how the program should be written in subprograms. Each of the five steps of top-down program design given in Chapter 7 will be applied.

STEP 1 Problem Definition

We wish to write a program for computing the trajectory of a rocket from initial launch to engine burn out, separation, and descent. The input data specifies the rocket configuration. Output consists of the input parameters and a table of computed parameters, such as, thrust, drag, weight, velocity, and altitudes as a function of time; and a summary of the total flight calculations, such as total flight time, maximum velocity, burn-out time, velocity and altitude. A complete problem statement is given in Problem 15.1.

STEP 2 Make a Data Table

The data table frequently referred to as a data base, is a key item of communication among those involved in a project program. Thus, our next step is to list all the input data that is required and all the output data that is desired. As we continue with Step 3 and 4, the data table is continuously revised to reflect additions to the list. A complete Data Base is given for the trajectory program in Problem 15.1.

STEP 3. Make a Top-Level Hierarchy Chart

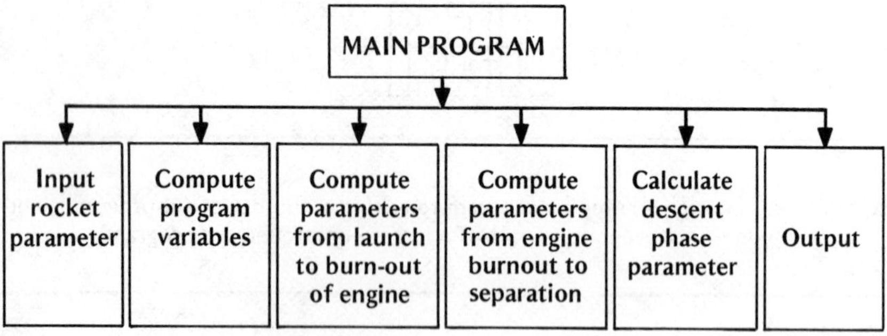

Figure 15.1-1. Top-level Hierarchy Chart for Rocket Trajectory

This top-level hierarchy chart breaks the trajectory of the rocket into phases where the calculations of the trajectory parameters would be similar. Input and output are separate functions as is the initialization of program variables. This chart gives an overview of the problem and begins to separate it by functions. Several refinements will be needed until all the individual functions that are needed to perform the calculations for the three center blocks are specified. The important idea here is that we have an overview of the whole program and a structure which can be broken down until the details of the problem come into focus.

Next, the top-level heirarchy chart is revised further breaking down each major block into simpler functions. This is shown in Figure 15.1-2.

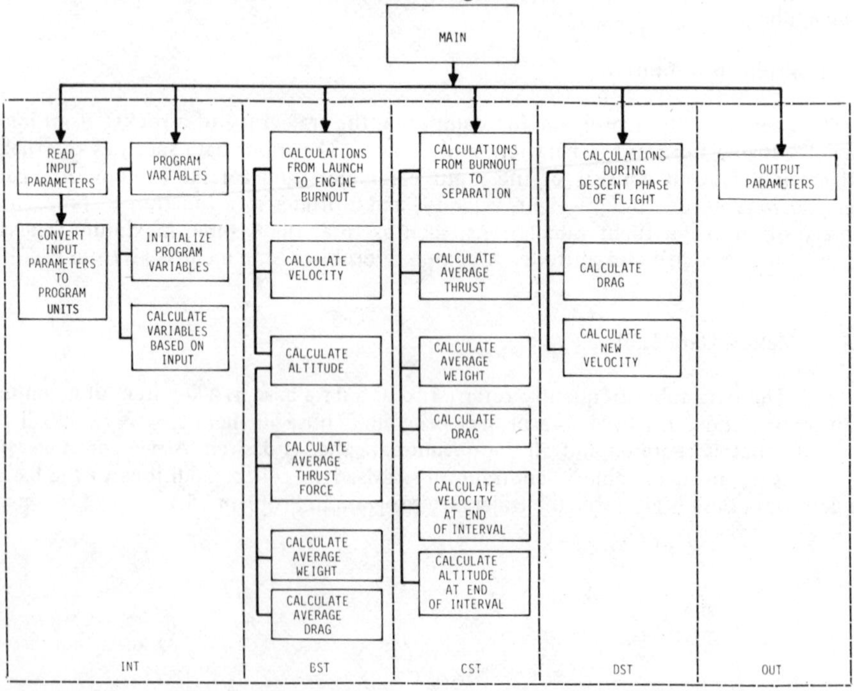

Figure 15.1-2 Revision I Hierarchy Chart for Rocket Trajectory

The revised hierarchy chart begins to show how to modularize our rocket trajectory program. The dotted lines were added after the functions were listed, and subprogram names have been added to show how the program is modularized into subprograms. The details of each of the subprogram and of the main program are now ready to be specified. These details are specified in Problem 15.1 and the next step, making the flow diagram, is left as an exercise. Additional columns have been added to the data table (Data Base) to show which subprograms use which data items, dimension size for arrays, initial values and Common location order.

STEP 4 Make Detailed Flow Diagrams

Sufficient information is given in Problem 15.1 to construct necessary flow diagrams.

STEP 5 Code the Program

The data table (DATA BASE) has been specified by the leading programmer. This table is given in Problem 15.1. Code each of the modules described below after completing flow diagrams.

CHAPTER PROGRAMMING PROBLEMS

TOPIC APPLICATION

a) Comprehensive Program
b) Production Programming
c) Use of COMMON

Problem 15.1

PROBLEM STATEMENT

The objective of this program is to show how a large programming task is coordinated among several programmers. The problem has been formulated to demonstrate the documentation and interface control typical of those methods used when extensive programs are to be written by several programmers working as a team.

The completed program will compute the trajectory of a small rocket launched vertically. The overall program should be written to print out a heading listing the configuration for a given rocket, print sample values of time, average, thrust, velocity and altitude followed by a performance summary.

The trajectory for this problem is divided into three phases:

Boost phase -- during which the rocket engine is firing.

Coast phase -- during which the rocket is continuing under its own momentum.

Descent phase -- during which a parachute is deployed automatically, and which reduces the velocity of the rocket to provide a safe descent.

In a large programming department the work of dividing a large job into smaller workable units is done by a senior programmer, whose title may be systems analyst, task leader, project programmer, or programmer/analyst. He/she divides the task into units called modules, writes a description of exactly what each module is to do, defines how data is to be passed from module to module, and sets standard procedures for each of the module programmers, who will write the detailed programs.

The program to be written to solve this problem is divided into six subroutines or modules:

1) MAIN (the main or calling program)
2) INT (read and initialize subprogram)
3) BST (boost phase subprogram)
4) CST (coast phase subprogram)
5) DST (descent phase subprogram)
6) OUT (write subprogram)

Figure 15.1-3 illustrates the trajectory to be analyzed. The boost, coast, and descent phases are separated by specific times: ignition, thrust termination, separation and impact as shown.

Boost phase -- occurs between ignition and thrust termination during which the rocket engine is firing

Coast phase -- occurs between thrust termination and separation during which the rocket is continuing under its own momentum

Descent phase -- occurs between separation (parachute deployment) and impact during which a parachute, deployed automatically, reduces the velocity to provide a slow descent

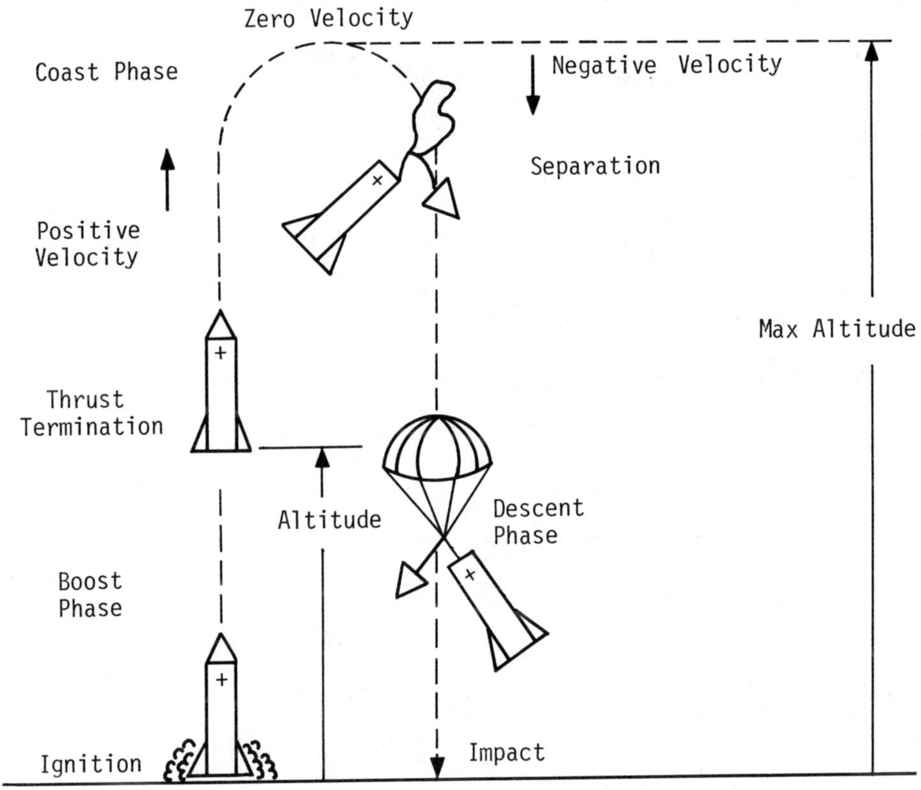

Figure 15.1-3 Model Rocket Trajectory

Your instructor will assign one of these phases, or the read/initialize program for you to program either individually or as a small group. You will also need to know the deck composition for your computer installation to compile the subroutines required. The MAIN or calling program may be written as follows:

```
12345 6 789...
        COMMON ...
        CALL INT
        CALL BST
        CALL CST
        CALL DST
        STOP
        END
```

PROGRAMMING STANDARDS

1) All variables except DO loop indexes or indexes used in that subprogram only

shall be assigned locations in COMMON (see data base in the following section)

2) All programs except OUT shall immediately on entry print the subprogram name and the programmers name left justified, i.e.,

```
          1
12345678901234...
INTJS  JOHN SMITH
```

preceeded and followed by a single blank line.

3) All outputs shall be printed by the routine OUT. Except for

   a) programmers identification described in item 2 above.

   b) error statements

Set print code to provide desired output format.

CODE	FORMAT
1	print heading
2	print sample values
3	print summary

4) Use the following statement subprogram for rounding if your computer does not provide this feature.

```
ROUND(X,K)=X+SIGN(.5*.1**K,X)
```

Where

X represents variable to be rounded

K number decimal places

This statement must be placed in the problem deck prior to any use of the subprogram name ROUND on the right hand side of the = sign.

INT Module

FUNCTIONAL DESCRIPTION

The object of this module is to initialize all variables, read in data, convert read in values to problem units, set constants, and to calculate quantities to be used by all subsequent modules.

PROCEDURE

1) Write COMMON statement.

2) Initialize variables (See DATA BASE) in COMMON not being read in from card data.

3) Read in constants (G,CDR,CDP,ROE)

4) Read in data (See data sheet in appendix)

5) Calculate burntime of engine

$$T_B = (NV)(D)$$

where T_B = burntime

D = time interval between thrust sample values

NV = number of entries in thrust table

6) Convert rocket weight, initial weight of rocket engine and propellant weight from grams to pounds. Use an arithmetic statement and multiply by 0.002205.

7) Calculate Wet Weight

$$W_W = W_R + W_P \text{ (pounds)}$$

where: W_W = Wet Weight

W_R = Weight of Rocket

W_P = Initial Weight of Rocket Engine

8) Calculate Area of the Rocket and Parachute

$$A_R = \pi\left(\frac{D_R}{2.0}\right)^2$$

where A_R = Area of Rocket

D_R = Diameter of Rocket

$$A_P = \pi\left(\frac{D_P}{2.0}\right)^2$$

where D_P = Diameter of Parachute

A_P = Area of Parachute

9) Convert area of the rocket and parachute from square inches to square feet by multiplying by 1/144.

10) Set IFLAG=1 and CALL OUT to print out heading

11) Return to calling program

BST Module

FUNCTIONAL DESCRIPTION

This module covers the time from launch to engine burn out. Figure 15.1-4 shows the forces acting on the rocket during this phase.

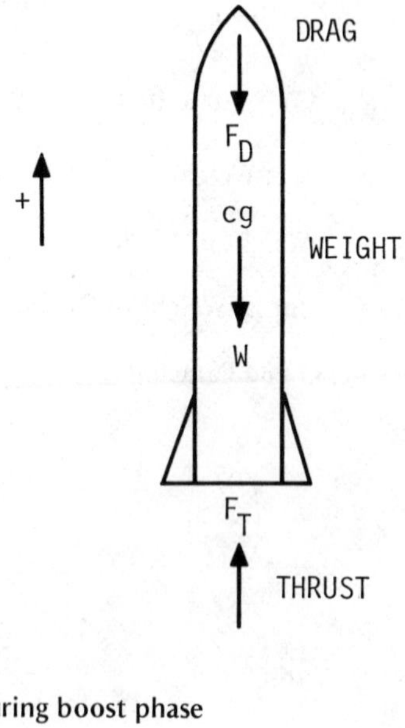

Figure 15.1-4 Rocket during boost phase

The sum of the forces

$$\Sigma F = F_T - F_W - F_D$$

where ΣF = resultant force (pounds)

F_T = thrust (pounds)

F_W = weight of rocket + engine (pounds)

F_D = drag force (pounds)

Using Newton's Law F = ma

$$\Sigma F = ma = \frac{F_W}{g} a$$

where m = mass of rocket
A = rocket acceleration
G = acceleration of gravity
= 32.2 ft/sec^2

The problem has been divided into small time intervals where the acceleration is assumed to be constant and average values are used. The acceleration can then be written as

$$a = \frac{\Delta V}{\Delta t}$$

ΔV = Change in velocity in ft./sec/
Δt = Time interval

Combining the above and using

$$\frac{(F_W)}{g} \frac{(\Delta V)}{\Delta t} = AF_T - AF_W - AF_D$$

where AF_T = average thrust force

AF_W = average weight

AF_D = average drag force

Solving for ΔV

$$\Delta V = \frac{g}{AF_W}(AF_T - AF_W - AF_D)\Delta T$$

The velocity during the flight can then be calculated in increments by

$$V_{new} = V_{old} + \Delta V$$

and the altitude can be calculated as

$$A_{new} = A_{old} + (\Delta V)(\Delta t)$$

Calculation of AF_T

AF_T must be recalculated for each interval. The average thrust during small time intervals can be determined by

$$AF_T = \frac{F_{TI} + F_{TE}}{2}$$

where F_{TI} = thrust at beginning of interval

F_{TE} = thrust at end of interval

The thrust curve will have the form of Figure 15.1-5. Thrust values for each time interval are supplied in tabular form.

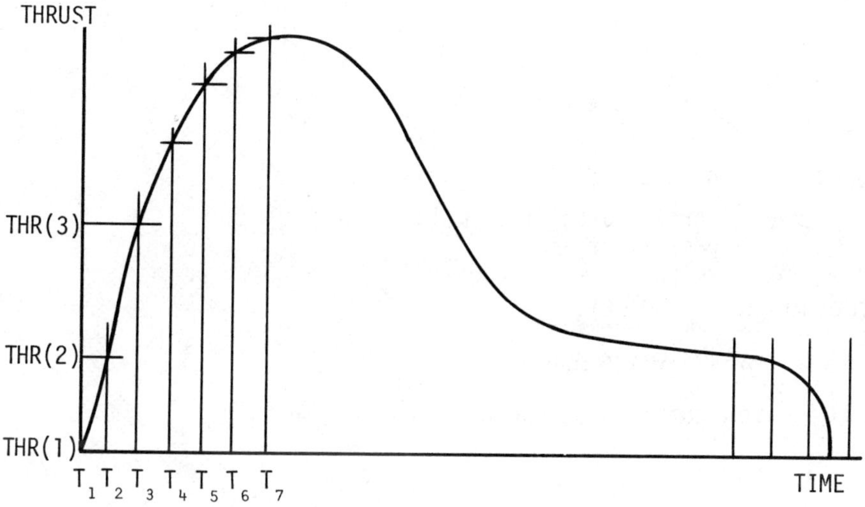

Figure 15.1-5

Calculation of AF_W

AF_W is calculated assuming a constant reduction of weight as the engine burns.

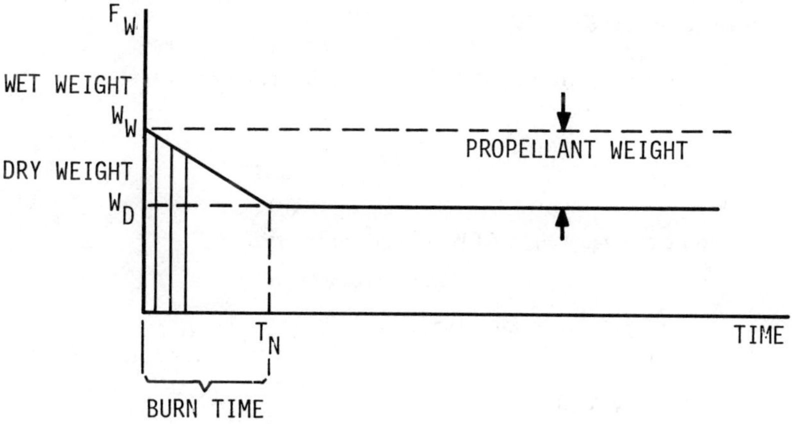

Figure 15.1-5 Weight Curve

$$AF_W = W_W - \frac{W_D}{N}(I - \tfrac{1}{2})$$

where I = interval
= 1, 2, 3, . . . N

Compute AF_D

The drag is given by the equation

$$AF_D = 1/2\ C_D\ A\ \rho V^2$$

where C_D = drag coefficient
A = surface area (frontal)
ρ = density of air
V = velocity

PROCEDURE (BST MODULE)

1. Write COMMON statement

2. Write ROUND Function Statement if required

3. Initialize

   Set IC = 1
   N = 1
   V = 0
   H = 0

4. Compute average thrust (AFT) for the first interval

$$AFT = TR(1)/2$$

   then go to step 6

5. Compute average thrust (AFT) for current interval except first

$$AF_T = \frac{TR(IC-1) + TR(IC)}{2}$$

6. Compute average weight AFW for current interval

$$AF_W = W_W - \frac{W_D}{NV}(IC-1/2)$$

7. Calculate drag AFD

$$AF_D = 1/2\ C_D A \rho V^2$$

8. Calculate change in velocity during interval

$$DV = \frac{g}{AF_T}(AF_T - AF_W - AF_D)\Delta t$$

9. Calculate velocity at end of interval

$$V_{new} = V_{old} + DV$$

10. If $v < O$ set V to zero

11. Calculate altitude at end of interval

$$H_{new} = H_{old} + (DV)(\Delta t)$$

12. If H<O set H to zero

13. Compare velocity with maximum velocity (VMAX) register

    If V > VMAX store new maximum velocity

14. Increment N by 1

15. Ready the following subscripted variables for print and round off if your computer does not provide this feature.

VARIABLE		ROUND TO
TIME	T(N) = (IC) (DELTA)	2 places
AVE THRUST	AVTR(N) = AFT	3 places
AVE DRAG	ADRAG(N)= AFD	3 places
AVE WT	AVWT(N) = AFW	3 places
VELOCITY	VEL(N) = V	2 places
ALTITUDE	ALT(N) = H	2 places

16. Set print code IFLAG = 2 and CALL OUT

17. If IC = NV go to 19
    IC < NV go to next step

18. Set

$$IC = IC + 1$$
$$N = IC$$

    then go to step 5

19. Set

$$BVEL = V$$
$$BALT = H$$

20. Remove remaining fuel

$$AFW = WW\text{-}WPP$$

21. Write thrust termination

22. Return to calling program

CST Module

FUNCTIONAL DESCRIPTION

This module covers the time from engine burn out to separation. Burn out occurs at TBURN = N*DELTA a quantity calculated by the INT program. The time covered by this module is determined by the delay time designed into the rocket engine and is read in by the INT program. The equations are the same as used for the boost phase with the thrust equal to zero and no further weight change. Values are to be printed every fifth iteration. Note that the direction of the drag force (with respect to the positive reference direction) changes when the sign of the velocity changes.

PROCEDURE

1) Write COMMON statement

2) Write ROUND statement (if required)

3) Test IC, time, velocity, weight and altitude to see if

T(N) = TBURN
IC = NV
Altitude H > 0
Velocity V > 0
Weight AFW > 0

If not print ERROR DETECTED IN OUTPUT OF BST PROGRAM and STOP.

4) Set NSTEP = 1
AFT = 0

5) Increment IC by 1

6) Calculate AFT and then set sign of AFT to the sign of the velocity using the FORTRAN supplied function subprogram SIGN. (Note: the equation for DV below has been formulated so that AFT must have the same sign as the velocity.)

Calculate change in velocity during interval

$$DV = -\frac{g}{AFW}(AFW+AFD)(\Delta t)$$

7) Calculate velocity at end of interval

$$V_{new} = V_{old} + DV$$

8) Calculate altitude at end of interval

$$H_{new} = H_{old} + DV(\Delta t)$$

9) Compare altitude with maximum altitude. If H ≤ HMAX, store new maximum altitude. If H HMAX calculate time to maximum altitude.

$$TMA = (IC-1)\Delta t$$

10) Increment NSTEP by 1

11) If time ≥ (TBURN + TDLY) go to step 17
If time < (TBURN + TDLY) go to next step
time = (IC)(Δt)

12) If NSTEP = 6 go to next step
If NSTEP < 6 go to step 5

13) Increment N by 1

14) Ready the following subscripted variables for print and round off if your computer does not provide this feature.

VARIABLE		ROUND TO
T(N)	= (IC) (DELTA)	2 places
AVTR(N)	= 0	3 places
ADRAG(N)	= AFD	3 places
AVWT(N)	= AFW	3 places
VEL(N)	= V	2 places
ALT(N)	= H	2 places

15) Set print code IFLAG = 2 and CALL OUT

16) Set NSTEP = 1
and return to step 5

17) Increment N by 1

18) Set IFLAG to 2 and CALL OUT

19) Ready the subscripted variables for printout as in step 14

20) Print out EJECTION POINT

21) Return to calling programs

DST Module

FUNCTIONAL DESCRIPTION

The purpose of this module is to determine the performance of the rocket during the descent phase of the flight. It covers the time from parachute ejection (TBURN + TDLY) to landing (ALT = 0). The time interval of this phase is determined by the altitude at ejection and rate of descent by parachute. Values are to be printed out after every 120th iteration.

PROCEDURE

1) Write COMMON statement

2) Write ROUND statement (if required)

3) Test IC, current time, velocity, weight and altitude to see if

$$T = TBURN + TDLY$$
$$IC = NV+TDLY/DELTA$$
$$\text{altitude} > 50$$
$$|\text{velocity}| < 100$$
$$\text{weight} > 0$$

If not, print ERROR DETECTED IN OUTPUT OF CST PROGRAM and call exit

4) Set NSTEP = 1

5) Increment IC by 1

6) Calculate drag

$$AFD\ SIGN(1/2\ C_{DP} A_p \rho V^2, V)$$

7) Calculate new velocity

$$V_{new} = V_{old} + \Delta V \quad \text{where} \quad \Delta V = -\frac{g}{AFW}(AFW+AFD)\ \Delta T$$

8) Compare altitude with maximum altitude. If H>HMAX store maximum altitude and set time as (IC) (Δt)

9) Increment NSTEP by 1

10) If H≤0 go to step 16
If H>0 go to next step

11) If NSTEP = 121 go to next step
If NSTEP < 121 go to step 4

12) Increment N by 1

13) Ready the following subscripted variables for print if your computer does not have the round-off feature.

VARIABLE			ROUND TO
TIME	T(N)	= (IC) (DELTA)	2 places
AVE THRUST	AVTR(N)	= 0.	3 places
AVE DRAG	ADRAG(N)	= AFD	3 places
AVE WT	AVWT(N)	= AFW	3 places
VELOCITY	VEL(N)	= V	2 places
ALTITUDE	ALT(N)	= H	2 places

14) Set print code IFLAG = 2 and CALL OUT

15) Set NSTEP = 1
and return to step 4

16) Increment N by 1

17) Ready the subscripted variables for print if your computer does not have the round-off feature.

VARIABLE			ROUND TO
TIME	T(N)	= (IC) (DELTA)	2 places
AVE THRUST	AVTR(N)	= 0.	3 places
AVE DRAG	ADRAG(N)	= AFD	3 places
AVE WT	AVWT(N)	= AFW	3 places
VELOCITY	VEL(N)	= 0.	2 places
ALTITUDE	ALT(N)	= 0.	2 places

18) Set IFLAG = 2 and CALL OUT

19) Set TFT = T(N)

20) Set IFLAG = 3 and CALL OUT

21) Return to calling programs

DATA BASE WORK SHEET   PROBLEM NO. 15.1   PROGRAMMER ______

VARIABLE NAME	TYP	DIM	USING SUBPROGRAM	INITIAL VALUE	UNITS	COMMON LOCATION		VARIABLE DEFINITION
RTYPE	A	5		read		1 to 5		Rocket Type
RLTH	R	1		read	inches	6	L_R	Rocket Length
DIAR	R	1		read	inches	7	D_R	Rocket Diameter
WRG	R	1		read	grams	8	W_R	Rocket Weight
WRP	R	1		0	pounds	9	W_R	Rocket Weight
DIAP	R	1		read	inches	10	D_P	Parachute Diameter
ETYPE	A	5		read	-	11-15		Engine Type
TOIMP	R	1		read	lb-sec	16		Total Impulse
TDLY	R	1		read	sec	17		Time Delay
TBURN	R	1		0	sec	18	T_B	Thrust Duration
WEG	R	1		read	grams	19	W_E	Initial Wt. of Rocket
WEP	R	1		0	pounds	20	W_E	Initial Wt. of Rocket
WPG	R	1		read	grams	21	W_P	Propellant Wt.
WPP	R	1		0	pounds	22	W_P	Propellant Wt.
DELTA	R	1		read	sec	23	ΔT	Time Interval
NV	I	1		read	-	24		Interval in Thrust Table

DATA BASE WORK SHEET PROBLEM NO. 15.1 PROGRAMMER ______

VARIABLE NAME	TYP	DIM	USING SUBPROGRAM	INITIAL VALUE	UNITS	COMMON LOCATION		VARIABLE DEFINITION
TR(N)	R	60	BST	read	pounds	25 - 84		Thrust Schedule
G	R	1		read	ft/sec^2	85	g	Acceleration of Gravity
COR	R	1		read	-	86	C_{DR}	Rocket Drag Coefficient
COP	R	1		read	-	87	C_{DD}	Parachute Drag Coefficient
ROE	R	1		read	slugs/ft^3	88	p	Density of Air
AR	R	1		0	ft^2	89	A_R	Frontal Area of Rocket
AP	R	1		0	ft^2	90	A_P	Parachute Area
PI	R	1		read	-	91	π	Const. = 3.1416
HMAX	R	1	CST OUT	0	-	92	H_{MAX}	Maximum Altitude
IFLAG	I	1		0	-	93		Print Code
WW	R	1		0	pounds	94	W_W	Wet Wt(Rocket + Engine)
N	I	1		1	-	95	N	Subscript for TR,AVTR,ALT, etc.
T(N)	R	175		0	sec	96-270	T_N	Time at End of Interval
AVTR(N)	R	175		0	pounds	271-445		Ave. Thrust During Interval
AVWT(N)	R	175		0	pounds	446-620		Ave. Wt During Interval

DATA BASE WORK SHEET PROBLEM NO. 15.1 PROGRAMMER ____

VARIABLE NAME	TYP	DIM	USING SUBPROGRAM	INITIAL VALUE	UNITS	COMMON LOCATION		VARIABLE DEFINITION
ALT(N)	R	175		0	ft	621-795		Altitude at End of Interval
VEL(N)	R	175		0	ft/sec	796-970		Velocity at End of Interval
ADRAG(N)	R	175		0	pounds	971-1145		Ave Drag During Interval
TMA	R	1	CST OUT	0	sec	1146		Time of Maximum Altitude
BVEL	R	1	BST OUT	0	ft/sec	1147		Burnout Velocity
BALT	R	1	BST OUT	0	ft	1148		Burnout Altitude
TFT	R	1	DST OUT	0	sec	1149		Total Time of Flight
DV	R	1		0	ft/sec	1150	ΔV	Calculated change in velocity during interval
V	R	1		0	ft/sec	1151		Calculated velocity at end of interval
H	R	1		0	ft	1152		Calculated altitude at end of interval
AFT	R	1		0	pounds	1153		Calculated average thrust during interval
AFW	R	1		0	pounds	1154		Calculated average weight during interval
AFD	R	1		0	pounds	1155		Calculated drag for the interval
VMAX	R	1		0	ft/sec	1156		Maximum Velocity
IC	I	1		1	-	1157		Iteration Counter

OUT MODULE

FUNCTIONAL DESCRIPTION

The purpose of this module is to program all WRITE statements, except for identification and event statements, required by the various modules. The program will provide for three sections of output.

A. ROCKET CONFIGURATION
B. SAMPLE VALUES
C. SUMMARY

Section A

Printing is to begin at the top of a new page. This section is identified by IFLAG = 1 and is called by the INT module.

Section B

This module will print the heading for sample values after skipping five lines from the end of Section A. After skipping two lines this module will provide the necessary WRITE statements for printing out sample values when called by the various modules with IFLAG set equal to two.

Section C

This section will print out the summary when called by the DST module with IFLAG = 3. Five lines will be skipped between sections B and C.

```
          OUTPUT FORMAT

          ROCKET CONFIGURATION

          ROCKET
               TYPE                   aaaaaaaaaaaaaaaaaaaa
               LENGTH                 nnn.nn INCHES
               DIA.                   nnn.nn INCHES
               WT.                    nnn.nn GRAMS

          ENGINE
               TYPE                   aaaaaaaaaaaaaaaaaaaa
               TOTAL IMPULSE          nnn.nn LB SEC nnn.nn N SEC
               THR. DURATION          nnn.nn SEC
    A          INITIAL WT.            nnn.nn GRAMS
               PROP. WT.              nnn.nn GRAMS nnn.nn POUNDS

          CONFIGURATION
               WET WT.                nnn.nn GRAMS nnn.nn POUNDS
               PAR DIA.               nnn.nn INCHES

          SAMPLE VALUES

               TIME     THRUST     DRAG       WT        VEL        ALT
              (SEC)     (LB)       (LB)      (LB)    (FT/SEC)     (FT)
           nnnnn.nn nnnn.nnn nnnn.nnn nnnn.nnn nnnnn.nn nnnnn.nn
    B      nnnnn.nn nnnn.nnn nnnn.nnn nnnn.nnn nnnnn.nn nnnnn.nn
           nnnnn.nn nnnn.nnn nnnn.nnn nnnn.nnn nnnnn.nn nnnnn.nn
             ...       ...      ...      ...      ...      ...

          SUMMARY

               BURNOUT VEL.             =nnnnn.nn FT/SEC
    C          BURNOUT ALT.             =nnnnn.nn FT
               MAXIMUM ALT.             =nnnnn.nn FT
               TIME TO MAX. ALT         =nnnnn.nn SEC
               TOTAL FLIGHT TIME        =nnnnn.nn SEC
               MAXIMUM VEL.             =nnnnn.nn FT/SEC
```

ROCKET ANALYSIS SHEET

ROCKET

TYPE	CHERØKEE - D RØCKET
LENGTH	16.60 INCHES
DIA.	1.325 INCHES
WT.	78.00 GRAMS 2.75 OUNCES
DRAG COEFF.	.65

RECOVERY

PAR. DIA.	18.00 INCHES
DRAG COEFF.	3.00

ENGINE

TYPE	D13 - 5 ENGINE
TOTAL IMPULSE	4.48 LB. SEC.
TIME DELAY	5.00 SEC.
THRUST DURATION	1.56 SEC.
INITIAL WT.	43.10 GRAMS 1.52 OUNCES
PROP. WT.	24.93 GRAMS
THRUST TABLE	(GRAMS) (See sheet 2)
TIME INTERVAL	0.04 SEC.

NUMBER OF THRUST INTERVALS 39

MISC.

ACCELERATION OF GRAVITY 32.2FT/SEC

AIR DENSITY 0.002378 $SLUGS/FT^3$

PI 3.1416

THRUST TABLE

END OF INT.	VALUE (POUNDS)	END OF INT.	VALUE (POUNDS)
1	0.21	21	2.97
2	0.70	22	2.97
3	1.85	23	2.97
4	3.99	24	2.97
5	6.29	25	2.97
6	7.80	26	2.97
7	8.76	27	2.97
8	9.13	28	2.97
9	7.79	29	2.97
10	4.38	30	2.97
11	3.31	31	2.97
12	3.12	32	2.97
13	2.98	33	2.97
14	2.97	34	2.97
15	2.97	35	2.97
16	2.97	36	2.05
17	2.97	37	1.05
18	2.97	38	0.49
19	2.97	39	0.00
20	2.97	40	

FORTRAN

A

KEYPUNCHING

APPENDIX A

The keyboard of an IBM 29 keypunch resembles the keyboard of a typewriter except that there are no lower case letters and there are special keys on a keypunch. A keypunch is normally in the alphabetic mode. In this mode, alphabetic and lower position characters are punched. To punch upper position characters and numerics, depress the NUMERIC key.

A picture of an IBM 29 keypunch is shown in Figure A-1.

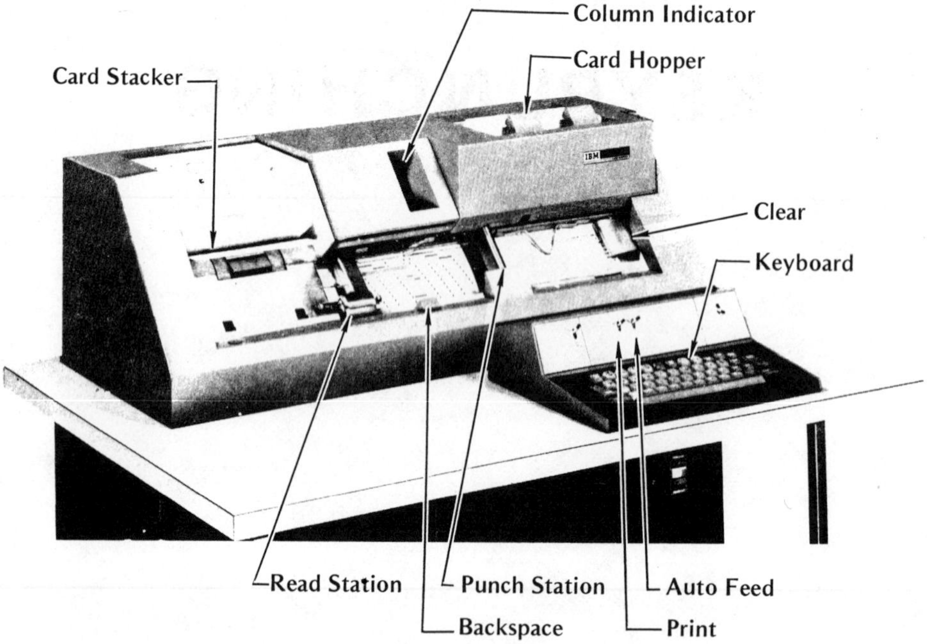

Figure A-1. IBM 29 Keypunch

Some special switches are:

AUTO FEED	--	With AUTO FEED (automatic feed) cards are fed automatically after being started by pressing down twice so there are two cards in the punch station.
PRINT	--	In the ON position, PRINT prints the characters that are punched across the top of the card.
CLEAR	--	Clears cards from the read and punch station.
BACKSPACE	--	Backspaces the cards in the read and punch stations one column as long as it is held.
COLUMN INDICATOR	--	Indicates the <u>next</u> column to be punched.

A keyboard of an IBM 29 keypunch is shown in Figure A-2 with an explanation of some of the special keys following it.

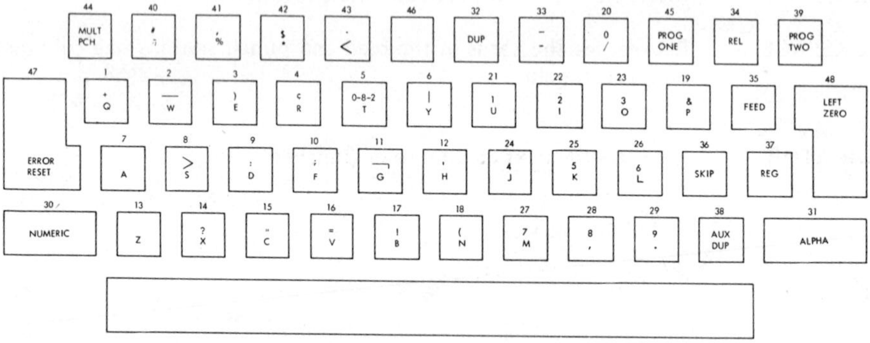

Figure A-2. Keyboard of an IBM 29 keypunch

SPECIAL KEYS USED TO PUNCH THE FORTRAN CHARACTER SET

1. MULT PCH -- Multiple punch. Allows special combinations to be punched in a column. It is not needed for the FORTRAN character set.
2. DUP -- Duplicate. Allows duplication of a card or portions of a card.
3. REL -- Release. Releases a card from the punch station.
4. FEED -- Feed. Feeds a card from the card hopper into the punch station.
5. REG -- Register. Registers a card in the punch station to allow punching into it.
6. NUMERIC -- Numeric mode. Puts the keyboard in the numeric mode so numerics and upper position characters can be punched.

7. SPACE BAR -- Space bar. Allows blank columns to be left in a card. It advances the cards in the punch and read station one column without punches each time it is depressed.

FORTRAN B

STATEMENT SUMMARY

STATEMENT TYPE	FØRM/EXAMPLE(S)	PURPOSE	PAGE
Arithmetic	123456789··· nnnnn v=e A=5.32 B=A+28.57	to perform arithmetic calculations and store the result	62

Arithmetic IF	nnnnn IF(e)nn_1,nn_2,nn_3
	IF(A-1.0)5,10,20
	IF(A**2-B**2)5,5,10
		to cause conditional branching based on a numerical value	248

BLØCK DATA	BLØCK DATA	to initialize variables in a common block	354
CØMMØN	CØMMØN$a_1(k_1)$,$a_2(k_2)$,...$a_n(k_n)$ CØMMØN A,B,D(30),IM(3,4),NX	to store values in common memory	
CØMMØN block	CØMMØN/name/$a_1(k_1)$,...$a_n(k_n)$ COMMON/ØUT/Y(100),RVT,IJ,KPQ	defines a common storage area under a given name	349
computed GØTØ	nnnnn GØ TØ (m_1,m_2,m_3,...m_n),iv GØ TØ (5,10,50,65),IFLAG GO TO (10,20,30,40),INDEX	to cause a branch based on an index value	245
CØNTINUE	nnnnn CONTINUE	to do nothing but provide a reference statement	78
CALL	nnnnn CALL name CALL name(a_1,a_2,...a_n) CALL PAGE CALL MTXA(X,Y,100) CALL SQRT(A,N)	to transfer control to the "called" subroutine	330
CALL EXIT	nnnnn CALL EXIT	to terminate execution and remain in ready state	75
DATA	DATA k_1/d_1/,k_2/d_2/,k_3/d_3/,...k_n/d_n/ DATA k_1,k_2,k_3...k_n/d_1,d_2,d_3,...d_n/ DATA A,B,C/1.,2.,3./ DATA A/1./,B/2./,C/3./	to assign values during compilation	47

STATEMENT TYPE	FØRM/EXAMPLE(S)	PURPOSE	PAGE
	1 2 3 4 5 6 7 8 9 ...		
DIMENSION	DIMENSION $name_1$($subscript_1$), $name_2$($subscript_2$),... DIMENSION X(100) DIMENSION I(50),NØN(50),BR(75)	to define storage requirements for arrays	182
DØ	nnnnn DØ n i=m_1,m_2,m_3 DØ 10 J=1,8 DØ 15 K=I,J,L	to define range of a DØ loop and loop index parameters	77
ELSE	nnnnn ELSE	defines a statement block to be executed if the IF block condition is false	287
ELSE IF	nnnnn ELSE IF(e) THEN ELSE IF(A.NE.B)	provides several IF blocks to be conditionally executed, within the main IF block	291
END	END	to define the end of the program	76
END IF	nnnnn END IF	defines the end of the IF block statements	284
EQUIVALENCE	EQUIVALENCE(a_1,a_2...a_n),(b_1,b_2...b_n) EQUIVALENCE(XIRST,XRIST)	to store several variables in the same memory location	352
EXTERNAL	EXTERNAL name ,...$name_n$ EXTERNAL SIN,CØS	to identify subprogram names as allowable subprogram arguements	343
FLØAT	...FLØAT(e)... R=FLØAT(I)	convert from integer to real mode	85
FØRMAT(read)	nnnnn FØRMAT(c_1,c_2,c_3,...c_n) 10 FØRMAT(I3) 10 FØRMAT(3F6.2,T20,I3,3X,3I6)	to specify location, field and type of input data	101
FØRMAT(write)	nnnnn FØRMAT(c ,c ,c ,...c_n) 10 FØRMAT('b',I3,I2) 30 FØRMAT(//1X,3F10.1,I2,3F8.2) 40 FØRMAT(2X,F3.1,T30,F4.1)	to specify location, field and type of output data	135

STATEMENT TYPE	FORM/EXAMPLE(S)	PURPOSE	PAGE
	1 2 3 4 5 6 7 8 9 · · ·		
FUNCTION	nnnnn name(a_1,a_2,a_3,...a_n) ATAN(ALPHA) ALØG(X) IABS(JJ)	to transfer program to the specified function subprogram	305
FUNCTION subprogram	type FUNCTION(a,b,c...) FUNCTION name(a,b,c...) FUNCTION RØØT(A,B,C) REAL FUNCTION IBS(X,Y) INTEGER FUNCTION ZIP(I,G,H)	to define a program as a FUNCTION subprogram	309
GØ TØ	nnnnn GØ TØ m GØ TØ 66	to cause an unconditional branch	243
IF THEN	nnnnn IF(e) THEN IF(A-B.GT.Ø)THEN	defines the start of a block of statements to be executed if the IF block condition is true	284
IFIX	nnnnn ...IFIX(e)...	to convert from real to integer mode	85
IMPLICIT	IMPLICIT $type_1$(a_1,b_1,...), $type_2$ (a_2,b_2,...),...	to override the explicit type specification rule	281
implied DØ	nnnnn ...(v(ix),ix=m_1,m_2,m_3)... READ(1,6)(UNIT(J),J=1,100) WRITE(3,7)(UNIT(J),=1,100) READ(1,8)A,B,(X(I),I=1,20)	to define a DØ loop interval to READ and WRITE statements	189
implied DØ for two dimensions	((v_i(i,j),j=1,n),i=1,m) ((X (J,J),J=1,N),I=1,M)	to define implied nested DO loops	212
INT	nnnnn ...INT(e)... I=INT(R)	to convert from real to integer mode	85
INTEGER type specification	INTEGER rn_1,rn_2,rn_3 INTEGER RØW INTEGER A,B,C	to override implicit real specification	46
INTRINSIC	INTRINSIC name ,...$name_n$ INTRINSIC ALØG10,ALØG	to identify system supplied subprogram names as allowable subprogram arguments	344

logical IF	nnnnn IF($e_1$reop e_2)s
	IF(A.LT.B)GØTØ 15
	IF(X**2.GT.Y**2)Z=X-Y
		to cause conditional branching based on a logical state	253

LOGICAL type specification	LOGICAL a,b,c LOGICAL T,F	to declare a LOGICAL variable name	259

STATEMENT TYPE	FORM/EXAMPLE(S)	PURPOSE	PAGE
READ (end-of-file)	123456789··· nnnnn READ(i,n,END=n_t)list 20 READ(1,30,END=99)A READ(1,30,END=99)B	to branch to statement n_t when end-of-file has been reached	99
READ(formatted)	nnnnn READ(i,n)vn_1,vn_2,vn_3,... 10 READ(1,8)X 200 READ(1,10)ITEM,XRAY	to input data in formatted form	98
READ(free format)	nnnnn READ,list READ,I,N READ,A,B,C,J,K	to input data in free format form	96
READ (unformatted)	nnnnn READ(i)list READ(9)A,B,C,D,E,F	to input data in unformatted form	123
REAL	nnnnn ...REAL(e)... R=REAL(I)	to convert from integer to real mode	85
REAL type specification	REAL in_1,in_2,in_3 REAL L REAL ITEM,NØ,ID,I1,I2,I3	to override implicit integer specification	45
RETURN	nnnnn RETURN	returns control back to the calling program	
statement function	name(a_1,a_2,a_3,...a_n)=expression FUNC(A)=3.*A**2+A-7 AVE6(A,B,C,D,E,F)=(A+B+C+D+E+F)/G	to define a function	317
STOP	STOP	to terminate execution	75
SUBROUTINE	SUBROUTINE name(a_1,...a_n) SUBROUTINE HEAD	to define a program as a subroutine subprogram	331
WRITE (formatted)	nnnnn WRITE(i,n)vn_1,vn_2,vn_3 WRITE(3,25) WRITE(3,10)X,Y,Z 300 WRITE(N,100)I,J	to output data in formatted form	133
WRITE (unformatted)	nnnnn WRITE(i)list WRITE(9)A,B,C,D,E,F	to output data in unformatted form	152

FORTRAN

TOPICS

APPENDIX C

Punched Cards

The only data on a punched card that is meaningful to a card reader is the punches or holes which it senses. The holes are interpreted and the data is passed through the proper channels to the computer in a standard code.

On an IBM punched card, data is stored in Hollerith code. A card is divided into 12 rows and 80 columns as shown in Figure C-1.

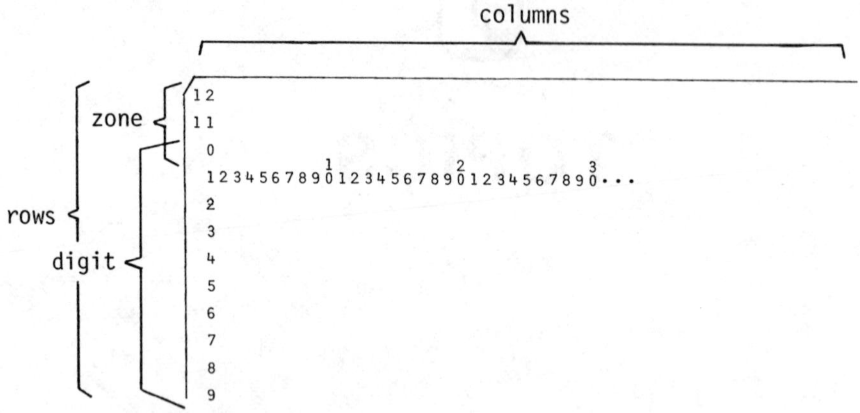

Figure C-1. Data Card Format

Each column may contain a character or a digit. A digit '5' would be stored by punching a hole in 5's row. Alphabetic and special characters are made by a combination of zone and digit punches. Table C-1 shows how alphabetic characters are made.

Table C-1
Coding of Alphabetical Characters

zone 12 and	zone 11 and	zone 0 and
1 2 3 4 5 6 7 8 9	1 2 3 4 5 6 7 8 9	2 3 4 5 6 7 8 9
A B C D E F G H I	J K L M N O P Q R	S T U V W X Y Z

EBCDIC

In order that different peripheral devices, such as printers, card punches, card readers, teletypes, and plotters, can communicate with a computer, standard codes have been established. All character sensitive I/O equipment will assume either extended binary coded decimal interchange code (EBCDIC) or USA Standard Code for Information Interchange (USASCII). The remainder of this Appendix shows how FORTRAN uses EBCDIC as the standard code to enable the computer to communicate with a card reader and a printer. There is a close similarity between the Hollerith code of a character on a card and the EBCDIC code of the character as it is stored in computer memory. However, the computer memory does not store 'punches' but rather stores data in binary notation in memory. The zone punch of the card appears as an EBCDIC binary code as given in Table C-2 whereas the digit punch is stored in computer memory as a binary value.

Table C-2
EBCDIC Binary Code

ZONE PUNCH	EBCDIC-BINARY CODE
12	1100
11	1101
0	1110
none	1111

For a 32-bit word computer, one character from a card takes eight bits so up to four characters from a card can be stored in a FORTRAN word. Figure C-2 shows how character data from a card would be stored in memory in EBCDIC code.

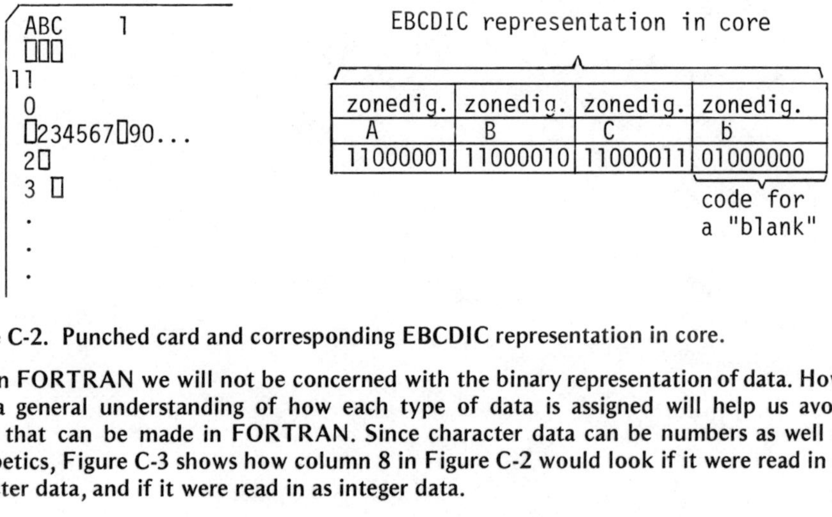

Figure C-2. Punched card and corresponding EBCDIC representation in core.

In FORTRAN we will not be concerned with the binary representation of data. However, a general understanding of how each type of data is assigned will help us avoid errors that can be made in FORTRAN. Since character data can be numbers as well as alphabetics, Figure C-3 shows how column 8 in Figure C-2 would look if it were read in as character data, and if it were read in as integer data.

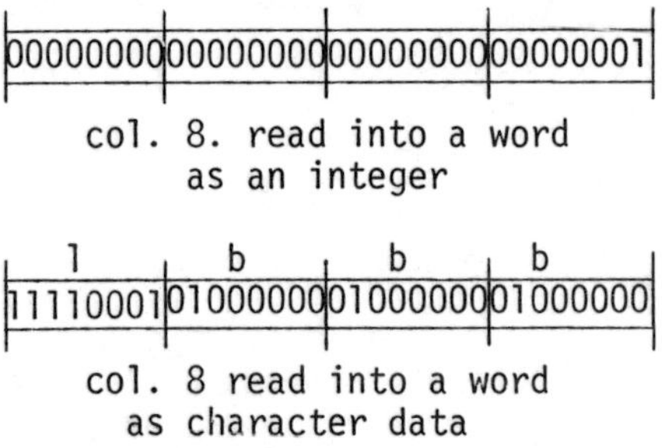

Figure C-3. Example of Binary Storage.

FORTRAN D

SORTING

Appendix D

The sorting of a random list of data into numerical or alphanumerical order is frequently required in the business applications of computers. Sorting problems occasionally come up in scientific work, too, although less frequently. Most scientific users of computers are not familiar with sorting methods. This section of the notes sets out three sorting methods. One is simple (and slow). The second is slightly more complicated, but it is usually more efficient than the first when long lists are to be sorted. The third is presented primarily for background information; it is the method used for sorting cards on a mechanical card sorter.

Definition of ascending order.

Let's define what is meant by having a list in order:

> A list is in ascending order if and only if every element of the list (except the last one) is less than or equal to its successor. The last element is excluded because it does not have a successor.

The definition gives us a test for the computer to use for telling whether a list is in order. It also gives a clue as to how to put the list in order. If an element is larger than its successor, we can bring the list 'closer' to being in order by interchanging that element with its successor. The following sort is based on that fact.

SORT BY PAIR INTERCHANGES (BUBBLE SORT)

Suppose we have the following list.

```
 5
 7
21
10
 4
 2
```

The computer can use the rule given above to determine that the list is not in order. The test is applied to successive list pairs as follows:

```
Is 5<7?      Yes
Is 7<21?     Yes
Is 21<10?    No
```

There is no need to go further—The list is not in order. However, further testing would show that three pairs, (21,10), (10,4), and (4,2) are reversed in the list. The same rule can be used to try to put the list in order:

```
Is 5<7?     Yes  - no action required
Is 7<21?    Yes  - no action required
Is 21<10?   No   - interchange 10 and 21
                   on the list
```

The list now is:

```
5
7
10
21
4
2
```

```
Is 21<4?    No - interchange 21 and 4
Is 21<2?    No - interchange 21 and 2
```

The list now is:

```
5
7
10
4
2
21
```

The last possible pair has been tested. Note that there were five comparisons required to test a list of six variables. Note also that only two pairs (10,4) and (4,2) are now reversed in the list. However the list is still not in order, so we repeat the process.

```
Is 5<7?     Yes - no action required
Is 7<10?    Yes - no action required
Is 10<4?    No  - interchange 10 and 4
Is 10<2?    No  - interchange 10 and 2
Is 10<21?   Yes - no action required
```

and the list now appears as:

```
5
4
2
7
10
21
```

Examination of the list shows two pairs (7,4) and (4,2) out of order. One might question whether the situation is improving, and ask how many times the process has to be repeated to get the list in order. The exact number of sweeps through the list which is required is not a constant. It varies according to how badly out of order the list is.

In this particular case, one finds that after the next sweep through the list one gets:

```
5
4
2
7
10
21
```

After the next

4
2
5
7
10
21

After the next

2
4
5
7
10
21

Which concludes ordering the list.

It can be shown by analysis that the maximum number of times through the list required to sort the worst possible case is n−1 sweeps where n is the number of list elements. A program that always sweeps that many times will always sort the list. Such an approach is wasteful of computer time, however, since a randomly ordered list will often require fewer than the maximum number of sweeps to get it in order.

The usual programming approach is to use a 'flag' variable. The programmer selects some variable (we will call it IFLAG) and set it to zero before starting a sweep of the list. If during the sweep a pair of variables is interchanged, the program sets IFLAG to 1, either immediately before or immediately after the interchange. This step is called 'raising the flag'. IFLAG is then tested at the conclusion of each sweep. If it is zero, no further sweeps need be made. If it is 1, i.e.,'the flag is up', the program should sweep again, (after setting IFLAG to zero). In this way only one extra sweep is made -- the one in which the flag does not go up.

This particular sorting method is sometimes called a 'bubble' sort. The name is most descriptive if the sort is done from the bottom of the list to the top, since the smaller list elements tend to 'bubble' upward through the list during each pass.

Detailed study of the given example will show that the largest number on the list is driven to the bottom of the list on the first sweep, that the next-to-the-largest number is driven to next-to-last on the second sweep, and so on. If very large lists are to be sorted, it may save computer time to write the program so that each successive sweep stops comparisons one element sooner on each successive pass. However, for short lists, (less than 500 entries) the extra data manipulation required to change the number of comparisons to be made on each pass uses about as much computer time as the redundant comparisons use.

A SORT-MERGE TECHNIQUE

The second technique which will be described here is really effective only on installations with four or more tape units, or similar devices. It is also adaptable to sorting card decks directly if a card reader is available with at least two input hoppers and two output stackers. The IBM 2560 is an example and is used with a 360/20 for sorting by this method.

The first step in the procedure is to split the original list into two lists. It can be done most simply by splitting the list roughly in half. However the following technique for forming two lists is a little more efficient, in that it saves one pass through list during the sort-merge.

Assume the input list, L, is to be split into two lists, A and B.

As an example, let L be as follows:

9
27
38
5
106
34
51
6
72

Arbitrarily put the first element of L into list A

L	A	B
27	9	(no entries)
38		
5		
106		
34		
51		
6		
72		

Continue to transfer elements from L to A as long as they are in ascending order. As soon as an element of L is detected to be smaller than its predecessor, however, switch to list B.

L	A	B
-	9	5
-	27	
-	38	
-		
106		
34		
51		
6		
72		

Continue transfering elements from L to B as long as they are in ascending order. As soon as an element of L is again detected to be smaller than its predecessor, switch back to A. Continue through L, and switch back and forth (toggle) between A and B until L is exhausted.

L	A	B
(empty)	9	5
	27	106
	38	6
	34	72
	51	

At this point L has been split into two lists.

The second step is to produce two new lists A' and B' from the lists A and B by the following rules.

Start: Examine the top element of A and of B. Pick the smaller of the two and transfer it to A'.

A	B	A'	B'
9	-		(no entries)
27	106	5	
38	6		
34	72		
51			

Next examine what are now the first elements of A and of B and pick the smaller of the two. If that one is larger than or equal to the most recent entry on list A', put it on list A'. If it is smaller than the most recent entry on A', toggle to list B'. Continue listing, toggling as required, until both lists A and B are exhausted. For the given example the result is:

A'	B'
5	
9	34
27	51
38	106
6	
72	

Using the same procedure as in the previous step, transfer the lists A' and B' to two new lists A'' and B''.

A''	B''
5	
9	6
27	72
34	106
38	
51	

The procedure is repeated as many times as necessary to produce a single list. In the example given the next sort merge will yield

A'''	B'''
5	(no entries)
6	
9	
27	
34	
38	
72	
51	
106	

This method of sorting is based on the same rule as the first one; the pair interchanges take place as lists A and B are merged. The more mathematically sophisticated student might wish to attempt as proof that this algorithm will always produce an ordered list (the proof is difficult) and to discover the maximum number of sort-merge steps required. Students interested in sorting may wish to consult one of the references below.

RADIX SORT

The radix sort is included here primarily for completeness, since it is most suitable for use on a mechanical card sorter that can test individual card columns. It is another example of a sort-merge technique, and is related to the previous example. The original list is first sorted into ten 'piles' according to the last (least significant) digit.

0	1	2	3	4	5	6	7	8	9
	51	72		34	5	106	27	38	9
						6			

In the mechanical card sorter the cards fall into a series of pockets much as is shown above.

The sorted cards are then merged into one stack with the cards from the lowest numbered pockets above the cards from the higher numbered pockets.

```
 51
 72
 34
  5
106
  6
 27
 38
  9
```

Note that the last significant digits are in order.

Next, cards are sorted again into ten piles, according to the next-to-least significant digit. Blanks are interpreted as zeroes.

0	1	2	3	4	5	6	7	8	9
05			34		51		72		
106		27	38						
06									
09									

They are again merged in order by placing stacks on top of each other from left to right.

05
106
06
09
27
34
38
51
72

Finally they are sorted on the most significant digit.

Blanks are again interpreted as zeroes.

0	1	2
005	106	
006		
009		
027		
034		
038		
051		
072		

The result of merging is an ordered list.

Radix sorting is impracticable in FORTRAN because numbers are ordinarily stored in binary notation. (A radix sort could be implemented using the alphanumeric capabilities of FORTRAN if it were mandatory to do so, however.) In other languages with decimal capability, particularly COBOL and BAL, a radix sort could be easily implemented but would probably show little or no advantage over other sort-merge techniques given in the references.

References:

(1) 'Digital Computer System Principles', H. Hellerman, McGraw-Hill, 1967

(2) 'Digital Computer and Control Engineering', R. S. Ledley, McGraw-Hill, 1960

(3) 'Sorting on Electronic Computer Systems', E. H. Friend, J. ACM, Vol. 3 pp. 134-168, 1956

(4) Comm. ACM, Vol. 6, No. 5, May 1963 (Several papers on sorting.)

FORTRAN

ROUND OFF ERRORS

APPENDIX E

INTRODUCTION

The term 'round-off error' is usually applied in computer work to the errors introduced by carrying only a finite number of significant figures in computations. The term 'round-off' is used even though numbers are often not rounded off in the customary grade-school sense, but merely truncated. Truncation is, after all, one way to round off a number (although not always the best one for accuracy).

Every digital computer has an upper limit on its basic accuracy. Round-off errors often cause programs to produce unexpected results. The following paragraphs exhibit the sources of the errors and give some practical programming tricks for avoiding surprises.

ROUND-OFF ERROR SOURCES

NON-TERMINATING FRACTIONS -- The major source of round-off error is, of course, arithmetic involving non-terminating fractions. As an example, the fraction 1/3 can be approximated by 0.3, 0.33, 0.333, 0.3333, and so on, but can never be written exactly with a finite number of digits. Most of us are accustomed to this, however, and are not startled when we obtain such results as

```
0.3x3=0.9
0.33x3=0.99
0.333x3=0.999
0.3333x3=0.9999
```

even though 3 x 1/3 is 1 exactly.

However, most scientific computers operate in a binary number system, rather than a decimal system. Many fractions which are terminating fractions in the decimal system are non-terminating in a binary system. (The reverse, however, is not true. If a fraction terminates in a binary form it will always terminate in decimal form.)

A simple example is the fraction 1/10. In binary notations it becomes

```
0.0001100110011001 1...
```

Regardless of how far the expansion is taken, multiplying this fraction by ten (i.e., the binary number 1010) yields

```
0.111111111111111...
```

Conversion of this number to decimal can yield 0.9999 ···, or 1, depending on the exact scheme used for conversion in the particular computer being used.

However, on any computer, the statements

A=0.1xB and A=B/10

may yield slightly different results (depending on the value of B). If, for example, B is equal to 10, the second statement will yield an A equal to exactly 1. The first statement will usually produce a binary value slightly less than 1.

MAGNITUDE FAULTS -- A second source of round-off error is the execution of additions or subtractions between very large and very small numbers. Although computers usually operate in a binary number system, the error source can be exemplified with a decimal example. Imagine an adding machine which has six significant figures or number wheels. We wish to do arithmetic, which sometimes uses numbers larger than 999,999 or smaller than 1. We can do so by keeping track of where the decimal point belongs on a piece of scratch paper as follows:

1) We will write all of our numbers as decimal fractions less than one and multiplied by some exponent of ten.

2) We will assume there is a decimal point between the left-most digit and the digit second from the left on our adding machine. Now, suppose we add 2 and 2 as follows.

Actual	Figures on adding machine	Figures on scratch paper
2	0.20000	1 signify that adding
+2	0.20000	1 machine results must
4	0.40000	1 be multiplied by 10

The scheme seems workable so far.

We consider the addition of 2 and 30. In the scheme set forth above, 30 is represented by 0.30000 in the adding machine and 2 on the scratch paper. Before adding, if the coefficients of 10 are made equal for both numbers (by shifting 2 to the right) the numbers will be aligned properly for addition in the adding machine

Actual	Adding machine	Scratch paper
30	0.30000	2
+ 2	.02000	2
32	0.32000	2

Suppose now that we attempt to add 2 to 2,000,000.

```
2,000,000  0.20000     ←shifted out of  7  ←increased by 6
       +2  0.00000(02)  adding machine  7   when mantissa is
                                            shifted six places
                                            to right
```

Note that even if 2 is added to 2,000,000 over and over (a million times) the answer will still be 2,000,000.

COMBINED ERRORS -- Both types of errors listed above can occur simultaneously; as an example, consider the following program:

```
      A=0.
      DØ20I=1,100
      A=A+1./3.
   20 WRITE(3,x)A
```

Imagine this program is being executed on a decimal machine which operates like the adding machine above. The first time through the DO loop we get

```
  0     0.00000   0
 1/3    0.33333   0
 1/3    0.33333   0
```

the second time

```
 1/3    0.33333   0
 1/3    0.33333   0
 2/3    0.66666   0
```

the third time

```
 2/3    0.66666   0
 1/3    0.33333   0
  1     0.99999   0
```

The fourth time through we shift our answer 1 place to the right so as to keep all numbers represented as fractions multiplied by exponents

```
  1      0.99999            0
 1/3     0.33333            0
 1 1/3   0.13333(2)dropped  Ø1 increased by 1
               shifted to      when we shift
               right
```

The fifth time through we must shift the .33333 to the right to align it with our previous answer

1 1/3	0.1333		1
1/3	0.0333(3)	dropped	1
1 2/3	0.1666		1

Note that the shift to the right caused some loss in accuracy. As the DO loop is executed over and over, the answer obtained will differ more and more from the actual answer. The table below shows how the error builds up through 100 steps.

Step	Actual	Machine answer	exponent
5		0.1666	1
6	2	0.1999	1
7		.2332	1
8		.2665	1
9		.2998	1
10		.3331	1
11		.3664	1
12	4	.3997	1
13		.4330	1
:		:	:
:		:	:
30	10	.9991	1
31		.1032	2
32		.1065	2
33	11	.1098	2
:		:	:
:		:	:
83	27 2/3	.2748	2
:		:	:
:		:	:
100	33 1/3	.3309	2

SUMMARY -- Only two sources of round-off errors have been discussed above. There are other related areas which arise in numerical integration, machine solution of differential equations, and related fields. For complex uses of computers, the analysis of error propagation is an important part of program design, and may even consume as much time as the writing of the program itself. The student should understand that the machine is not making a mistake. It is performing exactly as it was designed to perform. If a program gives the 'wrong' answer, the programmer is at fault. The following section gives some practical techniques for avoiding the effects of round-off propagation.

PROGRAMMING TECHNIQUES

Round-off errors often cause two major kinds of program running errors. The first is simply getting the 'wrong' answer in a repetitive computation after a variable has been incremented a number of times. The second error type (and one which is often more difficult to find) is a failure of the program to branch as expected at a decision point. As an example, one would expect the statement following to branch to statement 20.

```
IF (0.1 * A - A/10) 10, 20, 30
```

However, depending on the value of A, it will often branch to statement 10. Following are some programming techniques to avoid this sort of problem.

INTEGER ARITHMETIC -- The first practical trick to avoid round-off errors is to use integers wherever possible in arithmetic manipulations. As simple examples, consider the following two programs:

FLOATING POINT

```
   A = 0
   DØ 30 J = 1, 5
   DØ 40 I = 1, 100
40 A = A + 0.1
30 WRITE (3, 60) A
60 FØRMAT (F 12.8)
   STØP
   END
```

INTEGER

```
   DØ 30 J = 1, 5
   DØ 40 I = 1, 100
40 A = 0.1*(100*(J-1)+I)
30 WRITE (3, 60) A
60 FORMAT (F 12.8)
   STØP
   END
```

The output from each of these programs when run on a GE 420 is

FLOATING POINT	INTEGER
10.00000000	10.00000000
20.00000000	20.00000000
29.99999999	30.00000000
39.99999998	40.00000000
49.99999997	50.00000000

The advantage of this technique is that it is easily applied. The disadvantage is that computation time is significantly increased. Using typical values, statement 40 in the floating point program will require about 10 microseconds to execute on a moderately fast machine, whereas statement 40 of the integer program may require as much as 200 microseconds. In small programs this difference is of no concern. In large programs which are run repeatedly, the difference in computer usage costs can get significant.

Use of integers assures that IF statements will branch correctly. As an example the second partial program below is assured of branching correctly; the first is not.

```
A = 0.1*K
IF (A-30.) 10, 20, 30
```

```
A = 0.1*K
IF (K-300) 10, 20, 30
```

DOUBLE PRECISION ARITHMETIC -- When the range of a variable is such that integer arithmetic is impractical, round-off errors can be reduced many orders of magnitude by any of double-precision arithmetic. This technique has the same disadvantage as noted above. Double precision arithmetic takes longer to execute. When program speed is not an important consideration, double precision should always be considered for patching up an existing program, since usually the correction can be inserted by simply adding appropriate specification statements at the beginning of the program.

Correct branching at IF statements can usually be assured in the presence of round-off errors by the following tricks. A compiler supplied function which is called **ABS** returns the absolute value of its argument. The statement at the left below should be replaced with the two statements at the right (or their equivalent, depending on the exact nature of the problem being solved) when it is suspected that round-off errors will cause incorrect branching around zero.

```
IF (A - ALPHA) 10, 20, 30      IF(ABS(A - ALPHA)-DELTA) 20, 20, 40
                            40 IF(A - ALPHA) 10, 20, 30
```

DELTA is chosen to be larger than the largest round-off error and smaller than the smallest value of A -- Alpha that is significant.

REINITIALIZATION -- When execution time is important, a technique can be used in which incremental computations are mixed with periodic integer corrections. As an example, consider the following program, which is equivalent to the two programs discussed above, in the integer arithmetic paragraph, and which will run almost as fast as the floating point one, while retaining almost as much accuracy as the integer one.

```
   DØ 30 J = 1, 5
   A1 = 10*(J-1)
   A2 = 0
   DØ 40 I = 1,100
40 A2 = A2 + 0.1
    A = A1 + A2
30 WRITE (3, 60) A
60 FØRMAT (F 12.8)
   STØP
   END
```

SUMMARY -- A few of the sources of round-off errors and methods for dealing with them have been discussed above. The subject of error analysis and error propagation is an important field of study in numerical analysis, and is properly beyond the scope of a beginning course in programming. The student should, however, be alert to these problems, and examine any repetitive computation program carefully to assure that these effects are minimized.

ANSWERS TO PRACTICE SECTIONS

CHAPTER 1

Page 11:

READ, 3, STOP
2

Page 14:

Check with your instructor or computer installation

Page 15:

1) a)7 b)4 c)1 d)10 e)2 f)5 g)3 h)6 i)8 j)9

2) a) Requires little knowledge of the computer itself.
   b) FORTRAN is problem oriented allowing close translation of mathematical formula.

3) FORTRAN is a computer language in which the programmer requires little knowledge of the internal organization of the computer and is designed for ease in formula translation.
4) FORmula TRANslation

5) Translates the FORTRAN source program to an object program in machine language.

CHAPTER 2

Page 28:

1) %, @

2) +, –, *, /, **

3) a)F b)F c)F d)T e)T f)F g)F h)F i)F j)T

4) a)7-72 b)1 c)1-5 d)6 e)73-80

5) the process of finding errors (bugs) in the program

CHAPTER 3

Pages 54,55:

1) a)R b)X c)I d)R e)X f)R g)I h)R i)X j)R

2) a)R b)I c)R d)X e)R f)X g)X h)R i)R j)X

3) a)39 b)8.5 c)6 d)111.01 e)4.0 f)9 g)1.25 h)0.4

(CHAPTER 3, continued)

4) a)R b)I c)I d)I e)R f)I

5) *

6) READ

7) 0

8)

```
123456789...
      DATA PI,SUM,A,B,C/3.14159,0.0,3*(-1.0)/
```

CHAPTER 4

Page 66:

1) a) V
   b) I -- missing left parenthesis
   c) I -- expression starting in column 6
   d) V
   e) I -- missing variable or parenthesis set
   f) V
   g) I -- implied multiplication

2)

```
123456789...
      REAL M,KE
      Y=A*X**2+B
      F=M*A
      KE=1./2.*M*V**2
      A=B/(C+D)
```

3) a)9. b)1.67 c)10.5

Page 68:

1) a)7.0 b)4.05 c)7 d)4

2) a)0.0 b)0 c)12.0

Page 69, 70:

1)

```
123456789...
      PI=3.1416
      CR=57.296
      CM=6076.2
```

2)

```
12345|6|789...
     | |
     | |X=2.38
     | |Y=6.49
     | |ABAR=16.0
     | |BBAR=32.0
```

3)

```
12345|6|789...
     | |
     | |DATA X,Y,ABAR,BBAR/2.36,6.49,16.0,32.0/
     | |DATA PI,CR,CM/3.1416,57.296,6076.2/
```

Page 72:

1)

```
12345|6|789...
     | |
     | |E=A*EXP(A*T)
     | |S=SQRT(Y**3)
     | |V=SIN(X)+CØS(X)
     | |E=EM*SIN(W*T+P)
```

Page 74:

```
12345|6|789...
     | |
     | |REAL N1,N2
    1| |V=4.*T**3-18.*T**2+24.*T-10.
    2| |V=(64.*PI*(Y+8.)**2)/(3.*(Y-8.))
    3| |T=A*EXP(-X*SQRT(W/(2.*P)))
    4| |CL=P1-P2+Z*SQRT(P1*(1.-P1)/N1+P2*(1.-P2)/N2)
    5| |Z=-1./SQRT(X*X-A*A)-2.*A*A/(3.*SQRT((X*X-A*A)**3))
```

Page 82:

```
12345|6|789...
     | |
     | |INTEGER SUM
     | |SUM=0
     | |DØ 10 N=29, 67, 2
     | |SUM=SUM+N
   10| |CØNTINUE
     | |...
```

The loop will be executed 20 times.

Page 85:

To change an integer to real, use the **REAL** or the **FLOAT** function.
To change a real to an integer, use the **INT** or the **IFIX** function.

Pages 86-88:

1) a) V
   b) I -- implied multiplication
   c) I -- missing variable or parenthesis set
   d) I -- missing right parenthesis
   e) V
   f) V
   g) I -- expression on left side of equal sign

h) V
i) V
j) I -- invalid variable name

2)

```
12345|6|789...

a)   |  |...A/B+C/D...
b)   |  |...A/(B+C)...
c)   |  |...1./2.*X**0.5...
d)   |  |...5.*X*X+3.*X-18. ...
e)   |  |...A*(B+C)...
```

3)

```
12345|6|789...

     |  |Y=X*X/(X+5.)
```

4) A=4.0, N=4

5) N=2

6)

```
12345|6|789...

     |  |N=8
     |  |X=6.32
     |  |Y=23.58
```

7) To assign the value of 3.1416 to variable name PI for later reference.

8)

```
12345|6|789...

     |  |DATA N,X,Y/8,6.32,23.58/
```

9)

```
12345|6|789...
     |  |Y=(A*COS(X1)+B*SIN(X2))*EXP(A*T)
     |  |C=SQRT(A*A+B*B)
```

10) ----

11) To provide a means of program termination.

12) To define the end of a main program or subprogram.

13) IS=105

CHAPTER 5

Page 97:

LOT=27, SIZE=5.32

Pages 100, 101:

NOA will be read from card one
NOB will be read from card two

Page 106:

ID1=569, ID2=37, ID3=28

Page 113:

ITEM=68, COST=12.08

Page 116:

IN1=54, IN2=20, IN3=327

Page 117:

A=4677.78, B=6.4

Pages 123, 124:

1) IX=15, IY=993

2) ITEM=93, XRAY=732.

3) I1=15, I2=99, I3=23, I4=67

4) MASS=7.28, FORCE=5.49×10^1

5) 20 card columns

6) three data cards

7) a)530, b)53043.56, c)435, d)56, e)92, 5.

CHAPTER 6

Pages 153-156:

```
         123456789012345678901234567890123456789 ...
1) LINE 1 b23.4-16.0bb0.0bb892

   LINE 2 bb23.b-16.b0.826E-03bb892

   LINE 3 *********b0.00892

   LINE 4 b0.234E+02-0.160E+02b0.826E-03bb**
```

2)

```
123456789...

     WRITE(3,5)ANG
    5 FØRMAT('bTHEbLIFTbANGLEbISb',F5.1,'bDEGREES')
```

3) Statement label 10 -- three slashes at the beginning do nothing when preceeding a new page.

Statement label 20 -- record two is missing the carriage control character.

4)

```
123456789...

      WRITE(3,5)I1,I3,I5
    5 FØRMAT('1',I6/'0',I6/'0',I6)

    5 FØRMAT('1',I6//'b',I6//'b',I6)
```

5)

```
123456789...

      WRITE(3,5)XV,IN,YV,JN
    5 FØRMAT('1'/(/'b',T4,F6.2,T12,I3))
```

6)

```
123456789...

    8 FØRMAT('1',T8,F5.1,'bISb',F4.1,'bPERCENTbØFb',F5.1)
```

7)

```
                 1         2
        12345678901234567890123...
LINE 1
LINE 2  ONbHANDbb7bb47.12389
```

8)

```
                 1         2
        12345678901234567890123
LINE 1
LINE 2  ONbHANDb**bbb0.47124
```

9)

```
123456789...
      WRITE(3,5)E,I,P
    5 FØRMAT('1',T8,'VOLTAGE',T18,'CURRENT',T29,'POWER'
     +//T9,3(F5.1,5X))
```

10) blank, one advance
0, two advances
1, new page
+, no advance

(Chapter 6, Pages 153-156, continued)

11)

```
123456789...

      WRITE(3,5)I,AA,JU,B
    5 FØRMAT(///'b',2(I10,F10.3))
```

12)

```
123456789...

   18 FØRMAT('1',T57,'THISbISbPAGEb',I3,'bØFb',I3)
```

CHAPTER 8

Page 180:

1) WT

2) Array name, A
Element 8

3) NOEMP(1), BPAY(1)

Page 182:

a) LØAD'
b) CASH
c) VOLTS
d) NODEF

Page 184:

```
123456789...

a)    DIMENSIØN LØAD(50)
b)    DIMENSIØN CASH(31)
c)    DIMENSIØN VØLTS(200)
d)    DIMENSIØN NØ DEF(25)
```

Page 186:

a)V b)V c)V d)I e)I f)V (Parts (b) and (c) are invalid in FORTRAN '66.)

Page 192:

1)

```
123456789...

      DIMENSION Y(500)
```

2) X_1, X_2, Y_1, Y_2

3) JX_6, JX_7, JX_8, JX_9

4)
```
123456789...
      INTEGER SCØRE(100)
```

Pages 195-197:

1) a) $X_1, X_2, X_3, Y_1, Y_2, Y_3$
   b) 6
   c)
```
123456789...
   11 FØRMAT(6F8.1)
```
   d)
```
123456789...
      READ(1,11)(X(I),Y(I),I=1,3)
   11 FØRMAT(2F8.1)
```

2)

VARIABLE	FORMAT CODE	RECORD READ
X(1)	F5.3	1
X(4)	F8.1	1
X(7)	F6.1	1
X(10)	F5.3	2
X(13)	F8.1	2

3)
```
123456789...
      DIMENSIØN ITLE(7)
      READ(1,5)ITLE
    5 FØRMAT(T5,6A4,A2)
```

Pages 201-203:

1)
```
123456789...
      DIMENSIØN R(30)
      WRITE(3,5)R
    5 FØRMAT('b',F10.1)
```

2)
```
123456789...
      DIMENSIØN NRAY(64)
      WRITE(3,5)(NRAY(I),I=2,64,2)
    5 FØRMAT(('0',8(I6,3X)))
```

3)

```
123456789···
      DIMENSIØN IN(50),INSQ(50)
      READ(1,5)N,(IN(I),I=1,N)
    5 FØRMAT...
      IPD=1
      IPDSQ=1
      DØ 10 I=1,N
      IPD=IPD*IN(I)
      INSQ(I)=IN(I)**2
   10 IPDSQ=IPDSQ*INSQ(I)
      WRITE(3,15)N
   15 FØRMAT('1THEbNO.bOFbPOSITIVEbINTEGERSbISb',I2)
      WRITE(3,20)(IN(I),INSQ(I),I=1,N)
   20 FØRMAT('0',5X,'NUMBER',5X,'SQUARE'//
     +('b',5X,I4,7X,I4))
      WRITE(3,10)IPD,IPDSQ
   10 FØRMAT...
```

4)

```
123456789···
      DIMENSIØN Y(7)
      READ(1,5)X
    5 FØRMAT...
      WRITE(3,10)X
   10 FØRMAT...
```

```
123456789···
      DØ 15 I=2,8
      Y(I-1)=X**I
   15 WRITE(3,20)I,Y(I-1)
   20 FØRMAT('0',I2,5X,7Fw.d)    where w includes spaces
      between values.
```

CHAPTER 9

Page 209:

1) **1,1 1,2 1,3**
2,1 2,2 2,3
3,1 3,2 3,3

2) **9**

3) **1,1**
2,1
3,1
1,2
2,2
3,2
1,3
2,3
3,3

4)

```
123456789···
      DIMENSIØN A(3,3)
```

(Chapter 9, continued)

Page 212:

```
123456789...

      DØ 10 I=1,M
      DØ 10 J=1,N
      A(I,J)=0.
   10 B(I,J)=1.
```

Pages 215-217:

1)

```
123456789...

      READ(1,6)A
```

2)

```
123456789...

      READ(1,6)((A(I,J),I=1,3),J=1,3)
```

3)

```
123456789...

      READ(1,10)((A(I,J),J=1,3),I=1,3)
```

4)

```
123456789...

      SUMR1=0.
      DØ 20 I=1,3
      SUMR1=SUMR1+A(1,I)
   20 CØNTINUE
```

5)

```
123456789...
      SUMC3=0.
      DØ 20 J=1,3
      SUMC3=SUMC3+A(J,3)
   20 CØNTINUE
```

6)

```
123456789...
      WRITE(3,30)((A(I,J),J=1,3),I=1,3)
```

7)

```
123456789...
      WRITE(3,30)(A(I,I),I=1,3)
```

(Chapter 9, continued)

Page 219:

1) R(1,1) = 72.3
   R(2,1) = 60.0
   R(3,1) = 0.3
   R(1,2) = 83.9
   R(2,2) = 86.5
   R(3,2) = 0.0

2) R(1,1) = 72.3
   R(2,1) = 48.9
   R(3,1) = 60.0
   R(1,2) = 76.5
   R(2,2) = 0.3
   R(3,2) = 20.5

Pages 229, 230:

1) a)

```
123456789...
      DØ 20 I=1,3
      DØ 20 J=1,4
      DØ 20 K=1,5
      ARAY(I,J,K)=0.0
   20 CØNTINUE
```

b)

```
123456789...
      DATA ARAY/60*0.0/
```

2)

```
123456789...
      DIMENSIØN INMAT(3,4)
      READ(d_i, 10)INMAT
   10 FØRMAT(3I3)
```

3)

```
123456789...
      DIMENSIØN INMAT(3,4)
      READ(d_i,10)((INMAT (I,J),J=1,4),I=1,3)
   10 FØRMAT(4I3)
```

4)

```
            1         2         3
   123456789012345678901234567890123456789...
1
2    3    5    4    2
3   8    6    7    1
4   0
5
```

5 K(1,1)=96, K(1,2)=84, K(1,3)=23, K(2,1)=54, K(2,2)=21, K(2,3)=38

CHAPTER 10

Page 240:

1) branching, looping, terminating

2) T

Page 246:

```
12345|6|789...
     | |GØ TØ (100,200,300,400,500),M
```

Page 252:

1)
```
12345|6|789...
     | |IF(A-25)10,20,30
```

2)
```
12345|6|789...
     | |IF(IMØ)10,20,30
```

Pages 255, 256:

1)
```
12345|6|789...
     | |IF(IM.LT. 0.0) GØ TØ 10
     | |IF(IM.EQ. 0.0) GØ TØ 20
     | |IF(IM.GT. 0.0) GØ TØ 30
```

2)
```
12345|6|789...
     | |IF(A.GE.B) GØ TØ 23
```

3)
```
12345|6|789...
     | |IF(X.LT. 0.0) X=-X
```

Pages 257, 258:

1)
```
12345|6|789...
     | |IF(IX.GE.IY) GØ TØ 6
    5| |
```

2)
```
12345|6|789...
     | |IF(I.EQ.6) GØ TØ 10
     | |IF(I.EQ.7) GØ TØ 10
```

3)
```
12345|6|789...
     | |IF(I-6)5,10,5
    5| |IF(I-7)n,10,n
```

4)
```
12345|6|789...
   a)| |IF(I-100)7,8,8
   b)| |IF(I.GE.100) GØ TØ 8
```

CHAPTER 11

Pages 278-280:

1) a) LET
INP
PRI
GOT

b) 10, 11, 12, 13, 14, 15, 30, 14, 15, 30, 14, 15, 30, 16

2)

```
123456789...
      DATA IBLK/'b'/
      DIMENSIØN ICARD(80)
      READ(1,1)ICARD
    1 FORMAT(80A1)
      DØ 10 I=1,80
        IF(ICARD(I).NE.IBLK) GØ TØ 5
   10 CØNTINUE
    5 INDX=I
```

3)

```
123456789...
      DATA MINUS/'-'/, IDØL/'$'/,NMINUS/0/
      DIMENSIØN ICARD(80)
    5 READ(1,10)ICARD
   10 FØRMAT(80A1)
      ICØL80=ICARD(80)
      IF(ICØL80.EQ.IDØL) GØ TØ 90
      IF(ICØL80.NE.MINUS) GØ TØ 5
      NMINUS=NMINUS+1
      GØ TØ 5
   90 WRITE(3,92)NMINUS
   92 FØRMAT('bNUMBER ØF MINUS CARDS IS',I5)
      STØP
      END
```

4)

```
123456789...
      INTEGER DEG, UNIT
      DATA DEG/'DEG'/
      ...
      IF(UNIT.EQ.DEG)XLAT=XLAT/57.296
```

5)

```
123456789...
      DIMENSIØN MSG(3)
      INTEGER PØRK,BEEF
      DATA MSG/'COWb','HOGb','LAMB'/
      ...
    5 IF(MEAT.EQ.PØRK) GØ TØ 20
      IF(MEAT.EQ.BEEF)GØ TØ 10
      INDX=3
      GØ TØ 30
   10 INDX=1
      GØ TØ 30
   20 INDX=2
   30 WRITE(3,50)MSG(INDX)
   50 FØRMAT('bMEATbISbFRØMbAb',A4)
      ...
```

Page 282:

1)

```
123456789...
      IMPLICIT INTEGER(Z)
```

(Chapter 11, Page 282, continued)

2)
```
123456789...
      INTEGER ZØØ,ZULA,ZEBRA
```

3)
```
123456789...
      IMPLICIT INTEGER(A-Z)
```

4)
```
123456789...
      IMPLICIT REAL(M,N)
```

Page 286:

1) a)
```
123456789...
      IF(A.GT.B) THEN
      C=A
      ELSE
      C=B
      END IF
```

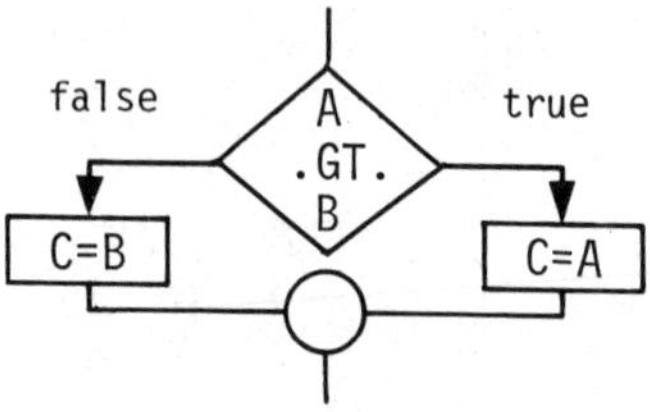

b)
```
123456789...
      IF(ISERNO.LE.0)THEN
      WRITE(3,10)
   10 FØRMAT ('bERROR')
      WRITE(3,20) CARD
   20 FØRMAT('b',...)
      ELSE
      NCARD=NCARD+1
      END IF
```

Page 290:

Extension of example program on page 289

CHAPTER 12

Pages 321-323:

1)T, 2)T, 3)F, 4)T, 5)F, 6)T, 7)T, 8)T

9)
```
123456789...
      SMALL=AMIN1(A,B,C,D,E,F)
```

10)
```
123456789...
      LARGE=MAX0(I,J,K,L,M,N)
```

11)
```
 123456789...
a)    Y=SIN(ATAN(SQRT(A*A+B*B))/ABS(C))
b)    Z=SQRT((A1-B2)/SIN(2*3.1416*RL))
```

12) 5

13) a) DEL and X for every fifth value of I, i.e., 5, 10, . . ., 300

b) 60

14)

```
123456789...
      REAL FUNCTIØN MATXS(A,B,N)
```

15)

```
123456789...
      INTEGER FUNCTION STEP (X)
      STEP=0
      IF(X.LT.-1.) GØ TØ 9
      IF(X.GT.+1.) GØ TØ 9
      STEP=1
    9 RETURN
      END
```

16)

```
123456789...
      FUNCTIØN SUM(A,J,M)
      DIMENSIØN A(100)
      S=0.
      DØ 5 I=J,M
    5 S=S+A(I)
      SUM=S
      RETURN
      END
```

17)

```
123456789...
C    SUBPROGRAM
      FUNCTIØN DØT(A,B)
      DIMENSIØN A(3),B(3)
      AB=0.
      DØ 5 I=1,3
    5 AB=AB+A(I)*B(I)
      DØT=AB
      RETURN
      END
C    MAIN PRØGRAM
      DIMENSIØN A(3),B(3)
      READ(1,5)A,B
    5 FØRMAT(6F5.1)
      PRØD=DØT(A,B)
      WRITE(3,6)PRØD
    6 FØRMAT('bDØT PRØDUCT=',F6.1)
      CALL EXIT
      END
```

18)

```
123456789...
      FN(A,B)=SQRT(SIN(A)+CØS(B))
```

19) 16

CHAPTER 13

Pages 336-337:

1) a)F, b)F, c)S, d)B, e)B (except for statement FUNCTIONS)

2)
```
123456789...

      SUBRØUTINE SKIP
      WRITE(3,5)
    5 FØRMAT('1')
      RETURN
      END
```

3)
```
123456789...

      SUBRØUTINE REVERSE(AR1,AR2,N1)
      DIMENSIØN AR1(50),AR2(50)
      DØ 5 I = 1,N1
      AR2(N1-I+1)=AR1(I)
    5 CØNTINUE
      RETURN
      END
```

CHAPTER 14

Pages 356, 357:

1) V, I, V, I, V, I, V, V, V

2)
```
123456789...
      EQUIVALENCE (AR1(1,1),AR2(1,1))
```

3)
```
123456789...
a)    CØMMØN A(10,10),B(10,10),C(10,10),IRØW,ICØL
b)    CALL MTXADD
c)    SUBRØUTINE MTXADD
d)    CØMMØN/ARY/A(10,10),B(10,10),C(10,10),IRØW, ICØL
```

4)
```
123456789...
      BLØCK DATA
      CØMMØN/SHIFT/DAMP(8)
      DATA DAMP/.1,.2,.3,.4,.5,1.0,2.0,3.0/
      END
```

5) Functions must have at least one argument.

INDEX